MUSIC IN WORLD CULTURES
Understanding Multiculturalism Through The Arts

James P. O'Brien, Ph.D.

DEPARTMENT OF MUSIC
THE UNIVERSITY OF ARIZONA
TUCSON, ARIZONA 85721

KENDALL/HUNT PUBLISHING COMPANY
4050 Westmark Drive Dubuque, Iowa 52002

Cover photos (top to bottom) by

James P. O'Brien
David Burckhalter. Courtesy of the University of Arizona Southwest Folklore Center
David Burckhalter

Copyright © 1994 by Kendall/Hunt Publishing Company

ISBN 0-8403-9122-6

All rights reserved. No part of this publication may be reproduced, stored in a retrieval system, or transmitted, in any form or by any means, electronic, mechanical, photocopying, recording, or otherwise, without the prior written permission of the copyright owner.

Printed in the United States of America
10 9 8 7 6 5 4 3 2 1

CONTENTS

Preface . . . . *vii*

Acknowledgements . . . . *ix*

Recordings . . . . *xi*

CHAPTER ONE — MUSIC OF ALL THE WORLD 1

    Melodic Structure: Scales 13
    Harmonic Structure: Chords and Texture 25
    Rhythmic Structure: Beat and Meter 31
    Formal Structure: Unity and Variety 33
    Instruments of the Western World 37
    Singing in Western Culture 40
    Key Terms and Concepts 43
    Self-checking Chapter Review 44
    Selected Bibliography 45
    Selected Discography 46

CHAPTER TWO — MUSIC OF THE INDIAN WORLD 47

    Melodic Structure: Raga 52
    Rhythmic Structure: Tala 66
    Formal Structure: Alap and Gat 70
    Instruments of Indian Music 73
    Singing in India 80
    Key Terms and Concepts 82
    Self-checking Chapter Review 83
    Selected Bibliography 84
    Selected Discography 86

CHAPTER THREE — MUSIC OF THE ARAB WORLD 91

    Melodic Structure: Maqamat 96
    Rhythmic Structure: Iqa'at 102
    Formal Structure 104
    Instruments of the Arab World 105
    Singing in Arab Culture 116
    Key Terms and Concepts 120
    Self-checking Chapter Review 121
    Selected Bibliography 122
    Selected Discography 123

CHAPTER FOUR — MUSIC OF THE CHINESE CULTURE 127

    Melodic Structure: Lu 135
    Harmonic Structure: Heterophony 140
    Instruments of China 140
    Singing in China: Opera and Vocal Music 154
    Key Terms and Concepts 158
    Self-checking Chapter Review 159
    Selected Bibliography 160
    Selected Discography 162

CHAPTER FIVE — MUSIC OF JAPAN 166

    Melodic Structure: Ritsu and Ryo Scales 171
    Genres of Japanese Music and Theatre 174
    Instrumental Genres 184
    Instruments of Japan 185
    Singing in Japan 197
    Key Terms and Concepts 198
    Self-checking Chapter Review 199
    Selected Bibliography 200
    Selected Discography 201

CHAPTER SIX — MUSIC OF INDONESIA 204

    Structure of Gamelan Music 209
    Melodic Structure: Slendro and Pelog Scales 211
    Musical Structure: Texture, Melody, and Rhythm 216
    Instruments of Indonesia 217
    Utility of Gamelan Music 224
    Key Terms and Concepts 229
    Self-checking Chapter Review 230
    Selected Bibliography 231
    Selected Discography 232

CHAPTER SEVEN — MUSIC OF OCEANIA ... 235

    Music of Polynesia ... 238
    Music of Micronesia ... 246
    Music of Melanesia ... 250
    Music of Australia ... 253
    Key Terms and Concepts ... 260
    Self-checking Chapter Review ... 261
    Selected Bibliography ... 262
    Selected Discography ... 263

CHAPTER EIGHT — MUSIC OF NATIVE AMERICANS ... 265

    Music of the Pueblo Indians ... 271
    Music of the Plains Indians ... 273
    Music of Athabascan Tribes ... 276
    Music of Eskimos ... 277
    Instruments of Native Americans ... 279
    Key Terms and Concepts ... 283
    Self-checking Chapter Review ... 284
    Selected Bibliography ... 285
    Selected Discography ... 286

CHAPTER NINE — MUSIC OF AFRICA (SOUTH OF THE SAHARA) ... 290

    Music of the Khoi-San Area ... 300
    Music of Eastern Africa ... 302
    Music of the Guinea Coast ... 304
    Music of the Congo Region ... 309
    Music of the Sub-Saharan Region ... 314
    Instruments of Africa ... 316
    Key Terms and Concepts ... 319
    Self-checking Chapter Review ... 320
    Selected Bibliography ... 321
    Selected Discography ... 323

CHAPTER TEN — MUSIC OF LATIN AMERICA ... 325

    Music of Mexico and Central America ... 328
    Music of the Caribbean ... 338
    Music of Spanish-Speaking South America ... 346
    Music of Brazil ... 351
    Key Terms and Concepts ... 355
    Self-checking Chapter Review ... 356
    Selected Bibliography ... 357
    Selected Discography ... 358

Sources of Material for World Music *361*

Index *366*

PREFACE

Today's university student is often subjected to a course of study, particularly in general education courses, that attempts to embrace all the past and present achievements of the Western world, including its art, literature, and music. In the latter, whether termed music appreciation, survey, or history, we usually try to expose the student to the grand sweep of music from Gregorian chant to the most recent innovations, realizing that even then, the course is delimited. Whether such a course is offered for one or more semesters, everything cannot be covered. In music, only perceptual frameworks can be developed for listening to and eventually appreciating much of the music of the European world. Developing an enthusiasm for doing so is perhaps the most important objective in such courses anyway--skills, concepts, and attitudes that will meet fruition much later in each student's life.

Why, then, an inclusion of world music in courses that already have difficulty in covering the achievements of Western culture? At the risk of perpetuating cliches, the answer is twofold: (1) because the world has shrunk and we now live in a global community in which pluralism and diversity are cultural norms, if not political mandates; and (2) because music is music and can be examined by understanding the same structures found in European-based music, melody, harmony, rhythm, timbre, dynamics, and form. There is a wealth of music that goes unsampled if the student is not exposed to it in a general education course and led to realize that although music is probably *not* a universal language, it is, at least, a universal occurrence and response. It consists of similar elements whether it comes from Europe, Asia, or Africa. Much as we begin to know the structure of English better when we study Spanish, Russian, or Arabic, we also begin to understand universalities in music when we listen to an Indonesian mode, Arab maqam, or Indian raga. Perhaps, we will not only learn to speak Spanish, but understand English better as well.

This book in intended for use with either general university students or music majors who have had some exposure to European art music, even if minimally. They should be able to apply the conceptual frameworks learned through the study of Western music to music of other cultures. The text is intended to present avenues which might not be traveled without some formal training in world music. Understanding and appreciating all music, whether European-based or not, should be the end result.

Many writings on music of other cultures explore scales, timbres, and tunings. This occurs here as well. One can appreciate minor tonality, however, in a Mozart symphony without knowing whether the scale is natural, harmonic, or melodic. Similarly, one can appreciate a raga in Indian music without specific awareness of the its name and theoretical constraints. Such complexities are better left to the specialist, not the general university student anyway. The development of broad concepts of world music, with some understanding of its utility, structure, and effect, is more of a priority than learning facts. Pursuing the music itself through selections from the discography will make these theoretical concepts come alive. Thoughtful users should not only understand the structure of each culture's music but recognize it by sound as well. The author sincerely hopes this occurs through use of this text.

James P. O'Brien
Tucson, Arizona

ACKNOWLEDGEMENTS

My first textbook, *Non-Western Music and the Western Listener*, was published in 1977. It was an early experiment in incorporating world music into general education and music appreciation. Although never a best seller, the book filled a need for many music departments in universities throughout the country and even the world. It attracted some favorable attention among professors who had similar commitments to world music in the curriculum. This book also involved me in the College Music Society's Wingspread Conference and Summer Institutes in the early 1980's as well as the International Society for Music Education's annual meetings. It provided a network of professional friends, many of whom continue to use *Non-Western Music and the Western Listener* to this day.

Music in World Cultures: Developing Multiculturalism through the Arts, my tenth book, replaces the earlier book. For seventeen years, I have wanted to do a second edition. By the time I finished the research, expanded the topics, and wrote the new manuscript, I felt it was sufficiently different to warrant being titled a new book. It is less scholarly, more user-friendly, more global, and, hopefully, better written.

In the seventeen years between the two books, many people have encouraged me to write again. Among these have been Tom Wisz, Jonathan Baile, and Paul Zagnoni, regional representatives of Kendall/Hunt. Bruce Kaufman, Senior Managing Editor, was the person who finally contracted and accepted the final manuscript.

I have also been encouraged by my department heads during the past seventeen years to continue the mission of world music. I thus owe thanks to Robert Werner, David Woods, Maurice Skones, and Dorothy Payne for their administrative support and encouragement as well as to my college deans, Robert Hull, Donald Irving, Pat van Metre, and Maurice Sevigny. The University of Arizona provided grant support to assist me with writing the manuscript and purchasing photographs. Special appreciation goes to Provost Jack Cole and Vice President Celestino Fernandez who awarded a teaching improvement grant to support this project as well as to William A. Welsh and Sue Keeth of the Office of International Programs who awarded two grants for travel to libraries to conduct photo research.

The archives and libraries in which I conducted research were helpful in accessing and obtaining necessary data, particularly the rich photo display contained throughout. I would like to thank the entire staff who gave me free access to recordings in The University of Arizona Music Library; Ken Moore, Associate Curator, Metropolitan Museum of Art; Mary Ison, Prints and Photographs Division, The Library of Congress; Jeff Place and Lori Elaine Taylor, Center for Folklife Programs and Cultural Studies, Smithsonian Institution; Lily Keiskes and Laveta Emory of the Freer and Arthur M. Sackler Galleries, Smithsonian Institution; Robert Lifson of the Field

Museum of Natural History, Chicago; Anita Jenkins, Eliot Elisofon Archives, National Museum of African Art, Smithsonian Institution; the Arizona Historical Society; Martha Lorantos, Music of the World; Yaleb Hachaichi, Office National du Tourisme Tunisien; Susan Wade Dewey and the Chicago Symphony Orchestra; Sarah Stoll and G. Leblanc Corporation; Peter Carrigan and the Australian Overseas Information Service; Larry Day and the University of Arizona Opera Workshop; Jim Griffith, Tucson Meet Yourself, and the Southwest Folklore Center, Tucson, Arizona, and David Burckhalter, Tucson photographer with a passion for capturing musicians. Special thanks is due David Belcheff, who created the maps used, and Alessandro Pezzati, Reference Archivist, of the University Museum, University of Pennsylvania, who was instrumental in providing photos and detailed captions as well. The clerical staff at the School of Music, especially Joe Swinson and Eileen VanKoughnet, were helpful and encouraging throughout this project, rejoicing when a chapter was completed or a photo obtained and always assisting however they could in special ways. Steve Crofts, long-time associate and friend at The University of Arizona, provided the final magic touch of organizing all materials, including photos, illustrations, and text, in camera-ready fashion.

Finally, my resident spouse, Shirley, and resident miniature pinscher, Peppin, helped me see the importance of "smelling the roses" often throughout the process, not allowing me to become too professorial, didactic, or obsessed by the project.

RECORDINGS FOR *MUSIC IN WORLD CULTURES*

Although there are no specific recordings to accompany this text, a discography follows each chapter. It is the intent that several examples from these lists be included in classroom presentation. In addition, one single compact disc is useful for individual student use:

> The Lyrichord World Music Sampler
> LYRCD 7414

This disc is available from:

> Lyrichord Discs Inc.
> 141 Perry Street
> New York, NY 10014
> Phone (212) 929-8234
> Fax (212) 929-8245

Selections are:

> Music from Bolivia
> Rhythms of Life (Zimbabwe)
> Ancient Egypt
> Calypsos (Costa Rica)
> "Far from the Land of Eagles" (Albania/Italy)
> "Soh Daiko" (Japanese Taiko Drums)
> Music of the Incas (Peru)
> Tibetan Ritual Music
> Ancient Art Music of China
> Australia
> Persian Love Songs (Iran)
> Japanese Masterpieces for the Shakuhachi
> The Kora and the Xylophone (West Africa)
> Korean Court Music
> Music of Bali—Gamelan Semar Pegulingan
> Solo Bansuri (India)
> Gypsy Passions: The Flamenco Guitar (Spain)

CHAPTER ONE

MUSIC OF ALL THE WORLD

Jazz, which is indigenous to American culture, is one type of world music. Miles Davis (1926-1991), jazz trumpeter. Courtesy of CBS Records.

Music of all the world is a large topic. It won't be covered here. This text will examine the music of several major cultures around the world, presenting structures and practices inherent in each. It will also highlight a few related cultures and suggest some readings and recordings that might be useful to gain an understanding of similarities and differences in all music the reader might encounter.

The symphony orchestra has been an important ensemble in European art music since the eighteenth century. Pictured are the woodwind section and violins of the Chicago Symphony Orchestra, Music Director-Daniel Barenboim. Photo by Jim Steere (1991). Courtesy of the Chicago Symphony Orchestra.

It is common for us to assume our music *is* the music of the world, that is, the art, folk, and popular music we hear, practice, and perform around us on the radio, cable TV, concert hall, or arena must also be the music heard in Japan, Singapore, Sri Lanka, and Lesotho. Although this music has spread to all regions of the earth as a type of cultural imperialism, it is not music of all the world. It is simply omnipresent. Long before European music left Lisbon, Paris, London, and Genoa, each region had its own music. Sometimes this music was a highly developed art form, standardized throughout a culture. Other times, it was folk-like, subject to change like much of society. In all cases, it represented certain ways of dealing with the structure and utility of organized sound, commonly defined as music, within a culture or region.

Before we begin to talk about structure and utility of music in China, Egypt, or Azerbaijan, it is well to re-examine the music of our own culture to review what we often take for granted. Any student who has begun the study of a foreign language ultimately asks the question: "How do we do it in English?" We know our native language so well, having mastered its syntax by rote at an early age, that we seldom think about its structure and utility. The way we speak and write often is intuitive. We don't think much about conjugations, declensions, idioms, and subject-verb agreement. We simply communicate. Only when faced with another system do we check out the validity and logic of our own. This also happens when students in a math class are suddenly faced

The gospel motivator is an important musician in African-American culture. Courtesy of the American Folklife Center, Smithsonian Institution, Photo No. 88-15071-25.

with the binary system of numbers. "How does it work in the decimal system?" By learning a new system, we also confirm and understand what we took for granted.

This process is no less true for the study of music of other cultures. There is nothing innately correct or perfect about our system of music, whether we consider its sound, organization, logic, or even notation. It works! But so do musical systems of other cultures. And the fascinating thing is that all systems work quite well. There is no inherent strength or weakness in any, only different solutions to the same problems. This is what this text is about.

Fittingly, then, we will first examine our own musical system as a point of reference for studying other cultures. This will provide questions which will be relevant throughout this text, including:

- What is the purpose or general cultural context of the music?
- How are musicians trained?
- What is the melodic structure?
- What is the rhythmic structure?
- What is the formal structure?
- What instruments are used? How?
- What is the role of singing?

In our own culture, whether American or European, music is used in a variety of ways. Let us consider several. Music is sometimes used purely for listening, that is, we turn the radio on or put a compact disk in our machine and then sit back and listen. What do we hear? Perhaps the music simply relaxes us because we enjoy the sound of the instruments, the vocal line, the words, the texture, and so on. Many listeners, particularly of popular music and jazz, simply enjoy the interpretation of a given performer. Such activity creates an ambience within our living environment that confirms us and improves our perceived quality of life.

Zubin Mehta, conductor, acknowledges Placido Domingo, tenor, following a moving performance. Courtesy of the New York Philharmonic.

Organized listening is the sole activity involved in going to a concert. In America and Europe, there are a variety of concerts we can attend. We go to opera, where a drama is played out in front of us with singing, acting, costuming, and staging. This usually occurs in a large theatre designed to stage such a production and includes the accompanying orchestra. Hundreds of people might attend, dressed somewhat formally to bring dignity and propriety to the perceived loftiness of the event. We can also attend a performance of a symphony orchestra, which presents more abstract music that relies less on story and drama, more on musical effect. Those who love opera because of its drama might not be attracted to purely orchestral music. To further enumerate similar experiences, we can attend solo voice or piano recitals, concerts of chamber music, or band concerts. Most all of these performances are regarded as peak musical experiences, requiring set dress, etiquette, and response to the music.

Opera requires listeners to accept certain conventions and customs. A performance of *The Impresario*, one-act opera by Mozart (1756-1791). Courtesy of Professor Larry Day, Western Ways Photo, and the University of Arizona Opera Workshop.

But concerts can also include jazz performances, whether in recital hall, night club, shopping mall, or street fair. Here, the atmosphere and attire are informal. The musicians might be dressed down and even talk or joke with their audience. There probably won't be a printed program delineating composer, composition, and opus number, but, rather, the pieces will be announced. People will respond more casually to the music, applauding after a good solo or clapping along with the beat of the music. At a rock concert, the involvement of the audience will reflect the nature of the music as well as the personality of the artists performing. People won't sit in their chairs, but will move around the auditorium (which is often an outdoor stadium), shouting, singing, waving, dancing, and generally interacting with the music in some hands-on manner. The audience doesn't need to have the pieces announced. They know all of these from cuts on the artists' albums.

Response to popular music is not as formal as with art music. Gladys Shelley, Nat King Cole, and Fred Astaire at a recording session. Courtesy of Ethel Gabriel

Jazz Opera

Symphony

Rock Chamber

Choir Night Club Lieder

Shopping Mall

These organized concerts, however, represent but a fraction of music in our lives where there is sharp focus on the sound, performers, and event itself. Music, however, pervades our every moment in much more subtle ways, ways we seldom even consciously recognize. Those who have religious affiliations find music is frequently an integral part of worship. Although this is not music purely for listening, it is certainly something we hear and in which we often participate, whether listening to a chancel choir deliver an anthem or singing a hymn-tune, folk-song, or chant ourselves, if only as response to a prayer. In Western culture, music has always been affiliated with religion. It is not surprising that much of the music of the Western world has some connection to religious practice, if only in its use of scales.

Then there is music which pervades our every waking minute--music on the clock radio, music on the car radio as we drive to work or classes, music in the bank building, dentist's office, restaurant, and, should we attend a film in the evening, music on the film track, or if we stay home and watch television, music on the tube. We never escape it. We'll probably fall to sleep to what the clock radio offers in the evening.

Worship

entertainment

Car radio

Clock Radio   Film Music

Concert

Television

Sporting Events

Theatre

What, then, is the utility of music in our culture? Certainly to enhance our aesthetic lives, but equally, to punctuate our day, call attention to products and services, relax as well as energize us, amuse us, make us part of a group, set the mood for visual images, remind us of something, as a background for exercise, genteel dining, or conversation, as ambience, and for no reason at all--just to provide an alternative to silence. It entertains, excites, elevates, and even annoys us. The utility of music is as pluralistic as the society from which it is derived.

Music entertains both performer and audience. Button accordion, a folk instrument. Courtesy of the American Folklife Center, Smithsonian Institution, Photo No. 91-15045-11.

We should not discount the omnipresence of music in almost every contact we have with electronic media, whether radio, television, or film. We sometimes listen passively, other times actively, and not at all occasionally. Music is omnipresent and multi-dimensional in our culture.

What is the role of musicians in European and American society? It depends what we mean by musician. Professional performers of art music play symphonic and chamber music on a regular basis in concert halls, music centers, and university campuses. We applaud them and admire their skill, but they hold no special place in society. After all, they have not been to outer space, have not discovered radium, atomic fusion, nor a cure for cancer. They are talented people who ply their craft well. The superstars of art music, those who attract a wide audience because of their charisma, stage presence, as much as their talent and musicianship, have a broader appeal and more name recognition. But society hardly values their contribution more than it does that of a philanthropist, professional athlete, entrepreneur, or film star. We watch them because of their compelling stage personalities and flamboyant technique.

The personality of the conductor is important to orchestral interpretation. Daniel Barenboim, Music Director of the Chicago Symphony Orchestra. Photo by Jim Steere. Courtesy of the Chicago Symphony Orchestra.

The same may be said of today's composer of art music. Their music may not be understood by concert audiences more attuned to music of the eighteenth and nineteenth centuries. They may be innovators without followers. They may be on the cutting edge of musical technology and development, but even sophisticated audiences will not rush to buy their products. They are rarely performed in public arenas.

The Grand Canyon Cowboy Band on the South Rim of the Canyon (1984). While working as cowboys and packers between the 1930s and 1950s, these men made extra pay by entertaining tourists in the canyonside hotels and on pack trips into the Canyon itself. Photo by Jim Griffith. Courtesy of the Southwest Folklore Center, Tucson, Arizona.

In more popular circles such as rock, jazz, or country-western, of course, performers are matinee idols, well known to their audiences because of astute marketing. Successful rock stars have to get radio stations to play their music. If enough do play it, success can come. Jazz performers have to play the clubs and festivals. Country-western singers have to convey some agony or joy with which their audience can identify. Much of it depends on luck and timing, not sheer talent, not to mention the "talk" shows to which one is invited. What we hear in the popular, rock, and jazz arena is often determined by the judgement of others--those who have a vested financial interest in the success of their music.

So the role of musician--performer, composer, and conductor--is rarely a highly regarded one in society. When great fame comes, it may be fleeting. Talent counts, but timing, exposure, and luck are frequently more important.

How are musicians trained in the Western world. Some music education occurs in public schools, particularly training in band and orchestral instruments as well as choral techniques. If one wants to learn guitar or piano, however, private instruction is necessary, as it is with orchestral instruments. The process begins early for some students and continues throughout their lifetime. Professional musicians often attend a university or conservatory to master their craft.

Performers often learn and master their craft in a university or conservatory. Student of string bass. Courtesy of the University of Arizona School of Music.

Rock and jazz musicians often have a more casual tuition. Jazz performers, to be certain, often master their technique and musicianship through formal instruction, often in a conservatory or university school of music. Many rock musicians, too, have some formal training, at least in the theoretical aspects of music. But for both, the real training comes through live interaction with other musicians, hearing, imitating, and mastering their craft through on-the-job training.

Since the training of Western musicians is as diverse as the music that results, some musicians learn to read music from written notation. Others develop a keen sense of hearing and play by ear. What characterizes each type of musician is difficult to assess since many performers and composers cross-over and do various types of music. A concert pianist may do jazz gigs in a nightclub and play keyboard in a rock group occasionally. Being a viable musician capable of making a living through performance requires one to develop a variety of skills and to perform a multitude of musical styles.

Street musicians in ninteenth-century America did not easily earn a living.
Courtesy of the Library of Congress Collections LCUSZ62: 11036.

All of this shows how pluralistic life has become in the Western world. We have many life styles, ideas, interests, aptitudes, and needs, and it is no wonder our music is so diverse. Most people become involved with only a few styles of music, however, ignoring many segments of music they do not understand or which do not interest them. We used to divide our music into "popular" and "classical", but these labels no longer apply. People follow Baroque chamber music, hard rock, cool jazz, Puccini operas, reggae, or new wave, but rarely all of it. Nonetheless, what unites our music is as important as what makes it different. Just as English has numerous dialects derived from the basic language, all of which can communicate at some level with the others, so too is our music derived from one common core. Pop culture's "The last time ever I saw your face" communicates as clearly as Shakespeare's "Shall I compare thee to a summer's day? Thou art more lovely and more temperate." Both are English and their sentiments are similar. Almost all Western music is premised on similar elements arranged in predictable ways. We will turn our attention to these so the reader can see what unites European and American music, not what divides it.

Melodic Structure: Scales

What do listeners remember about a musical selection? Most people would say the tune or melody. That's what is sung, if the piece is vocal, or at least remembered, if instrumental. Melody is what a composition is about--the main idea that is heard as foreground against supporting harmony and accompanying rhythm. If a composition is short, there may be only one melody. If the composition is long, there may be several melodies heard in succession. Significant melodies that unite a rather long composition are referred to as *themes*. Melody is something we hum, remember, and somehow store in our minds as the essence of a piece we find attractive. Rarely would a person awaken in night because they have a beat, timbre, or dynamic level going through their head. It's melody that makes us recall a certain musical selection.

Irving Berlin (1888-1989), American composer whose melodies are well known. Courtesy of the Library of Congress Collections LCUSZ62:37541.

What is peculiar about melody is that it is merely a succession of pitches we perceive as a unit. This unit has a syntax which is culturally inclusive, that is, in music of Europe and America, we have certain expectations how these melodies begin, grow, and end. This is largely because almost *all* melodies do about the same thing and are derived from the same source material, *scales*.

What is a scale? The simplest definition is a collection of pitches that are consistently arranged and become a catalog for creating melodies. Some definitions are in order for the reader to learn or review some basic concepts related to melody and scale. A good conceptual framework for discussing melody and its constituent structure is the keyboard:

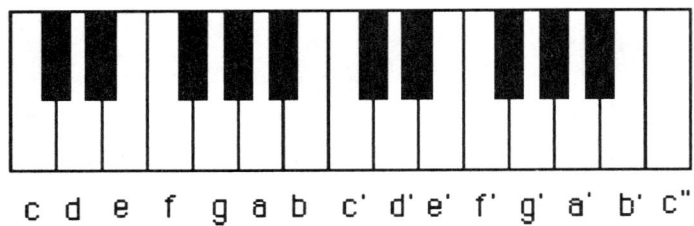

The pitches in Western notation are designated by letter names, a,b,c,d,e,f, and g, and then repeated both up and down the keyboard. These are given subscripts as well as upper-case letters to represent specific placement. c' indicates middle c, a pitch which vibrates c. 256 cps, as seen in this continuum:

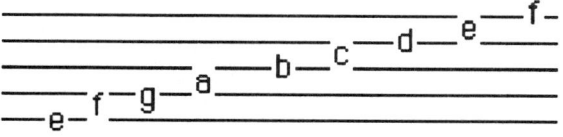

Between any two successive pitches of the same name, such as a to a', there is an *octave*, which means eight pitch names--a,b,c,d,e,f,g,a'--or seven different pitch names since the eighth is repetition of the beginning pitch. Thus, c' to c", B to b, d" to d', and AAA to AA are all octaves. Scales almost always are bound by an octave, that is, a scale begins and ends on a pitch of the same letter name.

Pitches and melodies are represented in notation by lines and spaces in a musical graph called a *staff*. It is typical to use a five-line, four-space staff, where each successive line or space represents the next higher pitch in sequence:

To standardize musical notation so it can be read easily and interpreted, certain positions of key pitches have evolved. These are identified by a *clef*, a musical symbol which identifies the position of either f, c', or g' on a staff.

The g clef, also called *treble* clef, is:

The f clef, *bass clef*, is:

The c clef may be used as:

or:

in which case it is referred to, respectively, as *alto clef* or *tenor clef*.

Referring back to the keyboard, there are additional pitches between many of the white keys which take their names from the basic letter designations. The black key between c and d is called c-sharp (♯) or d-flat (♭). Each black key similarly has a double designation used to show its function within a scale or composition. The smallest relationship or interval on a keyboard is called a *half-step*. There is a half-step between c and c♯, f and g♭, or b♭ and b. There is also a half-step between b and c as well as e and f, since half-step refers to the closest relationship possible. It is not a matter of black to white or white to black, but, rather, the closest pitch, either higher or lower, that is possible.

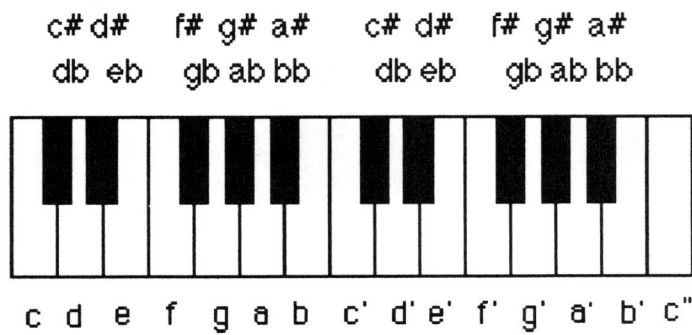

A *sharp* may then be defined as a pitch which is a half-step higher than a given pitch, a *flat*, a half-step lower. Half-steps are the *smallest* intervals we generally accept in Western music. In other words, country-western, rock, jazz, and art music generally do not use smaller intervals. Closely related to the half-step is the *whole-step*, which is simply two half-steps in the *same* direction, such as c to d, e to f♯, or a♭ to b♭.

Half-steps, whether sharps or flats, are notated on a staff by using the basic pitch name with the sharp (♯) or flat (♭) symbol. This may be placed before the actual note head or at the beginning of each staff line, in which case the aggregate sharps or flats are called the *key* signature.

Is it possible to hear intervals between pitches that are smaller than the half-step? Generally, yes, particularly in the middle of the audible frequency spectrum where our hearing is most acute. These pitches may sound "out-of-tune" to us, but only from our normal expectations. When a smaller interval is intended as part of a musical composition, whether Western or Eastern, it is certainly "in-tune". It is our ears that are out-of-tune!

Pitches which lie between half-steps are called *microtones*. When the half-step is evenly divided into two parts, each is called a *quarter-tone*. There is no standard way to indicate quarter-tones on staff notation, but many use this scheme:

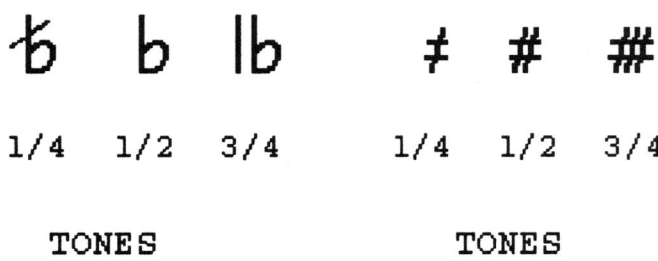

Many composers have invented their own system of indicating microtones when used with conventional Western notation. This necessitates that performers learn a new notation when they perform a composition requiring microtones. In music of the Middle East, India, or Asia, however, the tradition is aural. Notation is not as important for pitch since one learns to sound and interpret microtones, if not the entire melodic structure, by ear. When microtones are used in Western music, such as jazz, it is more in the nature of bending the pitch than sounding discrete tones which fall in the crack of our half-step system.

Although one cannot always discern pitches which lie between half-steps, it is important for having a mechanism to discuss microtones. This is accomplished by the *cent*, a unit which theoretically describes microtones as well as larger intervals. There are 1200 cents in an octave, 100 in a half-step.

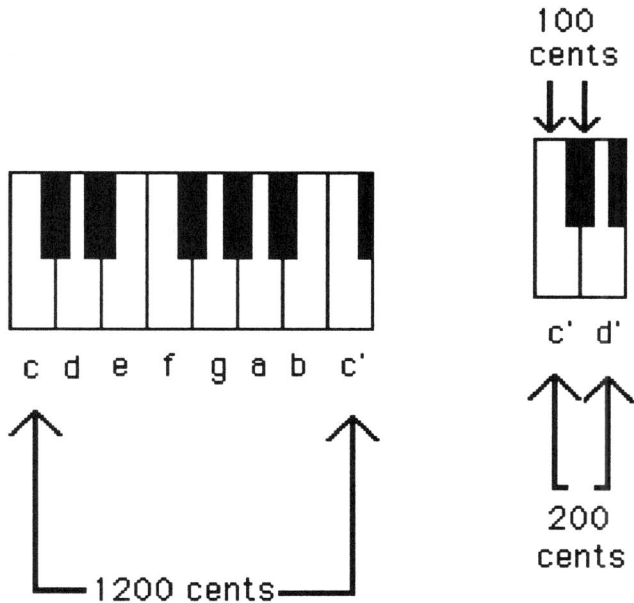

A quarter-tone is thus 50 cents, an *eighth-tone*, 25. It is not logical to use cents to describe large intervals, like the octave, but they are useful for intervals smaller than the half-step as well as those which do not clearly articulate with Western pitches. It is much like measuring distances with inches, feet, and miles. Cents are like inches, half- and whole-steps like feet, and octaves like miles. Each has a place when describing melodic structure. In melodies of European and American music, however, half- and whole-steps are an appropriate measurement.

After this lengthy discussion to provide vocabulary, we now return to the issue of scales. Most of our melodies are derived from two scales, *major* and *minor*. Each is bound by an octave and uses seven different pitch names. A scale which uses seven distinct pitches is called *heptatonic*. In addition, both major and minor have established successions of pitches which result in a basic scale with two half-steps and five whole-steps. Because of these relationships, it is typical that both major and minor use pitch names in sequence, with sharp or flat modification, that is a is followed by some version of b, b by some version of c, and so on. This structure is called *diatonic*. We can therefore say major and minor scales use five whole-steps, two half-steps, and are both diatonic and heptatonic.

Major scales are constructed in the following pattern:

1 1 1/2 1 1 1 1/2

Therefore, a major scale can be based on any pitch, including these:

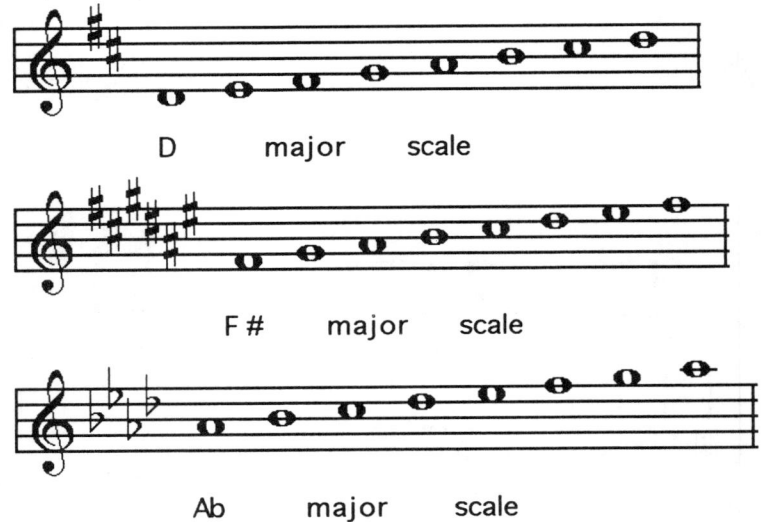

The initial pitch of a scale is called its *tonic*. For each tonic, there is a unique combination of either flats or sharps which are used to create the half- and whole-steps relationships. Only a major scale on c has neither flats nor sharps.

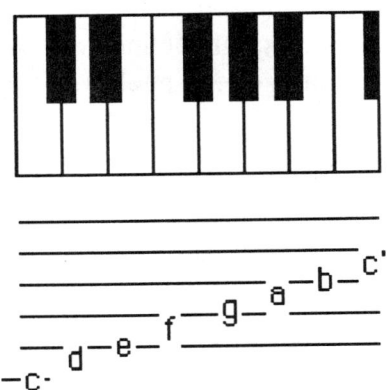

18

Since the combination of flats or sharps is consistent for every major scale, these are reflected in key signature. Each key signature identifies a specific tonic:

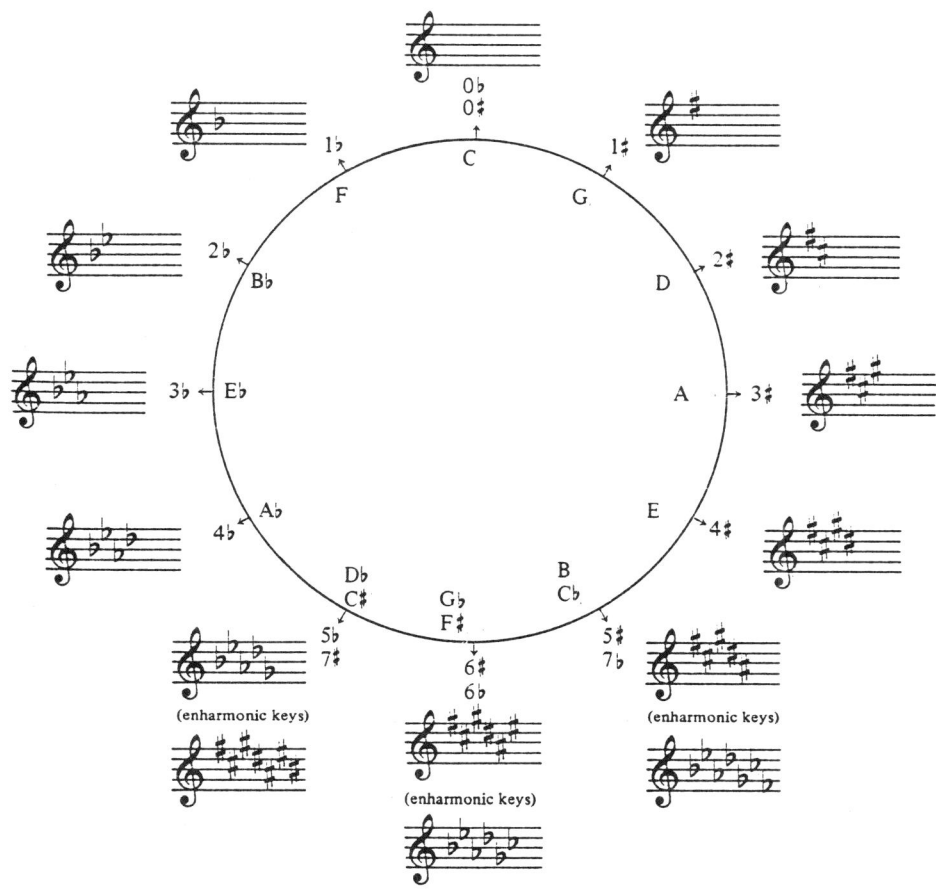

How do composers deal with scales? Undoubtedly, a composer first hears a melody and then notates it as part of a musical composition. The inherent relationships in the melody, particularly its beginning and ending pitch as well as intervals between successive pitches, will determine the scale on which it is based. This example:

clearly is based on this scale:

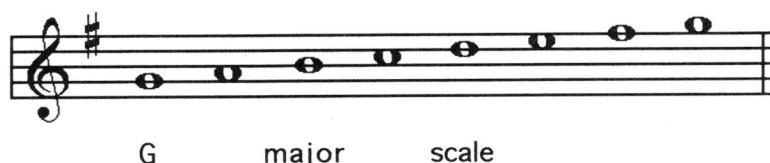

G major scale

Composers, however, are not so much concerned with scales as with writing attractive and memorable melodies. They may not even consciously discern the scale, but, rather, deal with the melodic material more intuitively. Most of us, when we speak or write, worry little about sentence structure. We intuitively know we need a subject and verb. Only when we stop to construct a sentence in a particular way might we become aware of sentence structure. Similarly, the composer will probably not consciously worry about scales and key signatures unless there is some reason to.

Minor scales are similar to major except they are used in various forms or *species*. The basic minor scale, which is diatonic and uses five whole- and two half-steps, is called the *natural minor scale*:

1 1/2 1 1 1/2 1 1

Here are several examples of the natural minor scale on different tonics:

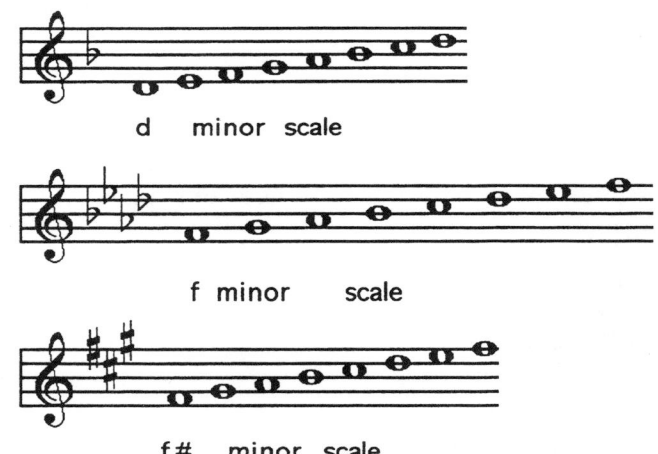

d minor scale

f minor scale

f# minor scale

As with the major, each natural minor scale has a given key signature for each tonic. Since these are the same key signatures used for majors, a major and minor are considered *relative keys* when they have the same key signature. These are:

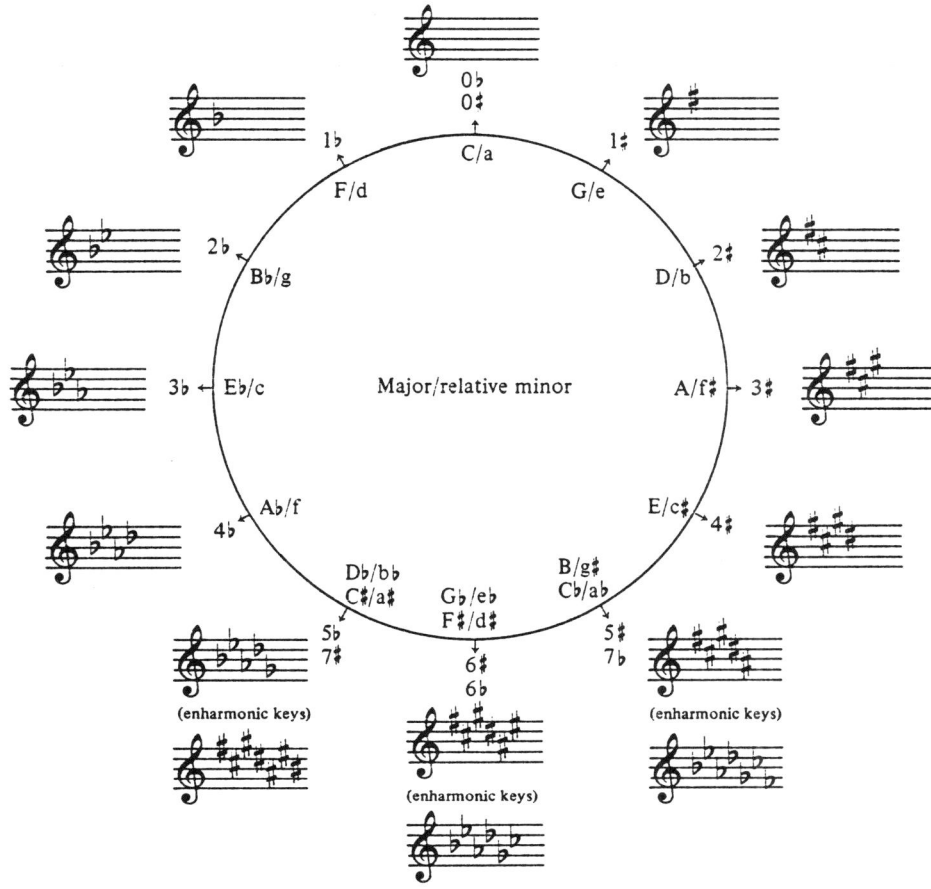

When one knows the major, the relative natural minor is determined by going to the major's sixth pitch, which becomes the tonic for the minor:

Conversely, when one knows the natural minor, the relative major is determined by going to the minor's third pitch, which becomes the tonic for the major:

The natural minor, however, is only one species of that type of scale. The *harmonic minor scale* has a slight modification which appears as an accidental (outside of the key signature) whenever it is used. The seventh pitch of the natural minor is raised a half-step:

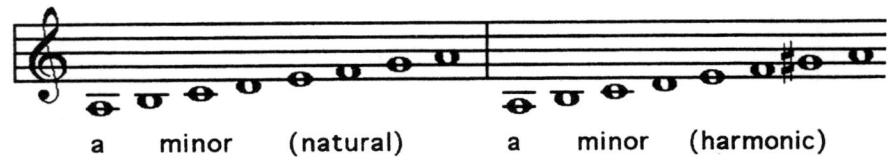

a   minor   (natural)   a   minor   (harmonic)

This does not change the basic key signature, however, since the chromatic alteration only appears as an accidental within a composition. The concept of relative majors and minors still applies, which means the key signatures above apply whether the minor scale is natural or harmonic. The harmonic minor scale is used in Western art music to create a stronger feeling of *tonality* in a composition since, by altering the seventh pitch upwards, a half-step relationship is created between it and the tonic, much like the major.

1 1/2 1 1 1/2 1 1/2 1/2

The natural minor scale is found more frequently in folk music. In either case, the composer probably responds intuitively to the scale, first hearing and notating a melody, and then deciding where it fits into the scheme of minor scales and key signatures.

The third minor scale, the *melodic minor*, is occasionally found in music. As with the harmonic minor, it has chromatic alterations which appear outside the key signature as accidentals. The sixth and seventh pitches are raised a half-step when the melody progresses upward, but are the same as the natural minor when the melody descends:

ascending

1 1/2 1 1 1 1 1/2

descending

1 1 1/2 1 1 1/2 1*

(*same as natural minor)

These are all examples of the melodic minor:

a minor (melodic)

These upward alterations are much like melodic ornaments that allow for smooth voice leading. Composers undoubtedly treat them intuitively more than consciously, as in this example:

Although major and minor scales are the basic materials from which composers derive their melodic ideas, they are certainly not the only possibilities. Major and minor, which are part of our system of tonality, have been around since the seventeenth century. Before then, *modality* was used, that is, the scales were called *modes*. Each mode, however, was diatonic and used five whole- and two-half steps. The modes are:

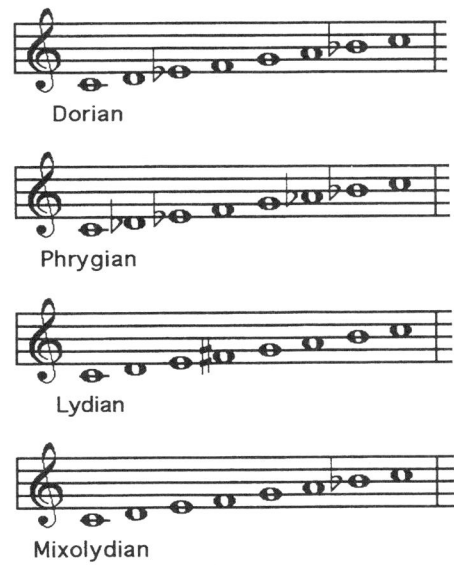

Although modality phased out in the Renaissance and Baroque periods of Western music, tonality phased in, twentieth-century composers have occasionally re-visited the church modes as a source of melodic material.

Similarly, composers of recent times have sometimes tired of major and minor, seeking new catalogs of pitches and relationships which could be used as a basis for melodies and themes. Among these scales is the *whole-tone scale*, which is *hexatonic*, that is, six-toned. Each successive pitch is separated by a whole-tone from its neighbor:

Whole - tone   scale

The *pentatonic*, five-toned scale, has been used too:

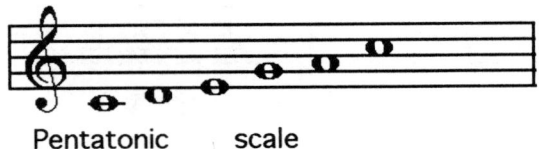
Pentatonic   scale

as well as the *chromatic* or half-step scale:

Chromatic   scale

The chromatic scale, however, has been a source for additional pitches to ornament a basic diatonic melody rather than as an independent structure. It has also supplied the basic pitches for *dodecaphonic* music, that is, twelve-tone music, which establishes a set ordering of the pitches as the basic melodic structure in a composition.

Although modes, whole-tone, pentatonic, and chromatic scales are used, the basis of Western music has remained *tonal*, major and minor for the past three hundred years. Major and minor provide sufficient means to structure melodies, particularly since a composer can move from one scale to another in one composition or movement, which is termed *modulation*. Using scales as a structural component of music is basic to European music theory, providing foundation not only of melody but harmony as well. Harmony is a rather unique phenomenon of music, found largely in Western music. It will be discussed it its own section.

Harmonic Structure: Chords and Texture

Harmony is an element which occurs by intent and preference in Western music. Although Gregorian chant, a monophonic style of liturgical singing, is the root of our heritage, harmony emerged around A.D. 1000 and has been part of our organized sound structure ever since. This is not to suggest we are the only culture which has harmony, only that this element is so integral to our musical thinking and sound ideal that it is difficult to imagine music *without* harmony. We have codified harmonic practice and often create our melodies to articulate with harmony. It is simply omnipresent in our musical structure. Other cultures may have harmony, but it is usually incidental to musical practice. In our culture, it is integral.

Harmony on the bagpipe occurs through the drone pipes. Courtesy of the American Folklife Center, Smithsonian Institution, Photo No. 88-15243-36.

What is harmony and how is it organized in Western culture? Harmony is defined as the simultaneous sound of two or more *different* pitches. Two pitches together make an *interval*, three or more a *chord*. Understanding intervals helps us understand chords.

Although half- and whole-steps are basic intervals, these units are insufficient for measuring large distances in melody or harmony. We therefore use a *numerical designation* for intervals. This is generally determined by counting the distance between (but including) the two pitches to be measured. C to c is an *octave* because it includes c, d, e, f, g, a, b and c, a total of eight pitch names.

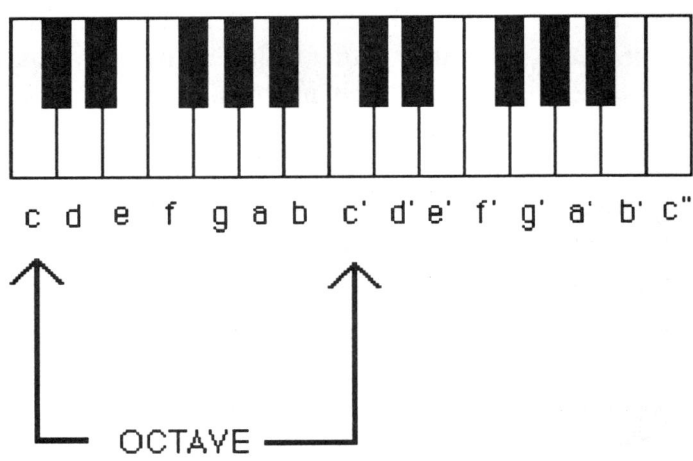

Similarly, intervals smaller than the octave are designated:

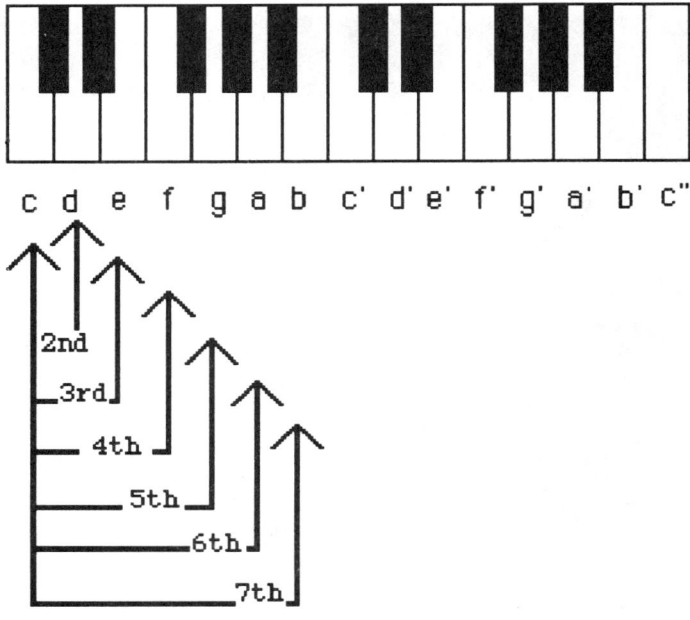

and those larger than the octave:

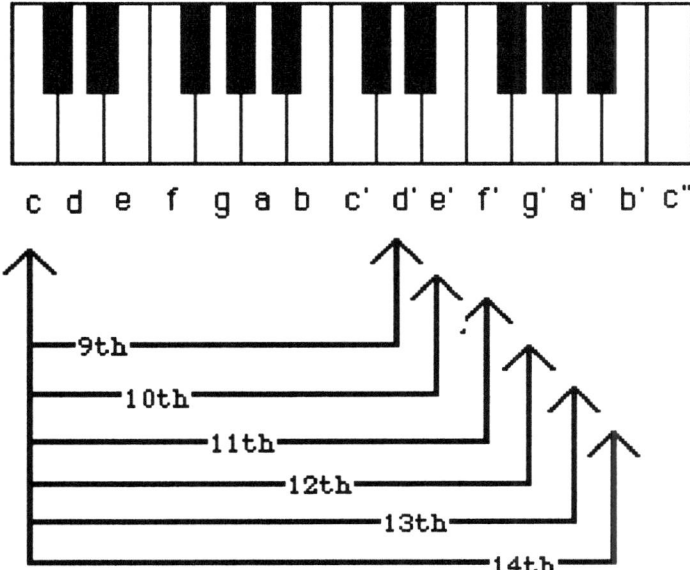

We rarely designate intervals which are larger than a double-octave (15va), but simply say "three octaves plus a third" to measure these large distances.

One can easily see this does not accommodate sharps and flats. This is because the numerical distance is only a rough measurement that is refined by adding a *qualitative designation* to an interval. The distance between c and e as well as c to e♭ is numerically a *third* in both cases. The former, however, is a *major third* (larger third), the latter, a *minor third* (smaller third).

Seconds, thirds, sixths, and sevenths are used in both major and minor sizes. Fourths and fifths, however, are called *perfect* in their most common use, rather than major or minor:

When a perfect or major interval is enlarged by a half-step, it is called *augmented*:

Conversely, when a perfect or minor interval is decreased by a half-step, it is called *diminished*:

All of these designations show how abstruse the discussion of intervals can be, which perhaps shows how studied and codified our entire element of harmony has become. However, intervals are the building blocks of chords and are therefore necessary to comprehend before we can talk about chords.

A chord is simply three or more pitches sounded together as a unit, usually in a way that is pleasing in sound. In Western culture, the interval of the third has become the constituent unit for chord building. This type of harmony is called *tertian*, which means, build in thirds. The basic chord has three pitches and is called a *triad*.

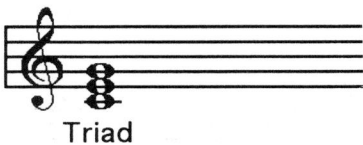

Triads are so basic to Western harmony that terminology has developed which describes each pitch. The pitch which is the foundation of the triad is called the *root*, the second pitch which is third higher than the root, the *third*, and the third pitch which is a fifth higher than the root, the *fifth*. Third and fifth thus describe the interval between the designated pitch and the root.

Although triads are basic to our harmonic practice, not any triad will do. These must clearly be related to the scale which encompasses the pitches of a melody in order for the harmony and melody to work well together. The structural pitches of a scale are its *tonic* (1) as well as its *dominant* (5) and *subdominant* (4). This is true, however, only for diatonic scales, that is, major and minor:

Therefore, the structural triads are those which use either the tonic, dominant, or subdominant as their root:

These are then referred to as the tonic (I), dominant (V), or subdominant (IV) triads. As harmonic practice evolved, composers treated the dominant chord slightly differently. To create more harmonic tension, which is described by the term *dissonance*, a fourth pitch was added to the dominant triad. This pitch was a third higher than the fifth and is known as the *seventh*, since it creates the interval of a seventh with the chord's root. The added pitch, of course, changes the dominant triad to a *dominant seventh* chord, which is designated as V7. This is the typical manifestation of most dominant chords.

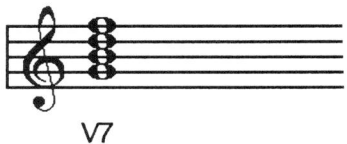

The I, IV, and V7 chords, whether derived from major or minor, are the backbones of harmonic structure, defining the *tonality* or key center of a composition.

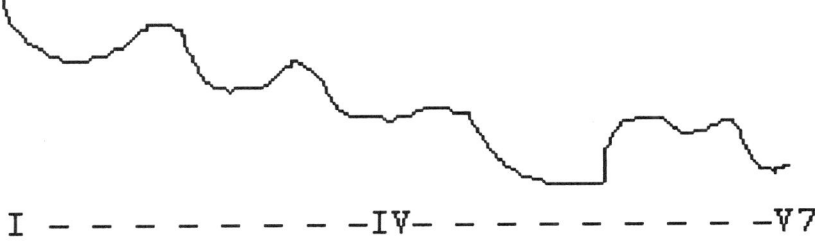

A short composition might remain in one tonality, a longer composition may change from one tonality to another as part of the musical structure. Changing tonality within a composition is called *modulation*. Modulation, particularly in compositions of any length, is a Western phenomenon. A symphony, for example, in C major, undoubtedly will begin and end in C major, but it may modulate to other major and minor keys throughout. Modulation provides contrast between and within the movements of a lengthy composition.

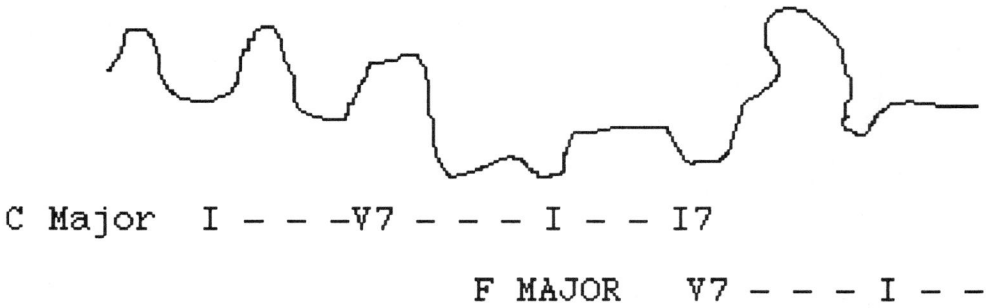

The consistency of major and minor scales and the harmony they generate, as described above, provide ample resources for Western composers to provide excitement and variety within compositions while maintaining a stable structural environment.

Since melody and harmony work together as part of our musical practice, there are established ways to describe how they articulate. This is generally referred to as *texture*, that is, the way melody and harmony work together. *Monophony* is a texture which is pure melody without supporting harmony.

A pure melody, however, if based on major or minor, may nonetheless suggest or outline harmony, so it is not necessarily devoid of harmonic content. *Homophony* is one melody supported by accompanying harmony:

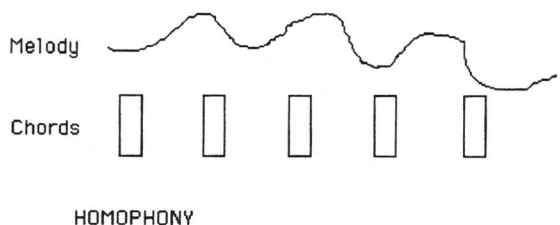

Polyphony is several melodies blending together to create harmony:

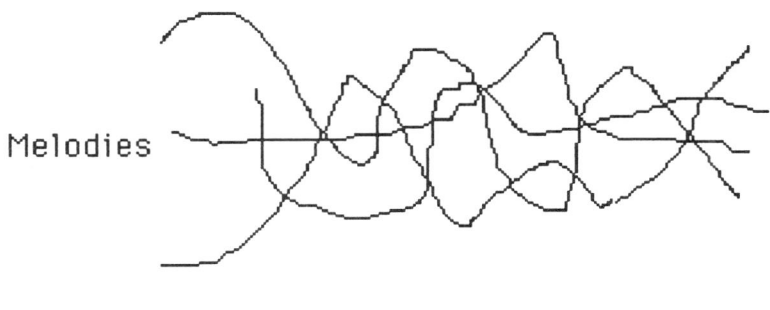

Although all three textures are used in Western music, homophony and polyphony are the most common.

Rhythmic Structure: Beat and Meter

The rhythmic structure of Western music is based on *beat*, an impulse that is regularly spaced throughout a composition, whether audible or inaudible. We measure musical events, particularly the flow of melody and harmony, against this consistent flow of beats.

When the beat is audible, it may be played by string bass, bass drum, tuba, or the pianist's left hand. Although this occurs, in art music it is more typical for the beat to be inaudible, felt but not heard. In either case, beat is the temporal device that measures musical events. *Tempo* in music is our perception of the spacing of the beat. The more frequent the beat, that is, the more that occur within a time span, such as a minute, the faster the tempo we associate with a composition:

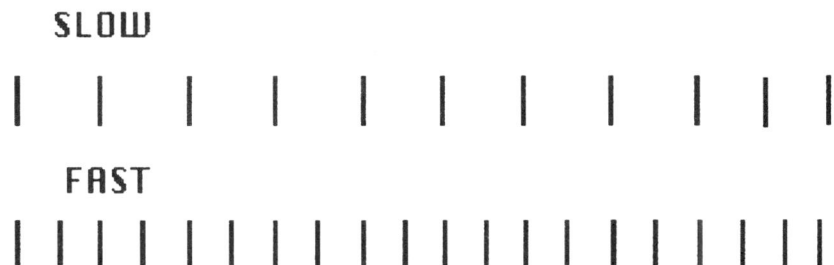

The beat can be suspended in a composition, that is, it may be performed *senza battuta*, without beat. This results in freer structuring of musical events, such as an improvisatory-like passage for instruments or recitative for voice. This, however, is only to provide contrast with sections in which the beat does occur.

The reliance on beat to structure musical events in Western music is easy to understand. The way the beats are stressed, however, provides additional structure. Our system of rhythm is *metric*, which means, beats are organized into a series where some are stressed, others, unstressed. *Accented beat* refers to these recurrences. *Duple time* is a stressed beat followed by an unstressed one:

DUPLE TIME

Triple is one stressed, two unstressed:

TRIPLE TIME

Quadruple is one stressed, three unstressed:

QUADRUPLE TIME

These are basic accent groupings which occur in a great deal of Western music. When accented beats are notated, they are reflected as *meter signatures*. Two-four ($\frac{2}{4}$) time means duple using the quarter note (♩) as the beat, three-four ($\frac{3}{4}$) means triple using the quarter note as the beat, four-two ($\frac{4}{2}$) means quadruple using the half note as the beat. These are typical meter signatures:

$$\frac{2}{4} \qquad \frac{3}{4} \qquad \frac{4}{4} \qquad \frac{6}{8} \qquad \frac{9}{8} \qquad \frac{12}{8}$$

In addition, composers sometimes use *asymmetric meters*, those which are not symmetrically arranged, including:

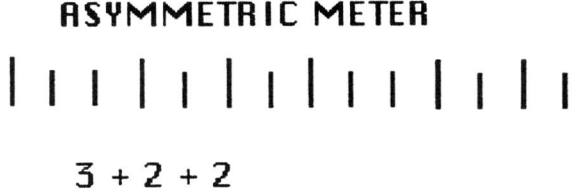

as well as *mixed meters*, where the accent grouping frequently changes:

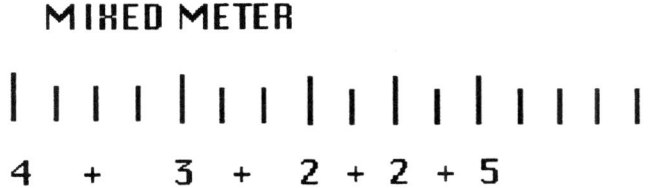

In both of these cases, however, it is not the basic beat which changes, only the way it is grouped. For a great deal of Western music, however, duple, triple, or quadruple time are typical.

Formal Structure: Unity and Variety

When music is vocal, words often unify a composition, providing focus and interest for listeners. When music is instrumental, however, ideas must be presented coherently and logically so that listeners can follow musical thought and development. In Western music, we often contrast *program* with *absolute* music. Program music, whether vocal or instrumental, has an extra-musical reference. When lyrics are included, such as in opera, oratorio, cantata, or lieder, words suggest a mood, convey an emotion, or simply tell a story. Although composers use musical elements to reinforce lyrics, without words, the extra-musical references can only be suggested.

Instrumental music can be programmatic too, suggesting a story or somehow conveying a visual image through title, themes, and organization. Without words, however, these references must be inferred. Music is not best at conveying stories and impressions since its dimension is aural, not verbal. Absolute music therefore has no extra-musical reference, relying on musical ideas purely to hold listeners' attention. Since all music, whether program or absolute, needs to have basic musical interest, we will discuss form as a musical phenomenon, devoid of lyrics.

Siamese dancers (Bangkok). Music for dance is usually programmatic. This dancing is governed entirely by tradition and the movements are learned from carvings of dancers on ancient temples. Photo by Baron Rodolphe Meyer de Schauensee. Courtesy of The University Museum, University of Pennsylvania, Neg. No. S4-14072.

Form operates on two levels, *micro-form* and *macro-form*. Micro-form refers to basic organization of music, beginning with the smallest unit of meaning, the *motive*. A motive is a small group of pitches or durations that are used as building block in a *phrase*.

In organizing musical material, phrases may be paired into a *period*, which is two phrases, the first called *antecedent*, the second, *consequent*. These are like question and answer, sometimes being similar to one another, other times, being different. The way a phrase ends, that is, whether it sounds rather incomplete or rather final, determines whether it is antecedent or consequent. The antecedent is often punctuated with an *incomplete cadence*, the consequent with a *complete cadence*.

ANTECEDENT

CONSEQUENT

Although there are various ways in which cadences may occur, it is typical for incomplete cadences to end on a chord other than the tonic (I) while complete cadences end on the tonic.

A larger section of music is often constructed of various phrases using a basic musical idea recognizable to listeners. This does not imply that all phrases are the same length nor that all are paired as periods, only that the basic building blocks of music are frequently the motive and phrase. When a melody becomes significant, it can be considered a *theme*, and most sections of music are somehow unified by a recognizable theme.

If a composition is short, such as a folk-tune or hymn-song, a few phrases may be all that it contains, using one theme.

However, if the piece is longer, additional themes may be used to provide contrast and maintain interest throughout. A composition does not need many themes to be enjoyable; rather, most composers have found that two or three are sufficient, particularly if they are used to provide unity and variety in an entire composition or even a single movement.

When we discuss form within a movement or in a multimovement composition, such as a sonata, we are examining macro-form. Musical ideas are often designated by a letter name in the order in which they occur. ABA, for example, means a composition has three sections with two basic ideas. The final section simply repeats the first. This is called *return* form, since there is a review or summary of the first idea, theme, or section at the end of the composition. It is well to remember that each section, A or B, probably consists of several phrases, demonstrating how micro- and macro-form both provide unity and variety within a composition:

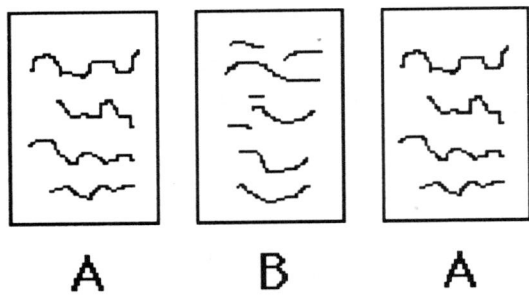

Return form includes all of the following schemes:

> ABABA
> ABACA
> ABACABA
> ABCDA
> ABACADABA

This is a useful way to organize musical ideas logically. Return forms are usually known by proper names, not merely a series of letters, and include rondo, minuet and trio, song form, and sonata-allegro form.

Another way to organize musical ideas is to maintain *one* idea, but slightly vary it upon each recurrence. This is called *processive form* and results in this type of scheme:

> A A1 A2 A3 . . .An

Processive form is often called *theme and variations* as well as other specific titles including divisions, passacaglia, and chaconne. Jazz improvisation is processive form that is created on the spot, without notation.

Although return and processive forms are the most popular types of macro-form in Western music, there are also *strophic* and *additive* form. Strophic is simply the repetition of the same idea over and over:

> AAAAA...A

It holds little interest in purely instrumental music but is frequently used in vocal music. The term "strophe" means a verse or stanza in poetry. When this type of poetry is set to music, as it may be in lieder or hymn-tunes, strophic form is often used. One stanza of music is used to support all stanzas of the lyrics, that is, we have one song with multiple verses.

Additive form simply means new ideas are continually introduced without repetition or variation:

> ABCDEF....

This may be found in Gregorian chant as well as avant garde compositions in which repetition is not important. The interest for listeners may simply be in the continual unfolding of new ideas with neither repetition nor variation. Like basic plots in a novel or play, however, return, processive, strophic, and additive provide sufficient plans for organizing musical compositions in most Western music.

Instruments of the Western World

There are only four ways sound can be made on acoustic instruments, whether the culture under consideration is East or West: strings; air column; drumhead; or self-vibration. There are therefore only four categories for classifying all the instruments of the world.

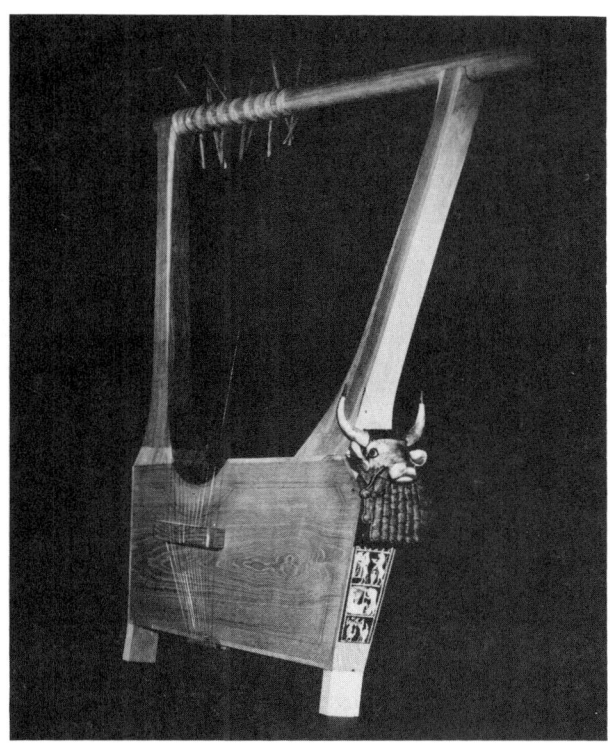

Ur (Iraq) bull-headed lyre (c. 2650-2550 B.C.) from Mesopotamia. This ancient chordophone was discovered in the death pit. The head is gold with lapis lazuli beard. Courtesy of The University Museum, University of Pennsylvania, Neg. No. S8-139328.

Those instruments which have an inherent sound when they are struck, scraped, rubbed, shaken, or stamped are called *idiophones* or self-vibrators. Those with a head made of animal skin or plastic are *membranophones*. Those which sound when a string is set into vibration are *chordophones* and those whose sound production depends on a vibrating air column are *aerophones*. In addition, the term *electrophone* describes instruments which depend on electrical energy for some or all or their sound production.

Western instruments are usually mass-produced in factories. Courtesy of G. Leblanc Corporation, Kenosha, Wisconsin USA.

Many instruments of the world are hand-crafted. Long drum, Chiang Mai, Thailand. Courtesy of © David Burckhalter (1989).

In the Western world, we group instruments more specifically by families, particularly in the orchestra, where instruments are classified as strings, brass, woodwinds, or percussion. The following shows both classification schemes:

CHORDOPHONES	AEROPHONES
String Family	*Brass Family*
'Cello	Baritone Tuba (Euphonium)
Banjo	Bass Tuba
Bass	French horn
Guitar	Trombone
Harp	Trumpet
Harpsichord	
Lute	*Woodwind Family*
Piano	Bassoon and contrabassoon
Ukulele	Clarinet
Viola	Flute and piccolo
Violin	Oboe and English horn
IDIOPHONES	Saxophone
Percussion Family	
Celesta	*Others*
Cymbals	Mellophone
Glockenspiel	Pipe organ
Gong (Tam tam)	Recorder
Maracas	**MEMBRANOPHONES**
Marimba	*Percussion Family*
Tambourine	Bass Drum
Tubular Chimes	Snare Drum
Vibraphone	Tambourine
Xylophone	Timpani
ELECTROPHONES	
Electronic pick-up	
Electronic organ	
Keyboard	
Synthesizer	

As we shall observe in all cultures, the melody and harmonic systems are reflected in the instruments of music. Our Western instruments are tuned to play half- and whole-steps, the same intervals used in melody and harmony. Keyboard instruments divide the octave into half-steps. Frets on a guitar are similarly arranged to sound half-steps. The harp uses a pedal mechanism to alter pitches by half-steps. Only in unfretted instruments, such as the string family, or an instrument which can sound variable pitch, such as the trombone, can microtones be played. Although lipping allows pitches to be aimed slightly higher or lower on all woodwinds and brass, they are also locked into the chromatic division of the octave.

Unlike our major and minor scales, the Burmese scale has seven equidistant pitches. Courtesy of The University Museum, University of Pennsylvania, Neg. No. S4-140744.

Singing in Western Culture

Greek singer with lauouto (lute), a chordophone which has four double courses. Courtesy of the American Folklife Center, Smithsonian Institution, Photo No. 88-15143-2.

Singing in Western culture cannot easily be delineated nor categorized. There are so many styles of singing, from the gentle, reedy sound of a folk singer to the raucous voices of rock, from the twang of a country-western star to the full resonance of an opera diva. Probably the only thing that unites these diverse vocal categories is that they, too, follow intervals associated with Western music, that is, half- and whole-steps. We generally do not accept voices that sing in the "cracks", at least on sustained, important tones of a melody. This does not mean that approaches to these pitches do not use microtones. In jazz, for example, it is common for singers to use *note bending*, particularly in moving from one important melodic note to the next, but once arriving, the pitch is expected to be sustained on a tone "in-tune" with our perception of pitch. Instruments of jazz similarly bend pitches for special effect. Even some operatic arias require *portamento*, gliding over pitches within an interval, to project the traditional style. Vocal inflections of rock are as varied as the artists who sing.

Performance by Figaro from Mozart's *The Marriage of Figaro*.
Courtesy of Professor Larry Day, Western Ways Photo,
and the University of Arizona Opera Workshop.

Although vocal qualities are difficult to categorize, we can identify basic *ranges* of the human voice. The highest voice, usually sung by women, is *soprano*, the lower female voice, *alto* or *contralto*. Male voices include the higher *tenor* and the lower *bass*. Although these voices suggest a certain quality, whether bright, nasal, or throaty, they are a convenient way to discuss voices in all music. There is a marked tendency in all cultures for instruments to model the human voice. If vocal production in a society, such as our classical vocal technique, focuses on sounding and sustaining clear, unwavering pitches, instruments associated with the same style will do the same. If pitch bending is indigenous, as in jazz, we will undoubtedly find saxophones and trumpets which accompany such singing to be similar. Nasality in a country-western singer's

Performance by I. K. Dairo, M.B.E.
Courtesy of Rakumi Records and Music of the World.

voice may be mirrored on a steel guitar. We will find that those cultures outside of Western music in which vocal quality is extremely nasal and vocal technique allows sliding between pitches will have instruments which do the same. After all, instruments are an extension of the human voice, undoubtedly the most basic, primeval instrument. Our technology, including musical instruments, simply extend our bodies, mirroring the societal norm.

Key Terms and Concepts

- Absolute music
- Accented beat
- Additive form
- Aerophone
- Alto (contralto)
- Alto (c') clef
- Antecedent
- Asymmetric meter
- Augmented
- Bass
- Bass (f) clef
- Beat
- Cent
- Chord
- Chordophone
- Chromatic
- Clef
- Complete cadence
- Consequent
- Contralto (alto)
- Diatonic
- Diminished
- Dissonance
- Dodecaphonic
- Dominant
- Dominant seventh chord (V7)
- Dorian
- Duple time
- Eighth-tone
- Electrophone
- Fifth
- Flat (♭)
- Half-step
- Harmonic minor
- Heptatonic
- Hexatonic
- Homophony
- Idiophone
- Incomplete cadence
- Interval
- Key signature
- Lydian
- Macro-form
- Major
- Major third
- Melodic minor
- Membranophone
- Meter signature
- Metric
- Micro-form
- Microtone
- Minor
- Minor third
- Mixed meter
- Mixolydian
- Modality
- Mode
- Modulation
- Monophony
- Motive
- Natural minor
- Note-bending
- Numerical designation
- Octave
- Pentatonic
- Perfect
- Period
- Phrase
- Phrygian
- Polyphony
- Portamento
- Processive form
- Program music
- Quadruple time
- Qualitative designation
- Quarter-tone
- Range
- Relative keys
- Return form
- Root
- Scale
- Senza battuta
- Seventh
- Sharp (♯)
- Soprano
- Species
- Staff
- Strophic form
- Subdominant
- Subdominant chord (IV)
- Tempo
- Tenor
- Tenor (c') clef
- Tertian
- Texture
- Theme
- Theme and variations
- Third
- Tonal
- Tonality
- Tonic
- Tonic chord (I)
- Treble (g') clef
- Triad
- Triadic
- Triple time
- Whole-step
- Whole-tone scale

Self-checking Chapter Review

Match Column II to Column I	
Column I	**Column II**
1. polyphony 2. scale 3. tertian 4. diatonic 5. aerophone 6. clef 7. hexatonic 8. modulation 9. whole-step 10. program music 11. tempo 12 triad 13. motive 14. idiophone 15. homophony	A. Music with extra-musical ideas, including stories or images B. Smallest unit of music meaning C. Catalog of pitches D. Self-vibrator E. Based on thirds F. Speed of the beat G. Uses pitches in sequence and has two half-steps and five whole-steps H. Two or more melodies interact to create harmony I. Produced through wind pressure J. Distance between C and D K. A chord with three tones built on thirds L. Six-pitched scales M. Changing scales or tonality N. Melody with supporting harmonic accompaniment O. Notational device for identifying pitches on a staff

Answers			
1.	H	9.	J
2.	C	10.	A
3.	E	11.	F
4.	G	12.	K
5.	I	13.	B
6.	O	14.	D
7.	L	15.	N
8.	M		

Selected Bibliography

Boyd, Jack (1991). *Encore! A Guide to Enjoying Music*. Mountain View, CA: Mayfield Publishing Company.

Danziger, Robert (1991). *The Revelation of Music: Learning to Love the Classics*. New Haven: Jordan Press.

Ferris, Jean (1991). *Music: The Art of Listening* (Third Edition). Dubuque, Iowa: Wm. C. Brown, Publishers.

Hoffer, Charles R. (1992). *A Concise Introduction to Music Listening* (Fifth Edition). Belmont, CA: Wadsworth Publishing Company.

Kamien, Roger (1988). *Music: An Appreciation* (Fourth Edition). New York: McGraw-Hill Book Company.

Machlis, Joseph (with Kristine Forney) (1990). *The Enjoyment of Music* (Sixth Edition). New York: W. W. Norton & Company.

May, Elizabeth (ed.) (1980). *Music of Many Cultures: An Introduction*. Los Angeles: University of California Press.

Nettl, Bruno, Charles Capwell, Isabel K. F. Wong, Thomas Turino, and Philip V. Bohlman (1992). *Excursions in World Music*. Englewood Cliffs: Prentice-Hall, Inc.

O'Brien, James P. (1987). *The Listening Experience: Elements, Forms, and Styles in Music*. New York: Schirmer Books.

Pen, Ronald (1992). *Introduction to Music*. New York: McGraw-Hill Book Company.

Politoske, Daniel T. (1992). *Music* (Fifth Edition). Englewood Cliffs, NJ: Prentice-Hall, Inc.

Sadie, Stanley (with Alison Latham) (1987). *Brief Guide to Music*. Englewood Cliffs, NJ: Prentice-Hall, Inc.

Seaton, Douglass (1991). *Ideas and Styles in the Western Musical Tradition*. Mountain View, CA: Mayfield Publishing Company.

Titon, Jeff Todd, James T. Koetting, David P. McAllester, David B. Beck, and Mark Slobin (1984). *Worlds of Music: An Introduction to the Music of the World's People*. New York: Schirmer Books.

Zorn, Jay D. (1991). *Listening to Music*. Englewood Cliffs, NJ: Prentice-Hall, Inc.

Selected Discography

Companion Recordings for *The European Musical Heritage*
(Sarah Fuller) Alfred A. Knopf, Inc.

Man's Early Musical Instruments
Folkways Records FE 4525

Musical Atlas (Sampler)
Odeon (EMI) C048-17838

Mustaphas: Soup of the Century
Rykodisc RCD 10195

Norton Anthology of Western Music (2nd ed.)
CBS Records, Inc.
CBS Special Products

CHAPTER TWO

MUSIC OF THE INDIAN WORLD

Indian woman.
Courtesy of the American Folklife Center, Smithsonian Institution,
Photo No. 85-15110-19.

The cultural region of India includes a large subcontinent in the Eastern hemisphere consisting of Pakistan, Bangladesh, Nepal, Sri Lanka, and India itself.

It also includes those areas where the culture has been transplanted by immigration throughout the world, including regions of the United States, the Pacific, and East Africa. Since this culture numbers over a billion people, nearly 20% of the world's inhabitants, its music is therefore significant in any discussion of music outside the Western tradition. Indian music is perhaps one of the few musical traditions of the world which has not been absorbed and changed much by its contact with the European world. Further, it is one that has been heard by many listeners outside of India.

India has always been a society characterized by various social strata, referred to as a *caste system* or *jati*. These are:

Workers and peasants	Shudras
Merchants and business people	Vaishyas
Military personnel	Kshatriyas
Religious leaders and intellectuals	Brahmans

This social stratification has allowed the culture to accept invading migrations from the North throughout its long history since each person's function in society was clearly defined through the caste system.

The two dominant religions of the area are Hinduism and Islam. The former is the older belief which is largely confined to the subcontinent while the latter is a world religion which was integrated into Indian culture in the past one thousand years. Only in Sri Lanka is there a significant population of Buddhists. The arts of India, especially music, have always been linked to religion and have thus changed little in the past millennium. Performers are judged not only by their skill, but by their claim to knowing ancient theories as well as having been trained by teachers whose pedagogy can be traced to generations past. Hearing Indian music thus involves listeners in a tradition which antedates the music Mozart and Haydn, even Palestrina and Josquin, by centuries.

Indian dancer prepares for performance by attaching bells to her ankles.
Courtesy of the American Folklife Center, Smithsonian Institution, Photo No. 85-0253-29.

In Indian culture, the *sangeet* represents three kinds of music, generally based on religious tradition. *Gita*, vocal music, includes religious chants and recitations used at Hindu shrines. Since singing really is the basis for learning all music, including instruments, gita is an important component of the sangeet. *Vadya* is instrumental music, whether used to accompany singing or as compositions in their own right. *Nrtta* is representational music, whether vocal or instrumental, used to accompany dance, narration and recitation, and full-scale drama, using human actors or puppets. It is generally confined to Hinduism since Moslems avoid such representations in their worship.

SANGEET

GITA	VADYA	NRRTA
VOCAL	INSTRUMENTAL	REPRESENTATIONAL

In Hindu mythology, nine feelings, called *rasas* are recognized, each of which can be portrayed through the arts. These are:

> love
> compassion
> valor
> tranquility
> terror
> anger
> surprise
> disgust
> humor

Only the first four are typically associated with music, however, the remainder being more suitable for other arts, particularly drama. This demonstrates that precise feelings are to be evoked through music. The sangeet, the three forms of music described above, thus has power to move humans (as well as animals, it is said). This is accomplished purely by the elements of the art form, not through direct representation. Artistic competence is thus judged by the ability of the performer to evoke the proper feeling and convey it to the audience.

Many of the feelings associated with music are linked to a special time of the year, if not day. This is due to the geography of the Indian subcontinent as it affects weather and the seasons. Although much of Southeast Asia has only wet and dry seasons, the plains, deserts, and mountains of India contribute to a slight variation in this pattern, creating three major seasons, winter, summer, and rainy season (monsoon). Agriculture, the basic economy of India, is ever dependent on weather. This has determined most human activity throughout its history, accounting for the timing of religious celebrations and festivals. Literature and the arts, not surprisingly, are cyclic as well, reflecting a right season to do this, a proper season to do that. In the United States, just as we consider "spring" the season to fall in love, the New Year a time to begin anew, in Indian culture, the arrival of the rainy season is the period of renewal. The summer sun parches the earth beyond endurance, and then the rains come. Rasas associated with the monsoon thus often express romantic feelings.

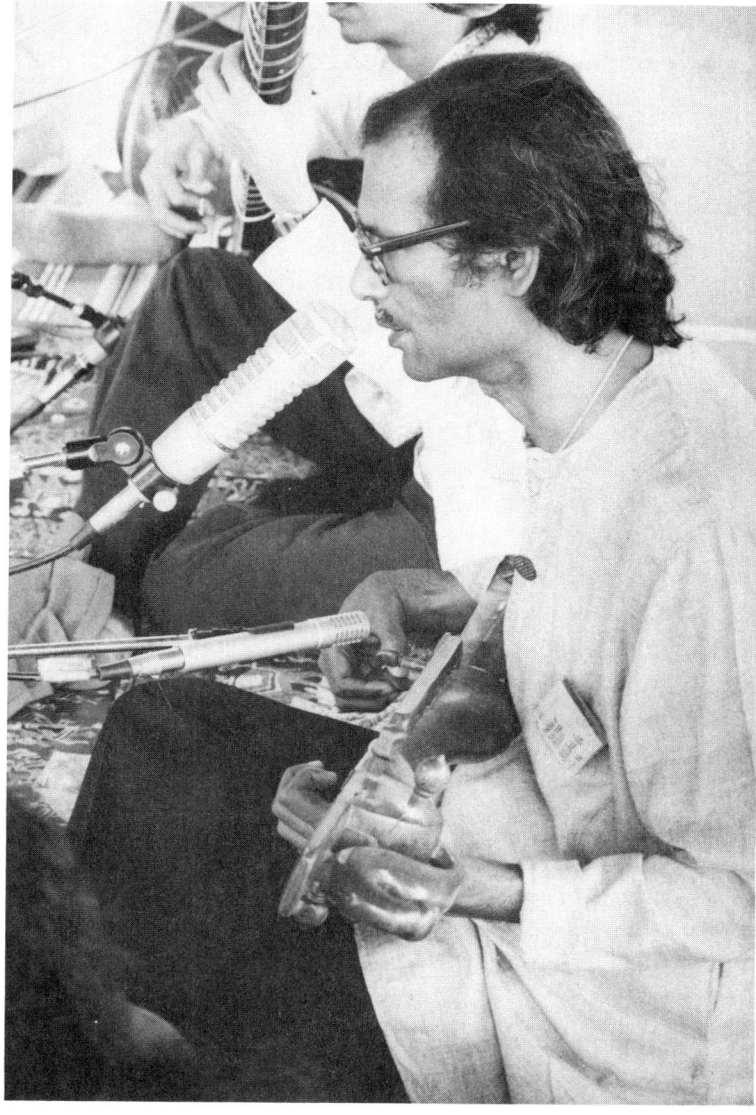

Indian music conveys set feelings known as rasas. Courtesy of the American Folklife Center, Smithsonian Institution, Photo No. 85-15110-10.

Training to become a musician involves more than merely mastering vocal or instrumental techniques. One must be able to evoke the appropriate rasa as well, a skill which takes years to cultivate and master. A student first seeks a master musician who consents to be his/her teacher. The two are then bound together in a *nara* (ceremony). This occurs symbolically by tying a string around the student's wrist three times. The student, known as a *shishya*, then offers a gift to the teacher or *guru*, after which the first lesson occurs. This symbolic and actual binding endures for life between the two, even obligating the student to serve the master with household and personal chores. Ravi Shankar, a world-famous sitarist, periodically returned to his guru in India for additional instruction and inspiration long after his reputation as a performer was established. Training is never complete!

In the guru-shishya relationship, instruction is approached systematically and slowly. The student learns scales and etudes through first singing material which is memorized by rote. This is gradually applied to the chosen instrument. Understanding the rasa associated with each exercise is as important, if not more so, than merely playing pitches correctly. The training might take twenty years or more, with the shishya then returning to the guru for additional training years thereafter.

Melodic Structure: Raga

Each feeling or rasa is evoked in music by its melodic framework. This framework is known as a *raga*, which translates basically as a melodic contour, tune, or simply scale. Or, to quote Sir William Jones:

> Raga, which translates as mode, properly signifies a passion or affection of mind: each mode . . . intended . . . to move one or another of our simple or mixed affections.[1]

Each raga should evoke the emotion or rasa with which it is associated. A raga connected to rain should convey the joyous feeling associated with the return of the monsoon. An ancient legend demonstrates the power of ragas. During Akbar's court in India (sixteenth century), a musician repetitively played a raga associated with fire. Eventually, he became warm, jumped into a fountain to cool himself, causing the water to boil. He was finally consumed by fire, and, according to tradition, turned to ash.[2]

Ragas are associated not only with seasons and elements, but with specific times of day. Some are appropriate to play in morning, others in afternoon, others, late at night. They have even been associated with miniature pictures called *ragamala* which give a visual representation of the rasa intended. A ragamala typically depicts rasa, hour, season, colors associated with these, as well as additional symbols known throughout the culture.

Ragas, then, are the melodic structure of Indian music. Like a scale, a raga is a catalog of pitches, at least as its basic structure. It is also a melodic contour which has a certain shape, both ascending and descending, as well as predominant pitches, intervals, and ornaments. These traits identify the raga and the rasa associated with it. It is the duty of musicians to convey this sentiment to their audience, not merely play notes. Tan-Sen, a famous singer of Mughal India, claimed he could plunge the world into darkness by singing an evening raga at noon, thus suggesting the power attributed to ragas.[3]

Ragas are derived from many sources in India, including local tribal songs, poetic chants, newly-composed songs, as well as music used in Hindu rites. At certain periods in history, ragas were grouped into families, reflecting the Indian penchant for hierarchial organization. *Raga shairveen*, appropriate from early dawn to sunrise, it was said, had five *raginis* (wives), all of whom were shy, lovely maidens similar in character to him. There were progeny of each marriage, *putras* (sons), each similar in character to the parents, that is, evoking a similar rasa.

Dhanashru Ragina represented in a ragmala. Courtesy of the Arthur M. Sackler Gallery, Smithsonian Institution, Neg. No. S1986.0462.

RAGA

| RAGINI | | RAGINI | | RAGINI | |
| PUTRA | PUTRA | PUTRA | PUTRA | PUTRA | PUTRA | PUTRA |

Although this poetic and whimsical classification scheme was used in Northern music, the term, ragini, never appears among South Indian theorists. Nonetheless, it shows the Indian tendency to personify elements of music and the arts in ways compatible with everyday experience and life. Thus, the pantheon of gods associated with Hinduism exhibits traits mirroring human more than divine emotions, an observation that aptly applies to ancient Greek religion as well.

Indian music, including its theory of ragas, derives from two traditions, united in concept, but separated by vocabulary and tradition. In a subcontinent as large as India, which has absorbed many waves of migration from Northern regions, it is not surprising to find numerous traditions. The main divisions are North (*Hindustani*) and South (*Carnatic*) styles. Both North and South India took Vedic traditions as a point of departure in music until the fourteenth century. Since then, differences have emerged, and, because of the influence of Moslems, traditions have mutated in the North. Music of the South is often used for devotion in Hindu temples and has therefore retained its strongly intellectual basis. Music of the North, used in the courts of the Moghul emperors, has become considerably more emotional and sensuous. Other distinguishing characteristics resulted from the use of different languages, such as Sanskrit and Tamil in the South, which has affected vocal styles. Music of the South is vocally oriented, instrumental music sounding like a transcription of a song. In the North, music is idiomatic, that is, sounds as if it were created for the instrument on which it is being performed. Although South Indian musicians transmitted their theoretical beliefs in writing, the tradition in the North has been oral. Nonetheless, both traditions share many of the same practices, particularly in use of ragas.

A raga, which is neither completely a scale nor a tune, but a melodic mold, is derived from a set of pitches called a *mela* or *thaat*. In this discussion, the term *mela* will be used, but this is synonymous with *thaat*, the former referring to Carnatic tradition, the latter, Hindustani. Each mela uses eight pitches or *swaras*. These do not represent absolute pitches, like C, F#, or Ab, but, rather, a set of relationships, identified by these names:

Sa Ri Ga Ma Pa Dha Ni Sa'

One thing that characterizes every mela is its outer boundary, Sa to Sa', which is always an octave, much like major or minor scales. Sa, however, is not a fixed pitch, but, rather, represents a pitch within range of the instrumentalists or singers, other pitches of the mela then being tuned relative to it. A fitting analogy to this might be in tuning a guitar. If one plays the guitar and has a piano or pitchpipe for tuning, the pitches used are:

Low---High

	E	A	D	g	b	e'
String #	6	5	4	3	2	1

However, if one has carried a guitar into the backwoods on a backpack, rendering it out of tune, and then attempts to tune it without a piano, the tuning will be relative. As long as the relationship between strings is maintained (from low to high, an interval of the fourth is used, except between strings 3 and 2, which is a third), the instrument will be in-tune with itself. This is all that is important, unless one is playing in a large ensemble, which occurs neither with guitar nor Indian instruments. The relative nature of tuning thus suffices.

The only pitch in a mela that is always a fixed distance from sa is pa, which is defined as a *perfect fifth* (702 cents) higher.

702 CENTS   498 CENTS

Sa   Pa   Sa'

1200 CENTS

The other pitches are thus somewhat variable within the mela. Each of the other five pitches has two basic positions (10 pitches) plus two adjustments slightly higher or lower for each of these (10 additional pitches), making twenty-two possible pitches in an octave, sa to sa'. This does not mean that all are used in a raga. Although each of the following can be *one* of *four* possible pitches, only one of each is used.

Ri Ga Ma Dha Ni

These twenty-two divisions of the octave are called *shruti*. Ri, for example, the second pitch in a mela, may be close to sa, an eighth of a pitch (22 cents) or quite wide (slightly larger than a whole-step, 204 cents). The interval between sa and ri, as one example, could be one of the following pitches, depending on the mela chosen:

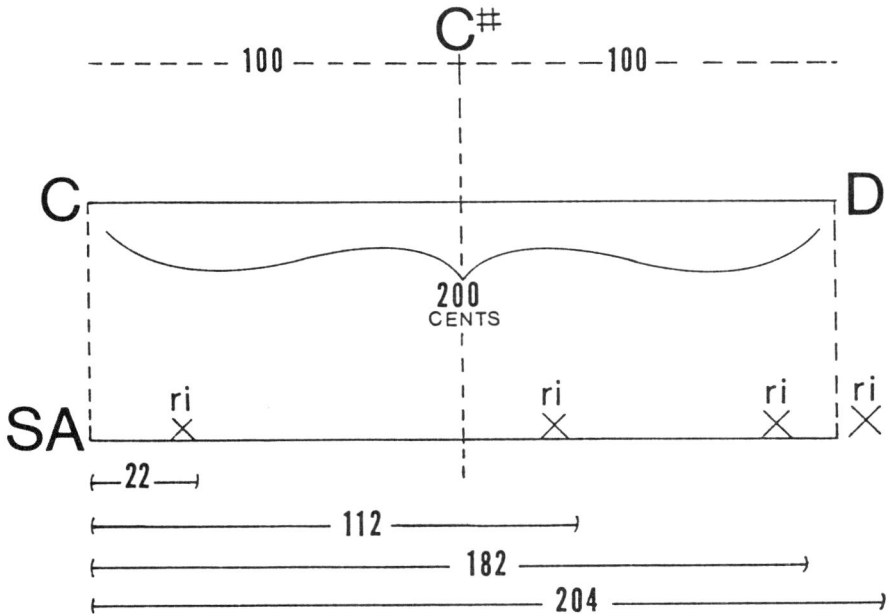

55

Thus, pitch choices in establishing a mela are:

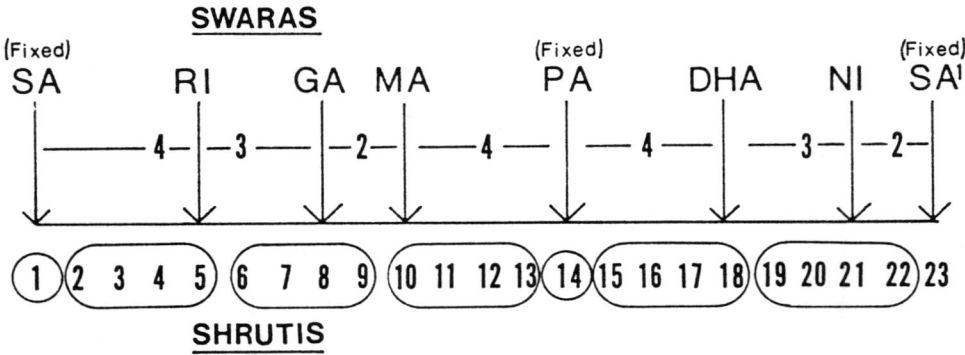

These are identified by the following names:

SWARA	SHRUTI	NAME	CENTS ABOVE SA
SA	1	SA	0
RI	5	SUDDHA RI	204
GA	8	SUDDHA GA	386
MA	10	SUDDHA MA	498
PA	14	PA	702
DHA	18	SUDDHA DHA	906
NI	21	SUDDHA NI	1088
SA	23	HIGH SA (TARA)	1200

In the Carnatic system, each mela is formed by joining two *tetrachords*, that is, four pitches with another four. This tetrachord:

might be joined with:

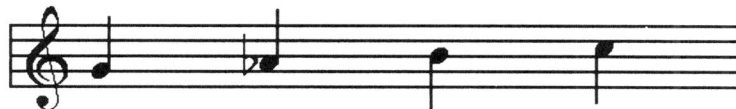

to create this mela.

Another mela is formed by simply changing the F-natural in the lower tetrachord to F♯:

There are six basic lower (*purvanga* = first limb [sa ri ga ma]) tetrachords, each of which can be varied by changing the F-natural to F♯. Each of these can be combined with six upper tetrachords (*uttaranga* = upper limb [pa dha, ni, sa']), resulting in source material for seventy-two melas in the Carnatic system (6 x 2 x 6 = 72). Fortunately, although each mela has been used to create ragas, only fourteen mela are truly significant. These are:

In the Hindustani tradition, ten thaat are considered significant. These are:

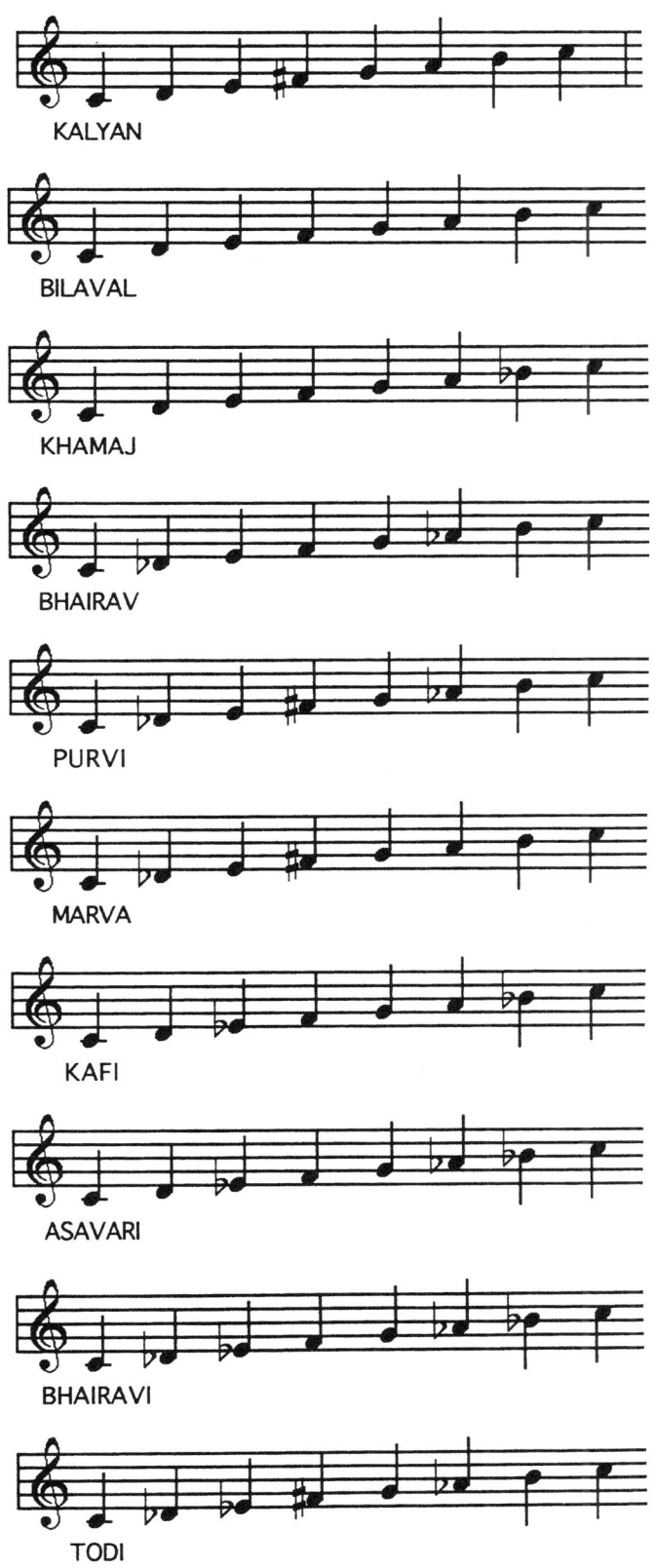

KALYAN

BILAVAL

KHAMAJ

BHAIRAV

PURVI

MARVA

KAFI

ASAVARI

BHAIRAVI

TODI

Although these are notated here with standard European musical symbols, representation is only approximate. For one thing, the microtones, although close to chromatic pitches, are not exactly the same, given that Western music divides the octave into twelve *equal* parts, Indian music into twenty-two *unequal* parts. Furthermore, sa, represented as C for this discussion, is not necessarily any given pitch. It is established by the ensemble and tuning of the mela or thaat is relative to it. The only pitch that is always a fixed distance from sa is pa, which is tuned a perfect fifth (702 cents) higher. This is true for every mela or thaat. It becomes obvious why Indian music sounds slightly "out-of-tune" to Western ears. Indeed, many of the pitches seem to fall in the "cracks" compared to our tuning. This points out that European music is probably not as melodically involved as that of other cultures, since the human ear can accept divisions far smaller than the half-step (100 cents) of the tempered scale. It also demonstrates that the Indian system represents a melodic structure considerably more intricate than ours.

String instruments, including this Tibetan pi-wang (hor-chin) with yak-tail bow, are able to play microtones required in the Indian musical system. Courtesy of © David Burckhalter (1974).

If the twenty-two shruti were placed in a continuum, low to high, the 1st (sa), 5th (ri), 8th (ga), 10th (ma), 14th (pa [fixed]), 18th (dha), and 21st (ni) shruti would be normal choices in a mela or thaat. These are referred to as *suddha* position. These can be raised or lowered, depending on which mela or thaat is used. Generally, a lowered shruti is referred to as *komal* (or *atikomal*, if lowered twice), a raised shruti as *tivra* (or *atitivra*, if raised twice). Most terminology, however, depends on which tradition is being observed, Carnatic or Hindustani, as well as the theorist. In short, the description of melas and thaats, as given here, suffices to understand the complexity and richness of the system. One needs only compare this system with our European major and minor scale, a system that applies, regardless of the initial tonic, to grasp which has the greater melodic complexity. In defense of Western music, however, major and minor are also the basis of a complex harmonic system, where chords, harmonies, tonalities, and modulation operate within most compositions as part of the musical structure. Indian music, by contrast, is virtually free of harmony.

Indian music theory represents a philosophical approach to the culture as much as a foundation for actual compositions. Each of the seven pitches of the mela, for example, represents various things, from being associated with a planet to denoting a person's age or the sound an animal makes. Sa, which is derived from the word "sadja", is permanent and thus never changes. It is associated with the moon, the sound of a peacock, as well as the age of a seventy-year-old person. Its basic temperament is considered happy, its color is pink, and it is harmonious in all ragas, occurring during all seasons of the year. Ri, or "rishabha", by contrast, is changeable. It fittingly has four shrutis. This is hardly surprising since it is associated with the planet Mercury (*mercurial* means inconstant or volatile). It is also happy but its color is pale green. It is appropriate only during the hot season and its sound is the cow calling its calf. All of these associations, which date from 4000 B.C., are outlined in the following chart:

SWARA NAME	MOOD	SEASON	COLOR	PLANET	AGE	SOUND
Sa Sadja	Happy	All	Pink	Moon	70	Peacock
Ri Rishabha	Happy	Hot	Green	Mercury	60	Cow
Ga Gandhara	Sad	Hot	Orange	Venus	50	Goat
Ma Madhyama	Restless	Rainy	Pink	Sun	40	Heron
Pa Panchama	Passionate	Rainy	Red	Mars	30	Cuckoo
Dha Dhaivata	Equable	Cold	Yellow	Jupiter	20	Horse
Ni Nishada	Happy	Cold	Dark	Saturn	10	Elephant

Although this lengthy discussion of melas and thaats is important in understanding Indian melodic structure, it does not result in musical compositions. It must be obvious that one mela or thaat may be the source for numerous ragas, each of which is related to the basic swaras. Compositions are based on ragas, each of which is derived from a mela or thaat. Raga, then, is a more specific term, mela or thaat, more general. It is much like saying a song is based on the C major scale:

C MAJOR SCALE

The sequence of notes in the scale is synonymous with mela, the actual tune, including its contour, pitch relationships, and ornaments, with raga. Each mela or thaat, then, becomes the parent scale for creating thousands of ragas. Although this is indeed mathematically possible, it is aesthetically untenable. How many feelings can humans convey through the arts? How many rasas are even recognized and used in music? Mathematics may help explain how music is structured, but it does little to motivate performers and audiences. Who worries about scales in a rousing jazz improvisation or a compelling performance of a Mozart concerto? Although there are theoretically thousands of ragas, only two hundred are in current use. Only thirty of these are considered popular and recognizable to Indian audiences. The following ragas, for example, are derived from melas of the same name:

Given the discussion so far, it is probably no surprise that there are numerous rules governing ragas. The first is the ascent, termed *arohana*, and the descent, *avarohana*. Unlike a major or minor scale, which uses the same pitches going up and coming down:

the movement of pitches in a raga, from low to high, arohana, may also be identical from high to low, avarohana, or it may be different:

RAGA MARU - BIBAG AROHANA   RAGA MARU - BIBAG AVAROHANA

Since a raga does not necessarily use all seven swaras derived from its parent mela or thaat, there may be a different number of pitches ascending than descending. In general, at least five pitches will be used, termed *odava*, but possibly six, *shadava*, or all seven, *sampurna*. Ragas are classified by their ascending and descending number of pitches. Odava-sampurna means five pitches ascending, seven descending, sampurna-shadava, seven ascending, and six descending, and so on. The above example is thus odava-sampurna (the ascending F-natural is an ornament).

There are other guiding principles for ragas. Two different pitches of the same name may never be chosen, such as two versions of ri. Ma and pa can never *both* be omitted in the same raga. In addition, each raga has a principal pitch, termed *vadi* (also *amsa*), which functions like tonic. The vadi requires a note in contrast, usually nine or thirteen shrutis higher, that is, respectively, the interval of a fourth or fifth. This is called *samvadi*, which functions much like dominant. The vadi, literally, "king", is considered the predominant note because it is accented, provides focus for the melody, and returns frequently, particularly at the end of a melodic cycle. The samvadi, literally, "minister", is considered consonant to the vadi. Two additional functions are designated in most ragas. The *anuvadi*, "servant", is a pitch which assists the vadi while the *vivadi*, "enemy of the king", provides dissonance within the raga. These functions, much like the tonic-subdominant-dominant relationships inherent in European music, provide reference points, either consciously or intuitively, for listeners. Many knowledgeable Indian listeners can perceive and appreciate how these pitches create the overall rasa or feeling in each musical composition.

The principle pitches assigned to a raga determine when it is appropriate to be performed. Generally, when the vadi is sa, ri, ga, ma, or pa, the raga is appropriate between noon and midnight. If vadi is dha or ni, it is appropriate between midnight and noon. Here are a few Hindustani ragas, showing many of the details discussed here:

THAAT	RAGA	PITCH #S	VADI	SAMVADI	APPROPRIATE TIME
Kalyan	Bhupali	5-5	Ga	Dha	7:00 p.m. to 10:00 p.m.
Kalyan	Chayanata	6-6	Pa	Ri	7:00 p.m. to 10:00 p.m.
Khamaj	Desh	6-6	Ri	Pa	10:00 p.m. to 1:00 a.m.
Bhairava	Bhairava	7-7	Dha	Ni	4:00 a.m. to 7:00 a.m.

A wedding procession in Kulu, India, showing the karna, a trumpet. Events, times, and feelings require certain ragas be used. Courtesy of © David Burckhalter (1977).

In addition to pitches, patterns of ascent and descent, and principal pitches, ornaments also characterize each raga. The concept of ornamentation is different than in the West. We think of ornaments as decoration, serving to enhance minimal melodies or to prolong a pitch on an instrument which does not have the power to sustain it. Ornamentation in Indian music, by contrast, it not decorative, but essential. It provides a dimension of music which is satisfied in Western music through the use of harmony. Indian ornaments, called *gamakas* in the South, *murchanas* in the North, include various vocal and instrumental techniques. Slowly sliding between pitches, which in our culture is termed *portamento*, is called *mind* in Hindustani music. Pitches are not sounded as precisely, but flow one into another rather fluidly. Mind thus refers both to how one approaches a pitch as well as exits it. In Carnatic music, the *kampita* is an ornament produced on a fretted-string instrument by slowly deflecting the string sideways, which has the effect of prolonging the pitch. A *nokku* is simply executing a kampita more quickly. Most ornaments involve sliding along or placing a fingernail on a string, slurring, trilling, arpeggiating, stressing, as well as turning around a pitch. Much like the visual art of the culture, which avoids heavy strokes and bold outlines, gamakas and murchanas give melodies gentle, diffused lines which turn, convolute, and deviate. Most, like colorations in jazz improvisation, are learned and mastered by rote imitation, each defining a specific raga.

Ornaments are played on Indian aerophones by finger movements and jaw position. This double flute is known as the gling-bu. Courtesy of © David Burckhalter (1974).

. . .most ragas are identifiable by specific ornaments, which, like the ragas and melas, have a special nomenclature. The thonk is a type of staccato and the varek, a twangy deflection of pitch. Minda is a slow portamento (glide) between pitches, kana is a brief pitch that precedes another or leads to a main pitch, and andolita is vibrato. In general, Southern Indian music prefers ornaments, Northern Indian, more sustained tones.[4]

Although nineteen gamakas are available, only ten are commonly used.

Hearing the differences among two-hundred ragas, including their pitches, patterns of ascent-descent, predominant pitches, and ornaments is undoubtedly overwhelming and unnecessary for anyone using this textbook. It probably helps little to say that only thirty ragas are truly popular anyway. Since the purpose of listening to Indian music, if not all music, is more than merely dissecting parts and investigating structure, grasping the overall sense and feeling of the music still applies. Although students of Western music might ultimately learn to identify cadences, progressions, harmonies, modulations, and forms, the joy of listening still is found in the uplifting quality of the actual sound of the music. This is equally true for Indian music. Although the vocabulary of the two cultures is different, the grammar of music only helps us understand how feeling is created. It does not create it.

Rhythmic Structure: Tala

The time structure of Indian music is no less interesting that its melodic, but, fortunately, perhaps easier to understand. Music of the Indian culture is based on a time cycle called *tala*. Each tala has a recurring cycle of regular beats or *matra*. Just as we think of scales when we discuss raga, we think of meter with tala. Meter, however, is not specifically accurate to describe what tala is any more than raga can be defined merely as a scale.

In European music, we use regular groupings of duple, triple, or quadruple time, at least commonly. Many of our Western rhythms evolved from dance, which requires repetition of set metric units. By contrast, a great deal of Indian music evolved from singing, which does not require a multiplication of metric units. Singing can be free, adding or deleting beats, or even suspending them at times. Thus, European time cycles are *multiplicative*, that is, groupings of a set number of beats are repeated throughout an entire movement or composition, such as 4 + 4 + 4 + 4, etc. Indian time cycles are *additive*, units being placed together to form larger cycles, such as 3 + 2 + 2 + 4 or 2 + 2 + 4 + 4. Unlike ragas, the classification of talas, in theory if not in name, is considerably more uniform between Northern and Southern Indian music.

A tala has three components: (1) the overall cycle of beats, called *avarta*; (2) the beat, called *matra*, as well as its tempo (*laya*); and (3) the division of the cycle into smaller units or partitions, called *vibhaga*. We will discuss each of these.

Avarta is the overall number of beats in a large cycle. The fewest number of beats observed in any tala is three, the greatest, one-hundred eight. Most talas, however, consist of a number between six and sixteen matra. *Teental*, for example, has sixteen beats, *dadratal*, six, and *tivratal*, seven.

Mridangam, double-headed drum, played by Trichy Sankaran.
Photo by Greg Plachta. Courtesy of Music of the World.

The movement of a tala depends on the speed the matra are counted, much as Western music. There are three layas generally observed. *Vilambita* is slow, with matra at sixty per minute. *Madhyama* is moderate, moving twice as fast as Vilambita, that is, 120 beats per minute. *Druta* is fast, with matra twice as fast as madya or four times faster than vilambita, that is, 240 beats per minute. Various talas are associated with different tempos. Dadratal and teental are used for fast, light music, rupaktal (7 matra) and ektal (12 matra) for slower, more serious music.

The third component of tala, vibhaga, is perhaps the most fascinating, the partitioning of cycles into metric units. This sometimes results in a symmetric tala, divided into repetitive units, at least mathematically. Teental is like this:

Teental   (16 matra)   4 + 4 + 4 + 4

By contrast, some talas are asymmetric, with partitions unevenly divided, including ektal or jhaptal:

Ektal   (12 matra)   4 + 4 + 2 + 2
Jhaptal   (10 matra)   2 + 3 + 2 + 3

In addition to the above talas, the following are also popular and frequently heard in Indian music:

Jhumratal   (14 matra)   3 + 4 + 3 + 4
Tivratal   (7 matra)   3 + 2 + 2
Dadratal   (6 matra)   3 + 3

There are theoretically an infinite number of talas. One-hundred twenty are generally known by musicians, but only thirty are commonly used, including those above.

None of this should suggest there is a "boom-chuck-chuck" accompaniment when a tala is used. Rather, the cycle of beats is an internalized framework which governs the performance, at least the concluding section, for musicians. It is neither physically nor aurally evident in most cases, but is evident to listeners frequently from patterns and physical gestures used by the drummer. Adital, which has 8 matra, subdivided 4 + 2 + 2, is counted:

X				X	O	X	O
1	2	3	4	5	6	7	8
CLAP	TAP	-	-	CLAP	WAVE	CLAP	WAVE
	WITH FINGERS ON PALM						

The downbeat of the tala, beat one, is called *sam*. Any beat which is clapped is *tali* (meaning "beat"), such as 5 and 7 in adital. A silent beat, indicated by a wave, such as 6 and 8 in adital, is *khali*, meaning "empty." The designation is usually "X" for tali, "O" for khali. Talas are thus defined by sounded and silent beats, including:

Caputal   (7 matra)   3 + 2 + 2

1	2	3	4	5	6	7
O	O		X		X	

Teental   (16 matra)   4 + 4 + 4 + 4

1	2	3	4	5	6	7	8	9	10	11	12	13	14	15	16
X				X				O				X			

Jhaptal   (10 matra)   2 + 3 + 2 + 3

1	2	3	4	5	6	7	8	9	10
O		X			O		X		

Although the description of counting talas refers to performance, particularly singing, the rhythmic structure is commonly kept by a percussion instrument, in which case the drummer does not merely beat the underlying matra, but, rather, adds rhythmic counterpoint to other instruments or singer. In this case, the tala is identified by rhythmic syllables or *bols*, such as:

TAN	NA	TI	RA
TINN	GHI	GA	DHU

In rupaktal (7 matra = 3 + 2 + 2), for example, we might hear:

Dhin	Dha	Trik	Dhin	Dhin	Dha	Trik
1	2	3	4	5	6	7

More than one bol may occur over a matra, as in keharvatal (4 matra = 2 + 2):

Dhagi	Nati	Naka	Ghina
1	2	3	4

or jumratal (14 matra = 3 + 4 + 3 + 4):

Dhin	Dha	Ti-ra-ki-ta	Dhin	Dhin	Dhagi	Ti-ra-ki-ta
1	2	3	4	5	6	7
Tin	Ta	Ti-ra-ki-ta	Dhin	Dhragi	Dhin	Ti-ra-ki-ta
8	9	10	11	12	13	14

Bols, learned by rote like drumming rudiments in the West, are a system for learning, performing, and remembering complex rhythmic patterns.

As with ragas, the point of listening to Indian music is never merely to identify the tala. Rather, understanding the relationship between rhythmic and melodic cycles, tala and raga, respectively, helps one understand the basic structure of Indian music and how improvisation occurs within these two dimensions.

Formal Structure: Alap and Gat

With a basic understanding of raga and tala, the formal structure of Indian music is not difficult to grasp. Form results from the combination of the music's melodic and rhythmic structure, raga and tala, respectively. This results in binary form, two-part, known, respectively, as *alap* and *gat*.

Indian music is largely improvised, based either on a raga or on a composition using a given raga. The former is called *anibaddha* (independent), the latter, *nibaddha* (dependent). In either case, it is never merely a memorized composition presented in recital, but variations and elaborations based on one or the other. Although the musician improvises, it is within the rules, structures, pitches, and ornaments typical of the raga. The objective is to reveal the feeling or rasa of the raga as profoundly as possible, not to surprise or shock, as often occurs in jazz improvisation. A performance ends only when all possibilities of further exploration are exhausted.

Many compositions begin with a slow section called *alap* (or *alapana* which literally means "an acquaintance." The tempo is usually slow and the flow is non-metric, free and rhapsodic. The purpose is to reveal the main characteristics of the raga, such as its vadi and other important pitches and intervals. Since the alap is an expository section, a fine musician will never rush through it. Typically, the lower tetrachord of the raga is exposed first, the purvanga. Gradually, the upper tetrachord, uttaranga, is introduced. The performer will emphasize the intervals, contours, and gamakas that uniquely identify the raga, only then moving into upper and lower octaves. Gradually, rhythmic flow assumes an indirect beat, the performer now grouping pitches into small rhythmic units of two or three adjacent pitches. This is known as the *jor* and it flows almost indistinctly from the opening section. The performer continues this exploration, giving heightened rhythmic impetus to the improvisation, which gradually moves into rapid plucking with increased beat division called the *jhala*. A sense of urgency becomes noticeable, characterized by increasing melodic activity, including the repetition of pitches, intervals, and contours, as well as increased emphasis on the metric flow.

SECTION 1 ALAP

alapana	jor	jhala
slow, free	metric	urgency
non-metric	increased activity	heightened activity

This eventually bursts into the second main section, the *gat*, which is characterized by the addition of the tala, the time cycle. This is often signaled by a descending glissando on the main melodic instrument, followed by the addition of drum accompaniment to establish and maintain the tala. The drummer seldom plays merely the strong and weak beats of the tala, although these are generally established in the first iteration of the cycle. Rather, rhythmic patterns, bols, are played within the framework of the tala:

SECTION 2 GAT

Time Cycle (Tala)
established
Drum plays bols
Momentum builds

In the gat, momentum generally builds again into another jhala where the performers create dissonance in an interesting manner. Unlike Western music, where dissonance results from chords that seek resolution to more stable harmonies, in Indian music, the absence of harmony necessitates another structure for creating tension. This occurs in the interplay between raga and tala. Both represent unique cycles which are in congruence when the vadi of the raga occurs with the sam of the tala, that is, the "tonic" of the scale with the "downbeat" of the rhythmic grouping.

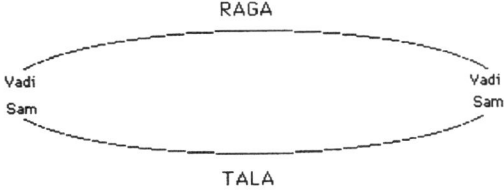

Tension occurs when the two cycles are "out of synch", that is, their main events do not occur at the same time. This generates excitement and makes listeners anticipate the return of some type of congruence, thus resolving the perceived dissonance or conflict. Skillful performers can cleverly built interest in a performance in this way.

Much like jazz, an Indian composition has no predetermined length. It is really up to the performers. Proficient musicians can continually build excitement within the constraints of raga and tala, allowing a single composition to last for several minutes, if not hours. Only when the musical possibilities are thoroughly explored and exhausted does the composition end. Appreciative audiences applaud not only at the conclusion, but whenever exciting moments occur within the course of the performance.

In a Western sense, Indian compositions are like continuous variations, using basic melodic and rhythmic materials to improvise variations that run together without clear sectioning. Unlike Western music, however, the variations do not hold interest because of changes in timbre, harmony, or dynamics, but, rather, through development of melody and rhythm as represented, respectively in raga and tala.

Maharajah Sir S. M. Tagore's Indian orchestra. Several Indian instruments are seen: Center front, pakhavaj (two-headed drum); front row, left to right, sitar, large bowed lute, small bowed lute, three dilrubas, another large bowed lute, and tamboura (far left); back row, left to right, pungi (flute), bin (stick zither, and two shahnai. Courtesy of Field Museum of Natural History, Chicago, Neg. No. A86409.

Instruments of Indian Music

Ensembles in Indian culture are small and there is no grouping comparable to the symphony orchestra. By Western standards, Indian ensembles are a form of chamber music, presented in small rooms and recital halls. This can also be interpreted to mean that each performer has a specific function in the ensemble and is therefore not playing the same part as another musician. In many ensembles, three performers are used to fulfill three functions: (1) melodic instrument; (2) drone; and (3) rhythmic instrument. We will examine a typical and popular ensemble of North India, which uses sitar, tamboura, and tabla.

Sri Lankan sitarist at Tucson Meet Yourself.
Photo © David Burckhalter.
Courtesy of Jim Griffith and the Southwest Folklore Center, Tucson, Arizona.

The *sitar*, a chordophone, is one of the most popular of all Indian melodic instruments. Its silvery sounds have become familiar to many listeners in Europe and America and many Westerners have attempted to learn it. The sitar was allegedly invented by Amir Khusro, a poet-musician of the Delhi court in the thirteenth or fourteenth century. It is said he combined the ancient Indian vina, an instrument with numerous strings, with the Persian sehtar, an instrument with only three, and the sitar resulted. In the eighteenth century, instrument makers added three or four melodic strings, which were eventually enhanced with sympathetic strings, between eleven to fifteen in number. Sympathetic strings, used in instrument construction in many Asian regions, enhance the overall resonance of an instrument. Although they are not part of Western violins and guitars, their effect can be observed in the piano. The numerous strings in a piano, one, two, or three per key, depending on the register, vibrate in sympathy throughout the range of the instrument. This makes the timbre rich and sonorous. For the same reason, sympathetic strings are part of the sitar.

Sitars typically have six or seven main strings used for melody or drone. They are divided into three areas. The top two strings, most distant from the performer, are the principal melody strings. The middle two strings are used for reinforcement and elaboration in the alap. The bottom two or three strings, closest to the performer, the *chikari*, are drone strings, generally not fingered, only struck or plucked. The tuning is often:

The sympathetic strings are tuned to the basic mela or thaat, thus reinforcing pitches played on the seven main strings.

The sitar is fretted, that is, it has pitch divisions along its neck. There may be nineteen or twenty frets, which sit rather high on the neck. These are too high to be depressed to the actual neck, but pitches are distinctly made simply by stopping any string against the fret. The way pitches flow together in Indian music reflects sitar technique, where the performer slides along the string, parallel to the neck, as well as ornaments by pulling the string sideways, perpendicular to the neck. The sitar frets are tied onto the neck with gut or silk string and are therefore moveable. This allows the performer to set pitch divisions, which, as we have seen, are microtonal, necessitated by the chosen mela/thaat and raga. Since each raga may use a slightly different positioning of pitches, depending where ri, ga, ma, pa, dha, and ni lie, it is important that frets can be repositioned. This occurs, of course, not during performance, but before. It also shows that changing ragas within a composition or even within a set of compositions for recital is difficult. Once the frets of the sitar are set to accommodate the pitches of a given mela or thaat, only ragas derived from the parent scale may be performed. Melodic intricacy, it appears, has a side effect. There is simply no way to build an instrument which can play all pitches, all melas, or all ragas without re-tuning or re-setting frets.

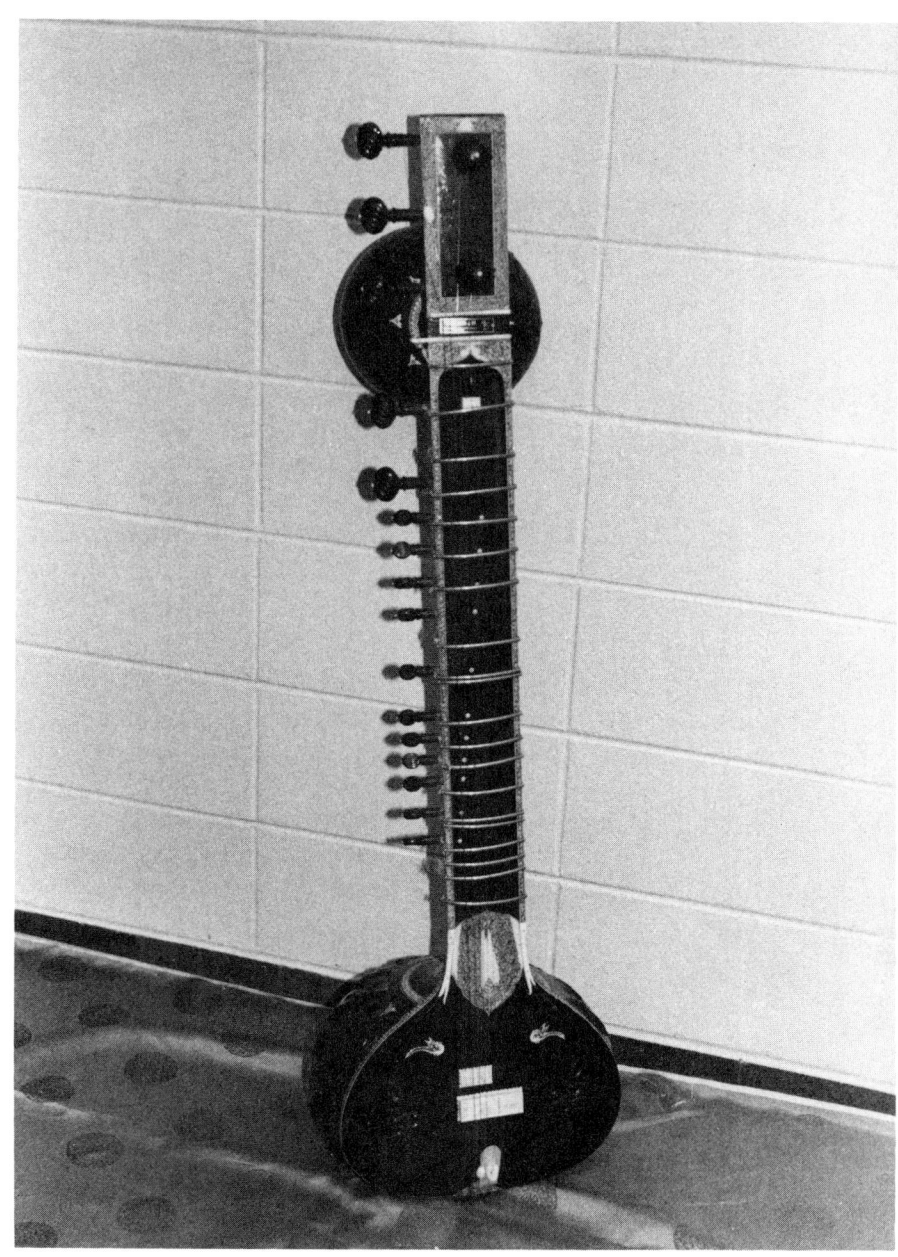

North Indian sitar, showing moveable frets, main and sympathetic strings, as well as double resonators. Courtesy of K. H. Han, Northern Illinois University.

    The sitar is often accompanied by another chordophone, the *tamboura*, which plays drone. Simpler than the sitar, it has four strings (sometimes six) tuned to sa and pa (sometimes including ma) and no frets. Its function in ensemble is providing a drone, the reference point against which melodic improvisation of the sitar occurs. The simpler playing technique of the tamboura is part of the shishya-guru system of music education. A student of the sitarist participates in the ensemble by playing tamboura. Here, he or she can observe the technique of the master, participate in music making, as well as master the feeling of the raga. It is a simple system of music education which occurs both unofficially and officially throughout the world.

Tamboura, a drone instrument with four unfretted strings.
Courtesy of K. H. Han, Northern Illinois University.

The sitar and tamboura are similar instruments and may have evolved from the same ancestor. Although they appear to be much like instruments of the violin or guitar family, in reality, they are zithers, long stick-like instruments. The actual stick is hollow whereas it is a solid structure with the violin or guitar. The gourd resonators, which are placed at the base or both ends, merely reinforce the basic sounds. The hollow neck itself, of course, provides a means to attach the sympathetic strings within the instrument.

Tamboura performer.
Courtesy of the American Folklife Center, Smithsonian Institution,
Photo No. 85-15110-15.

The final function in Indian music, time keeping, is accomplished by a drum. There are two main types. In the South, the *mridangam*, a two-headed drum about two feet long, is used. The larger head is played by the left hand, the smaller, the right. The right head usually has a small circle of black manganese dust, boiled rice, and tamarind juice. This affects the tonal quality of the head and is also used in tuning. Each hand and head thus sounds different bols. Although the shell of the mridangam was frequently constructed of terra cotta (clay or pottery) in earlier times, it is now made of wood.

Daya (smaller drum) and baya (larger drum), collectively known as tabla.
Courtesy of the American Folklife Center, Smithsonian Institution,
Photo No. 87-9946-18.

In the North, two drums are used collectively called *tabla*. The smaller drum, *daya*, played with the right hand, has a wooden shell, the larger, *baya*, a brass or terra cotta shell. As with mridangam, the tabla player is able to vary the drum sound by where he/she hits the hand, palm, or points of the fingers. Animal parchment, whether calf, sheep, or monkey skin, is used for the heads, not plastic, and the basic tuning is done with the side cords, the fine tuning with the black circle of paste (and spit). The right hand drum or head is often tuned to sa, the left, pa, which functions much like tonic-dominant.

The alternating dryness and humidity of Indian weather creates havoc for instrumentalists in tuning. The strings of the sitar and tamboura are more flexible than drum heads, ever sensitive to changes in heat and humidity. In practice, all performers ultimately tune to the drum, demonstrating the pragmatic as well as relative nature of Indian systems of temperament. In ensembles of three performers, it is important only to be in tune with one another.

Drummers function as time keepers in Indian music, remaining silent in the opening alap, but then establishing the time cycle in the gat. This, as we have seen, is accomplished through bols typical of a tala as well as improvisation within its overall cycle of matra. In past centuries, the role of drummers was passive. More recently, they have developed considerable virtuosity through imitating and countering the melodic instrument, such as the sitar, generating dissonance and excitement through cross-rhythms.

Sarangi, a bowed chordophone with 4 melodic and 24 sympathetic strings. Courtesy of the American Folklife Center, Smithsonian Institution, Photo No. 86-312-18.

There are numerous other Indian instruments, including:

CHORDOPHONES	AEROPHONES
Dilruba	Bansuri
Ektar	Nagasvaram
Gottuvuadyam	Pungi
Sarangi	Shahnai
Sarod	Sruti-Box (Surpeti)
Surbahar	Tippera
Vichitra Vina	**MEMBRANOPHONES**
Vina (bin)	Bholak
Violin	Dholak
IDIOPHONES	Naqqara
Jaltarang	Pakhavaj
Kanjira	Tavil

Although each cannot be discussed here, those who are interested in pursuing Indian culture and its music beyond the discussion here, might pursue instrumental music in which these are used.

Singing in India

The basis of a great deal of world music is the human voice. This is certainly true in India, where singing is the core experience in music education. Instrumental study follows rather than precedes vocal tuition. It is generally not surprising in any culture to find that voices and instruments do similar things. If instruments play microtones, are nasal, and slur between pitches, so does the voice. Williard noted the quality of Indian singing as:

> The peculiar nature of the melody of Hindoostan not only permits but enjoins the singer, if he has the least pretention to excel in it, not to sing a song throughout more than once in its naked form; but on its repetition . . . to break off sometimes at the conclusion, at other times at the commencement, middle, or any certain part of a measure and fall into a rhapsodical embellishment called Alap . . . .[5]

The singer, functioning as the main melodic instrument, much like sitar, sarod, or sarangi, accompanied by a tamboura or shruti-box to provide the drone, first sketches the raga, emphasizing vadi and samvadi. The raga is fully exposed before the drum enters and establishes the tala, after which the song progresses to its finale.

There are several main types of singing, three of which come from North India. The first, *dhrupad*, is solemn, generally presenting one feeling or rasa. It develops slowly, with little ornamentation. The lyrics present subjects associated with heroic endeavors or religious themes. Since dhrupad takes a singer of tremendous stamina and a vocal range of three octaves, men generally sing it. Dhrupad is one of the oldest traditions of North India.

Khayal, love songs, by contrast, are performed by women. This style is lighter and is now considered the norm for Indian classical singing. The overall style is freer, employing elaborate vocal ornamentation. Two or three feelings may be developed successively in khayal, instead of merely one, as with dhrupad.

Thumri, a third style of singing, developed during the eighteenth and nineteenth centuries. It is sensuous and lively, using simpler ragas and time cycles. Many musicians consider it simpler to sing than khayal and dhrupad. In thumri, the singer may change ragas (and feelings) as the song develops. Since lyrics are minimal, the short, terse melody is used as basis for improvisation. Both thumri and khayal are improvised, but thumri uses ornaments that are quicker and lighter, reflecting its popular nature. Thumri also incorporates word-painting to some degree, the singer conveying actions of the song and sentiment of the words in melodic movement and articulation. Although dhrupad, khayal, and thumri each have their own vocabulary of ragas and talas, the tendency is now to intermix all three styles.

Ghazal, another genre of North Indian singing, is recited poetry in the Urdu language, usually in five or more couplets. The subject matter is amorous and erotic, reflecting male-female attraction, on a sensual level, as well as to God, on a spiritual. In centuries past, it was sung by dancing women and courtesans, but is heard now in private concerts in homes as well as on radio. The ragas and talas of ghazal are usually not complicated.

South Indian vocal styles are also numerous, but the most important are *padam*, *varnam*, and *kiranam*. Padam, which is used for temple worship, is the oldest tradition. It is sung in slow tempo while dancers interpret the words of its devotional text. Varnam is used either for accompanying dancing or singing alone. Although it is considered somewhat an etude or study piece, developing a singular raga in each composition, many singers begin a concert with varnam. Kiranam (also *kriti*) is a devotional group song where a leader intones a few phrases and the entire group responds on a refrain. Kiranam are also used as concert pieces.

In both South and North vocal styles, the audience expects the singer to be sweet and entertaining as well as to have the ability to affect all those who hear. Mastering the feeling of the raga is as essential as presenting flawless technique. Objectionable mannerisms include singing with fear or with the mouth wide open, craning the neck like a camel, gesturing frantically with the hands, singing with short breaths or with eyes tightly closed, as well as braying like a donkey.

Key Terms and Concepts

Additive
Alapana
Antibaddha
Anuvadi
Avarta
Avarohana
Arohana
Baya
Bol
Carnatic
Caste system
Chikari
Daya
Dhrupad
Druta
Gamaka
Gat
Ghazal
Guru
Hindustani
Jati
Jhala
Jor
Kampita
Khali
Khayal
Kiranam (Kriti)
Komal
Laya
Madhyama
Matra
Mela
Mind
Mridangam
Multiplicative
Murchana
Nibaddha
Nokku
Nara
Odava
Padam
Perfect fifth
Portamento
Purvanga

Putra
Raga
Ragamala
Ragini
Rasa
Sam
Sampurna
Samvadi
Sangeet
Shadava
Shishya
Shruti
Sitar
Suddha
Swara
Tabla
Tala
Tali
Tamboura
Tetrachord
Thaat
Thumri
Tivra
Uttaranga
Vadi
Varnam
Vibhaga
Vilambita
Vivadi

Self-checking Chapter Review

| Match Column II to Column I ||
Column I	Column II
1. raga	A. drone instrument
2. vadi	B. feeling
3. matra	C. daya-baya
4. dhrupad	D. downbeat
5. rasa	E. opening section of a composition
6. sam	F. melodic material of Indian music
7. gat	G. beat
8. swaras	H. vocal composition
9. sitar	I. ornament
10. tala	J. rhythmic syllable
11. bol	K. sa, ri, ga, ma, pa, dha, ni, sa'
12 tamboura	L. main pitch
13. alap	M. melodic instrument
14. tabla	N. Indian time cycle
15. gamaka	O. second section of a musical composition

Answers			
1.	F	9.	M
2.	L	10.	N
3.	G	11.	J
4.	H	12.	A
5.	B	13.	E
6.	D	14.	C
7.	O	15.	I
8.	K		

Selected Bibliography

Bandoypadhyaya, Shripada (1958). *The Music of India* (Second edition). Bombay: D.B. Taraporevala Songs and Company, Private Ltd.

_____ (1977). *The Origin of Raga*. New Delhi: Munshiram Manoharial Publishers Pvt. Ltd.

Bhattacharya, Arun (1978). *A Treatise on Ancient Hindu Music*. Calcutta: K.P. Bagchi & Company.

Cohn, Jerry (1965). *An American Student and North Indian Music*. Madison: University of Wisconsin research paper in conjunction with Benaras Hindu University.

Danielou, Alain (1968). *Northern Indian Music*. New York: Frederick A. Praeger, Publishers.

Deva, B. Chaitanya (1973). *An Introduction to Indian Music*. New Delhi: Ministry of Information and Broadcasting, Publications Division.

_____ (1981). *The Music of India: A Scientific Study*. New Delhi: Munshiram Manoharial Publishers Pvt. Ltd.

Fyzee-Rahamin, Atiya Begum (1925). *The Music of India*. London: Luzac and Company.

Holroyde, Peggy (1972). *The Music of India*. New York: Praeger Publishers.

Keesee, Allen (1968). *The Sitar Book*. New York: Oak Publications.

Kuppuswamy, Gowry and M. Hariharan (eds.) (1980). *Indian Music: A Perspective*. New Delhi: Sundeep Prakashan.

Popley, Herbert A. (1950). *The Music of India* (Second edition). Calcutta: Y.M.C.A. Publishing House.

Purcell, William A. (1966). *An Introduction to Asian Music*. New York: The Asia Society.

Rosenthal, Ethel (1928, 1990). *The Story of Indian Music and Its Instruments*. New Delhi: Low Priced Publications.

Sambamoorthy, P. (1956). *South Indian Music Book II* (Fifth edition). Madras: The Indian Music Publishing House.

Schramm, Harold (1969). *Traditional Indian Melodies for Sitar*. New York: Southern Music Publishing Co., Inc.

Shankar, Ravi (1968). *My Music, My Life*. New York: Simon and Schuster.

Shirali, Vishnudass (1936). *Hindu Music and Rhythm*. Paris: Uday Shan-kar and Company

Sinha, Purnima (1970). *An Approach to the Study of Indian Music*. Calcutta: Indian Publications.

Tagore, Raja Sir Sourindro Mohun (compiler) (1965). *Hindu Music from Various Authors* (Vol. XLIX). Varanasi: The Chowkhamba Sanskrit Series Office.

Wade, Bonnie C. (1979). *Music in India: The Classical Traditions*. Englewood Cliffs, New Jersey: Prentice-Hall, Inc.

Selected Discography

A Concert of South Indian Classical Music
Nonesuch Explorer Series H-72040

Anthology of Indian Music, The
World Pacific Records #26200

Ashish Khan: Young Master of the Sarod
World Pacific Records WPS-21444

Bengal
Odeon C064-17840

Bhimsen Joshi: Hindu Classical Singer
EMI (The Gramophone Company of India, Ltd.)
EASD-1501

Bismillah Khan
Odeon Records MOAE 120

Classical Indian Music
London STS 15094

Classical Indian Music
Odeon Records

Classical Music of India
Folkways Records FI 8366

Classical Music of India
Nonesuch Records H-72014

Drums of India, The
World Pacific Records WP-1403

Exotic Sitar and Sarod, The
Capital ST-10497

Festival of India
Music of the World CDT-121

Folk Music of India
Folkways Records 4409

Genius of Ravi Shankar, The
Columbia CS-9560

Great Music of India, The
The Music of India Co.

India
Columbia 91-A-02021 (Volume 12)

India
Odeon Co. 64-17859
Musical Atlas
UNESCO Collection Volume 6

Indian Folk Music
Columbia Masterworks KL-215

Indian Sitar, The
Musical Heritage Society, Inc. MHS 3028

Indian Street Music (The Bauls of Bengal)
Nonesuch Explorer Series H-72035

Laya Vinyas: The South Indian Drumming of Trichy Sankaran
Music of the World CDT-120

Music from Soundtrack to *Gandhi*
RCA ABL 1-4557

Music from South India (Kerala)
Folkways Records FE 4365

Music of India: Morning and Evening Ragas
Angel Records #35283/Capital Records DT 2721

Music of India: Traditional and Classical
Folkways Records FE 4422

Music of Southern India, The
Nonesuch Records #72003

Music of South India: The Ten Graces Played on the Vina
Nonesuch Explorer Series H-72027

North India Instrument Music
Philips 6586-020

North India: Instrumental Music (Sitar, Flute and Sarangi)
Philips 6586-009

North India: Vocal Music (Dhrupad and Khayal)
Philips 6586-003

Pannalal Ghosh
Odeon MOAE 102

Pannalal Ghosh, Flute
EMI The Gramophone Company of India, Ltd. EALP 1354

Raga Darbari
EMI The Gramophone Company of India, Ltd. ECSD 2824

Ragas from South India
Folkways Records FW 8854

Ragas of India, The
Folkways Records FL 8368

Ragas--Songs of India
Folkways Records FG 3530

Ragas--Streams of Light
Limelight Records (Mercury) LS-86056

Ramnad Krishnan: A Concert of South Indian Classical Music
Nonesuch Records H-72040

Ravi Shankar: Improvisations
World Pacific Records ST-1416

Religious Music of India
Folkways Records FE 4431

Sarangi: The Voice of a Hundred Colors
Nonesuch Records H-72030

Sounds of India, The
Columbia CS 9296

Sound of the Sarod
World Pacific Records WPS-21435

Three Ragas
Capital Records DT-2720

UNESCO Collection: A Musical Anthology of the Orient
Barenreiter-Musicaphon
  Volumes I-IV, BM L-2006, 2007, 2019, and 2021
  Volume I: Vedic Chants
  Volume II: Dance and Theatre Music of South India
  Volume III: Dhrupads
  Volume IV: Carnatic Music

West Meets East
  Volumes I-III
  Angel S-36418, S-36026, SFO-537200

Endnotes

1. Sir William Jones, "On the Musical Modes of the Hindoos," *Hindu Music from Various Authors*, (compiled by Raja Sir Sourindro Mohun Tagore) (Varansi: The Chowkhamba Sanskrit Series Office, Volume XLIX, 1965), p. 142.

2. Herbert A. Popley, *The Music of India*, (2nd edition) (Calcutta: Y.M.C.A. Publishing House. 1950), p. 66.

3. Atiya Begum Fyzee-Rahamen, *The Music of India* (London: Luzac and Company, 1925), p. 88.

4. Popley, *op. cit.*, pages 84-87.

5. Captain N. Augustus Williard, "A Treatise on the Music of Hindoostan", Tagore, *op. cit.*, page 48.

CHAPTER THREE

MUSIC OF THE ARAB WORLD

Arab traditions are widespread throughout the Middle East and Asia.
Azerbaijani drummer.
Courtesy of the American Folklife Center, Smithsonian Institution,
Photo No. 88-15025-18.

The Arab world shares many qualities of the Indian, representing, as it does, not one country, but several, including Iraq, Saudi Arabia, Egypt, Kuwait, Qatar, Bahrain, Lebanon, Syria in the eastern regions of the Middle East, Morocco, Algeria, and Tunisia in the western. The culture has been transplanted to many regions of the globe, allowing one to hear Arab music in many cities of the United States.

The Arab tradition in music is not singular, but is often mixed with Persian and Turkish influences as well, particularly in timbres, melodic structures, and even performance. This is not to suggest that all music of the Middle East is the same, but, rather, that it derives from a common repertoire and practice, reflecting an interchange of cultural ideas throughout the history of Islam, due to changing political structures in the Arab world. The same observation might be made of European music. Gregorian chant, Mozart symphonies, Wolf lieder, Gillespie improvisations, Reich motives, and Mick Jagger gyrations have a common heritage. What they share is more prevalent than what makes them different. The discussion in this chapter, although generic, is intended to describe a wide body of practice and theory in the Middle East, largely Arab, but not excluding Persian and Turkish influences.

Music of the Middle East, which shall simply be termed Arab music in this chapter, can be traced to pre-Islamic times, when caravan songs (*huda*) were an important part of music making as was music presented by dancing slave-girls. Pre-Islamic society drew distinctions between songs that men and women sang, as well as between serious music and music for entertainment.

During the first century of Islam (seventh century), Arab music was infused with ideas derived from Persia and Byzantium. The main centers of early Islam were Mecca and Medina, where the Umayyad caliphate ruled between A.D. 661 and 750, establishing an Arab empire. Where formerly there had been only nomadic, warring tribes, the Umayyads brought social and cultural integration to the entire region. Music for entertainment, dominated by dancing girls in pre-Islamic times, was taken over by enuchs, usually non-Arab males. Because of the immoral behavior of this group of performers, music was not highly regarded in early Islamic culture, and a separation emerged between the religious use of music and its role as entertainment, the former being considered art music, the latter, folk music. The term used to describe these, respectively, became *thaqil* ("heavy" style) and *khafif* ("light" style). Thaqil was influenced by Persian and Byzantine practice since musical theorists traveled to these regions to learn and assimilate these practices into Arab music. Since Byzantine music, like Indian, was derived from ancient Greek practice, it is not surprising there are many commonalities among the theories and practices of all these cultures.

Caravan at watering hole near Ruwala (c. 1952).
Photo by Carleton S. Coon.
Courtesy of the University Museum, University of Pennsylvania, Neg. No. 50194.

When the Umayyad caliphate was overthrown by the Abbasids in A.D. 750, the power of Islam shifted to Iraq, specifically Baghdad. Music was subjected to additional Persian influence because of its geographical propinquity. This period, which lasted from the eighth to thirteenth century, is considered the "Golden Age of Islam", when Arabic-Islamic thought, literature, music, and culture became standardized and almost universal throughout the Arab world. As Bishai states:

> The rulers of the empire during these two periods were of Arab descent and, in spite of family feuds and dynastic quarrels, they believed that their own prosperity and the prosperity of their own people scattered throughout the Arab empire depended mostly on the prosperity and welfare of the local populations living under their rule. Accordingly, they encouraged trade and promoted creative arts, supplying as much protection and security to the professional sector of their domain as possible.[1]

One of the cultural endeavors accomplished during the Abbasid caliphate was the translation of numerous Greek treatises into Arabic, including those dealing with music theory. An academy was established at Baghdad to centralize learning and scholarship, thus fostering and solidifying Arab thinking. Important scholars of these periods who wrote on music include Al-Kindi, Al-Farabi, Ibn-Sina, Al-Isfahani, and Al-Maraghi.

A Prince and a Princess Listen to Musicians. Hafiz. Iran, 19th Century. Courtesy of the Arthur M. Sackler Gallery, Smithsonian Institution, Neg. No. S1986.47153.

During the Mamluk (1258-1517) and Ottoman (1517-1798) periods, Arabs were ruled by non-Arabs, leading to a general decline in culture from the zenith of the Golden Age. The modern era dates from the end of the caliphate in 1924. After World War I, modern Arab nations were formed, still known by names given in the opening paragraph above, if not by the same boundaries of the 1920s.

Much like India, music in the Arab world is considered a powerful evoker of feelings and moods, not merely something nice to hear. The musician is expected to follow scales and themes that are well established in the culture yet to improvise and shape these personally to show his creativity. The tradition is not written, but passed aurally, master to student, whether the music is art or folk. Nonetheless, the status of music in Arabic-Islamic culture is tenuous at best. There is little liturgical music in Islam and musicians are not highly regarded. Some strict Muslim rulers have prohibited music. Only the chanting of scriptures from the Koran and a call to worship (*adhan*) by the muezzin from the top of a minaret, both purely vocal, are part of worship. In the culture, nonetheless, it is considered an honor to be able to perform these two types of religious music.

The omnipresence of Islamic thought in society provides a blending of religious themes in secular music, particularly in mystical brotherhoods, where Koranic stories are told in song, often extolling the prophet of Islam, Muhammad. Secular music includes caravan songs, characterized by repeated tunes that convey the pulsation and repetition of a moving group of people and animals. They are performed as special entertainment at private parties. Popular music, which uses colloquial Arabic lyrics, conveys themes of women, love, and wine. It is performed in nightclubs. Classical songs are based on Arab literature, following meters of the language itself. These are known as *ghazal* and have subjects ranging from love and other related human emotions to praises of individuals and their great deeds. Instrumental music compliments vocal or occurs independently, using instruments that occur throughout the Arab world, even when known by a variety of names.

Tashkent musicians and dancers from Sartovsk. The trumpet is much like the Indian karna, the double drums, similar to tabla. Photo by Bolojinsky. Courtesy of the University Museum, University of Pennsylvania, Neg. No. S4-140745, Object #19656.

The structure of Arab music, indigenous to all genres, will be our primary focus in this chapter.

Melodic Structure: Maqamat

Maqamat (maqam, singular) are the melodic materials of Arab music, much as ragas are in Indian. Although Arab scholars have attempted to categorize and label all magamat, there is universal agreement in neither nomenclature nor number. In the eastern Arab countries, over 100 have been identified, in the western, far fewer. Rather than attempting merely to enumerate, we will define and try to build an understanding what a maqam is and how it functions in musical compositions.

The pitch system of Arab music divides the octave into more intervals than the Western. While we distinguish twelve half-steps, each 100 cents, in our octave, some Arab scholars have cited 17 divisions in the octaves, others as many as 25. Twenty-four is also a common number used, which translates as quarter tones (50 cents) from a Western perspective. Since the quarter-tone is not used, except in deriving a flattened third, it is good to think of the Arab systems as consisting of twelve half-steps plus five intervals that are three-quarters of a step, thus, seventeen divisions in the octave. These are acoustically derived, that is, from the division of a vibrating string on a musical instrument, specifically the *ud*, an instrument similar to the Western lute. The complication arises from the neutral third used in Arab music, an interval a quarter-tone smaller than the Western major third but a quarter tone larger than a minor third.

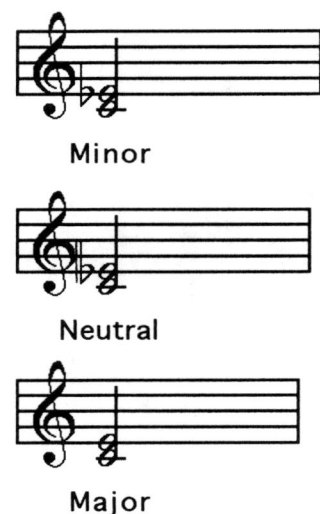

Minor

Neutral

Major

This is a typical interval used throughout the Middle East, sounding a bit different to Western ears because it is slightly flat or sharp to what we expect. There are also specific names to specify half-steps, three-quarter-tones, and whole-steps, respectively, *muganeb sagheer* (small distance), *muganeb kabeer* (big distance), and *bu'd tanee ny*. Western notation, therefore, can only approximate Arab intervals, using additional symbols for quarter-and three-quarter tones:

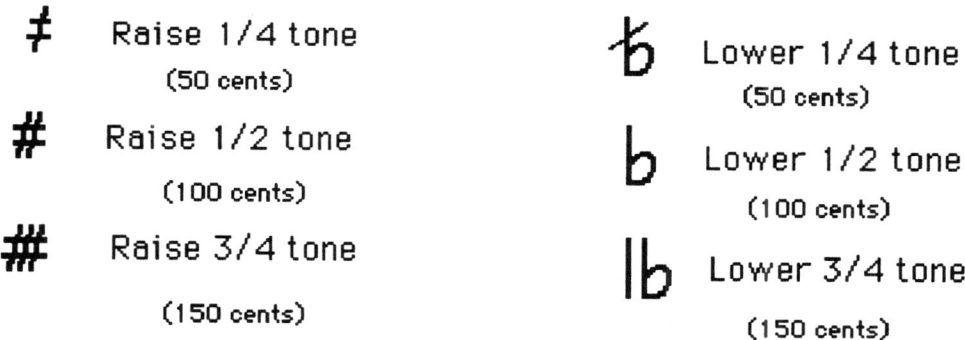

These intervals are integral to maqamat and therefore to the sound of Arab music, much like the varying intervals (shruti) used in Indian ragas. The intervals, however, are always used as part of a four- or five-pitched melodic structure, not as isolated musical events.

Maqamat can be described by the pitches used, including their range and intervals, lower and upper parts, as well as beginning and ending pitches. The lower and upper parts, either tetrachords or pentachords, are known as *ajinas* (*jins*, singular, meaning "genre"). Seventeen ajinas are recognized and used, each consisting of three, four, or five pitches:

A maqam consists of at least two ajinas placed in succession, using the same jins at different pitch levels or simply different ajinas. Although two ajinas make an octave, it is not uncommon to go beyond the octave with yet another jins. This may be a repetition of one already used or yet another one:

Some maqamat use different ajinas in the *same* octave, thus somewhat complicating the understanding and classification of Arab modal theory. Since the system is melodic, however, it is the mold of the melody and its progression from low to high that is ultimately important in understanding the structure, not in citing ajinas. Nonetheless, these are twelve main modes, originally termed *shudad*, now, magamat, which provide melodic material for all Arab music:

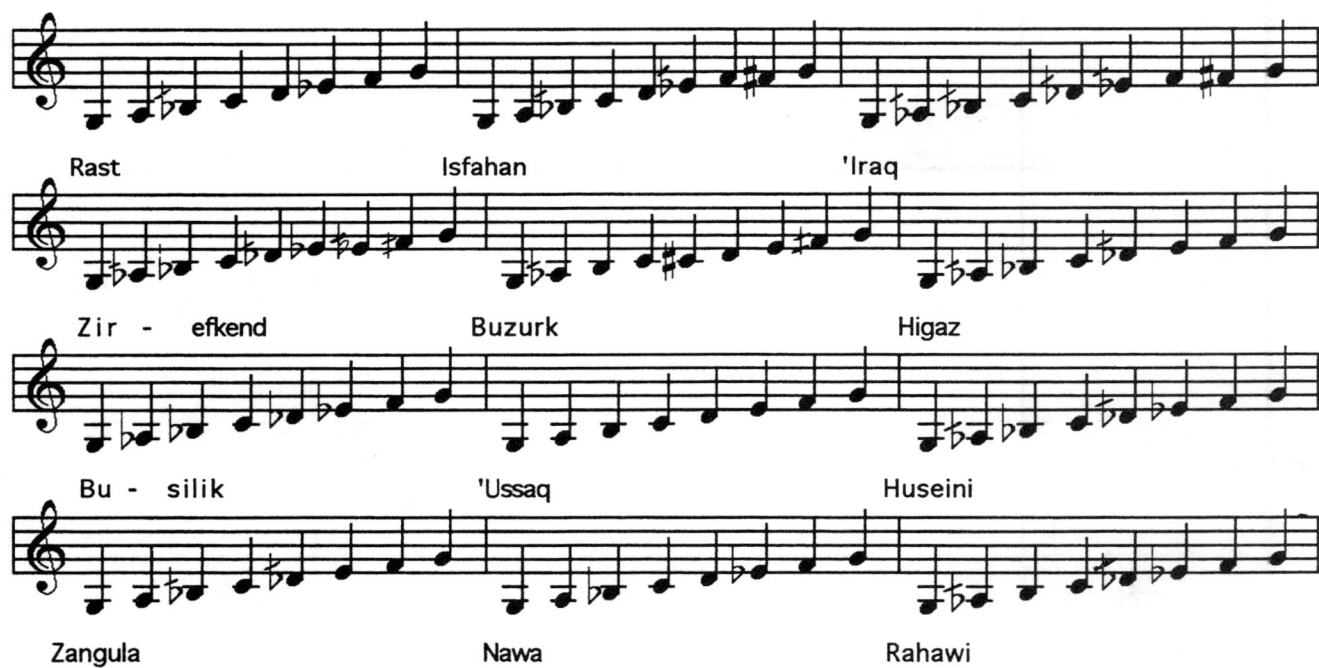

These function like the Carnatic mela and Hindustani thaat, providing the essential pitches used in melodic improvisation. In addition, the beginning pitch of a melody, known as the *mabda*, and its final resting place or tonic, *qarar*, are important. A pitch which provides contrast to the qarar at the interval of a fifth higher (sometimes a fourth or third) is the *ghammaz*, which acts somewhat like a dominant. The *zahir*, leading tone, may lie either above or below the qarar, depending on the maqam used, and occurs near cadences to propel the melody to its final resting place.

Tuvin (Tashkent) long lute (c. 1890). Photo by Bolojinsky. Courtesy of the University Museum, University of Pennsylvania, Neg. No. S4-140735, Object #19664.

The names of pitches are:

1	yaga
2	asheeran
3	agam asheeran
4	'aeirag
5	rast
6	doukah
7	seekah
8	giharka

Much like Indian ragas, the paternal maqamat enumerated above are associated with non-musical aspects of Arab society, particularly the horoscope, as well as times of the day.

Rast	Ram	sunrise
Isfahan	Bull	
'Iraq	Twins	nine o'clock
Zir-efkend	Crab	
Buzurk	Lion	
Higaz	Virgin	midnight
Bu-silik	Balance	afternoon
'Ussaq	Scorpion	sunset
Huseini	Archer	end of night
Zangula	Capricorn	
Nawa	Water carrier	before night prayer
Rahawi	Fish	morning

Healing properties have also been associated with these main maqamat. Isfahan can cure colds, Rahawi, headaches, 'Iraq, heart disorders, and Rast, problems of the eyes.

Melodic improvisation is based on a maqam, recognizing its range, ajinas, intervals, and important pitches. Although it can occur either vocally or instrumentally, the tradition is basically rooted in instrumental practice, given the derivation of maqamat from fret positions on the ud. This contrasts with Indian practice which is vocally derived, particularly the Carnatic tradition.

The maqam develops in a rhythmically free style, depending on the musician, since motives and patterns are not part of the maqam, only the fixed tonal space. This allows for a great deal of creativity in exploring tonal levels, which begin in the lowest jins and progress into higher registers. Since each jins has a central pitch, a phrase centers around this pitch. Arab melodic progression is typically conjunct, since the musician moves gradually from low to high pitches as the improvisation develops.

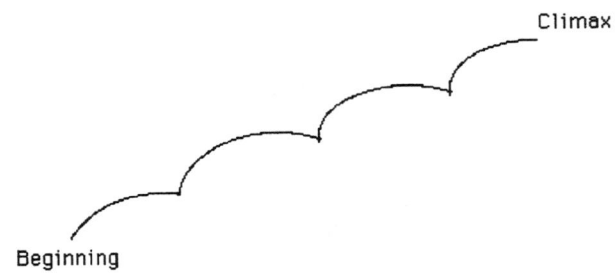

The composition ends when exploration of the highest significant pitch is complete.

The principle of maqamat is indigenous to most music of the Middle East, pointing out the common cultural heritage of Persians, Arabs, and Turks. In Iran, they are called *dastgah-ha* (*dastgah*, singular). Five are recognized, each representing a specific sentiment or feeling, not unlike Indian rasas, and adjustment of intervals in each doubles the number. The addition of two independent modes, Nava and Rast Pandjgah, brings the total number of dastgah-ha to twelve, as it is in Arab music. Although Iranian and Arab modes may share the same name, they can differ in feeling, intervals, and pitches. The neutral (flattened) third is typical in both, however.

In Iranian music, the dastgah is developed through short melodic gestures that are presented progressively higher in the mode. These are called *gusheh-ha* (*gusheh*, singular). The entire composition is a set of variations on these melodic motives.

Azerbaijani musicians.
Courtesy of the American Folklife Center, Smithsonian Institution,
Photo No. 88-15047-26.

In Azerbaijan, a former Soviet republic, the melodic mode is called *mugam*. Azerbaijan, which was also once part of the Persian empire, has a cultural connection to Turkey, which again demonstrates the homogeneity of musical practice in this region of the world. There are seventy mugams, which have names synonymous with Persian dastgah-ha. In Azerbaijani music, the mugam is explored freely in a non-pulsed improvisation called a *bardasht*, which is much like an Indian alap. This is followed by a rhythmic section, similar to the gat, called a *reng*.

In addition to these two examples, melodic modes and molds, similar to magamat, dastgah-ha, and mugam, are used in Turkey, North Africa, and Egypt, where they are known as *makam*, *taba*, and *nagham*, respectively.   All of these refer not only to the actual mode used, but to the realization of a piece of music, whether vocal or instrumental. Maqam, meaning "assembly place", fittingly describes the tradition of Arab as well as Persian and Turkish music, where this type of composition was performed, beginning in the eighth century with the Abbasid caliphs. Much like Indian music, this music represents a tradition many centuries old, which helps one understand its varying vocabulary and practice within a basic conceptual structure.

Rhythmic Structure: Iqa'at

Darabukka, hour-glass drums. Courtesy of Office National du Tourisme Tunisien.

The time cycles of Arab music are arranged as a series of strong and weak beats, not unlike Indian practice, but considerably simpler in execution. There are over a hundred *iqa'at* (*iqa*, singular), as they are called, in eastern regions of the Middle East, far fewer in North Africa. Each iqa has a series of strong beats, *naqarat*, repeated throughout a musical work (or sections of it) divided into smaller parts, *ajza*, which, in turn, have several units each. In the thirteenth century, for example, Safi-al-Din identified several cycles, including:

THAQIL THANI (16 BEATS)
3 + 3 + 2 + 3 + 3 + 2

THAMAL (12 BEATS)
2 + 2 + 2 + 2 + 2 + 2

HAZAJ (12 BEATS)
4 + 3 + 3 + 2

Although iqa'at were originally defined as meters to accompany recitation of poetry, they are now delineated as syllables on a drum, including *dum* (strong beat), *tak* (weak beat), *mah* (a beater stronger than dum which may follow it), as well as *ka*, *kah* (*ke*), and *ta*, all weaker beats than tak. Strong and weak beats, however, are not simply produced by force, but by timbre. Dum is a muffled beat while tak is clear. This depends where the syllable is sounded on the drum, rim or head, as well as whether the striking hand is closed or open. These attacks can also be effected on other instruments, such as how a string is plucked or air expelled by a wind instrument or the voice.

In ancient theory, two types of cycles were recognized, *conjunct* and *disjunct*. If two cycles run together with attacks of equal duration, they are conjunct:

KHAFIF AL-HAZAJ

THAQIL AL-HAZAJ

If separated by a rest, usually double the time between two attacks in either cycle, they are disjunct:

AL-RAMAL

Disjunct cycles were used predominantly in music practice, providing interest for both performers and listeners. Similarly, symmetrical arrangements of strong and weak beats, indigenous to European music, are not as common as asymmetrical patterns.

In naming iqa'at, the type of attack (*naqrah*) determines its classification. If the initial attack is heavy, *thaqil* is used, if light, then *khafif*, a distinction observed earlier to designate "heavy" and "light" styles of music as well. Nomenclature of iqa'at, as with maqamat, is not consistent because two distinct cultural groups may use the same name to represent different cycles. Since Arab time cycles are part of performance vocabulary, rather than written theory, they continually change, depending on the performers who use them. Although the discussion here is general, it should suffice for understanding basic concepts inherent in rhythmic practice in the Arab culture. Even the basic term, iqa'at, varies by culture. In Egypt, it is called *durub*, in Turkey, *uzal*, and in Syria, *taqm*.

Formal Structure

Egyptian dancer and musicians. Photo by Maison Bonfils (c. 1870). Courtesy of the University Museum, University of Pennsylvania, Neg. No. S4-139920.

There are both single and multimovement forms in Arab music, the latter often incorporating vocal and instrumental selections in the same composition. The *nawba* is like a Western cantata, consisting of several movements, eight or nine, which alternate between vocal and instrumental sections. What frequently distinguishes a nawba is one unifying maqam with changing iqa'at in each subsequent movement, moving from complex to simpler ones as the work progresses. Although the term referred to a group of musicians in tenth century literature, it was later used to designate an actual type of composition. Nawba meant a suite in four movements during the Abbasid caliph, consisting of vocal pieces, the first and last in Arabic, the second in Persian, and the third in either language. Presently, in Egypt and Syria, there are eight movements. The first is a *taqsim*, also performed occasionally as a solo piece, which is a virtuoso instrumental movement. The performer explores the maqam chosen for the entire suite in this initial movement, using either a free or measured rhythm, much like an Indian alap. When this is accomplished by a singer, usually on the words "ya layli", it is called a *layali* (which translates as "beauty of the night." A layali is often followed by a *mawal*, a love song in four, five, or seven verses set as a virtuoso vocal cadenza. Other important movements in the nawba include a *muwashshahat* (also *tawshih*), a strophic song with a refrain. Muwashshahat can be sacred as well as secular and are characterized by one meter that prevails from beginning to end. The poetry is arranged in couplets with a refrain in which soloist and chorus alternate. The *qasida* is an improvised vocal movement on verses of an Arabic poem, usually of some length, with variable rhythm but only one rhyme scheme. The singer is accompanied by a string instrument in both of these movements. After the qasida, which is the climactic movement, lighter, more folk-like movements follow, including *tahmila*, an instrumental piece in which soloist alternates with ensemble musicians, and the *dawr*, a vocal folk piece. The entire nawba uses an accompanying ensemble of string, wind, and percussion instruments. The term nawba refers both to compositions largely improvised as well as set pieces from standard repertoires. In Morocco, Algeria, and Tunisia, for example, the term refers to a repertory more than improvisational compositions. Even the term nawba is not universal, *wasle* being used in Syria and Egypt, and *fasil* in Turkey. The homogeneity of the genre lies in the use of soloists and ensemble musicians in a multimovement composition.

Instruments of the Arab World

Undoubtedly the best known Arab instrument is the *ud*, a lute. Our word, "lute", comes from "al-ud", and it is undoubtedly the forerunner of the European lute, imported into Western countries during the Crusades. The instrument was known to the Arabs as early as the seventh century, as well as the Persians, where it was called *ud farisi* (Persian lute), existing both as a long-necked instrument, the older type, and short-necked, which is more typical of the modern ud. In

Ud, both a solo and accompanying instrument. Courtesy of Office National du Tourisme Tunisien.

the eighth and ninth centuries, the instrument was shaped somewhat differently by Arab instrument makers and called *ud al-shabbut* (shabbut lute). Uds of this period generally had four strings tuned in fourths, A-d-g-c'. The lowest string, A, was called *bamm*, the highest, c', *zir*, meaning, respectively, low and high. A fifth string was added above zir by the ninth century in Muslim Spain, a fourth higher than c'. The highest pitch thus became f':

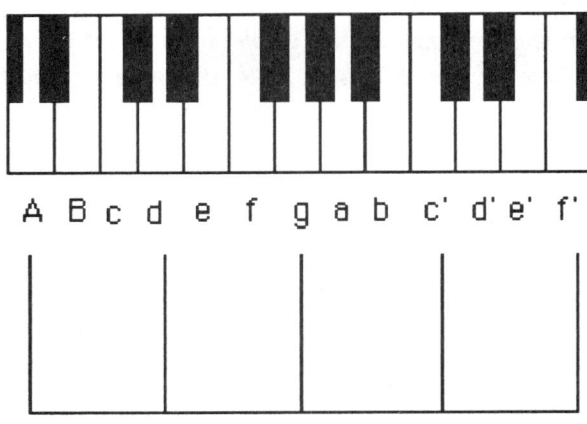

Bedouin musicians playing at a wedding on fiddle (left) and double pipe (right). (c. 1905). Photo by Jessie Tarbox Beals. Courtesy of the University Museum, University of Pennsylvania, Neg. No. S4-140731.

The four string model, however, continued to be the norm in the Middle East. Some regions made uds with frets, others without.

The modern ud is used in a variety of Middle Eastern countries, where it is configured and tuned slightly differently from region to region. Five-string instruments with double courses are common, tuned d-e-a-d'-g', and an eleventh, single string may be added on top. In western Arab countries, Morocco, Algeria, and Tunisia, the four-string instrument is used, double-strung, and tuned G-e-A-d. The ud may have moveable gut frets or be fretless, which allows greater flexibility in pitch focus and ornamentation for the performer. The strings are either gut or wound metal. As we have observed, the ud is used both as a solo instrument and as accompaniment for other instruments and vocalists in nawba.

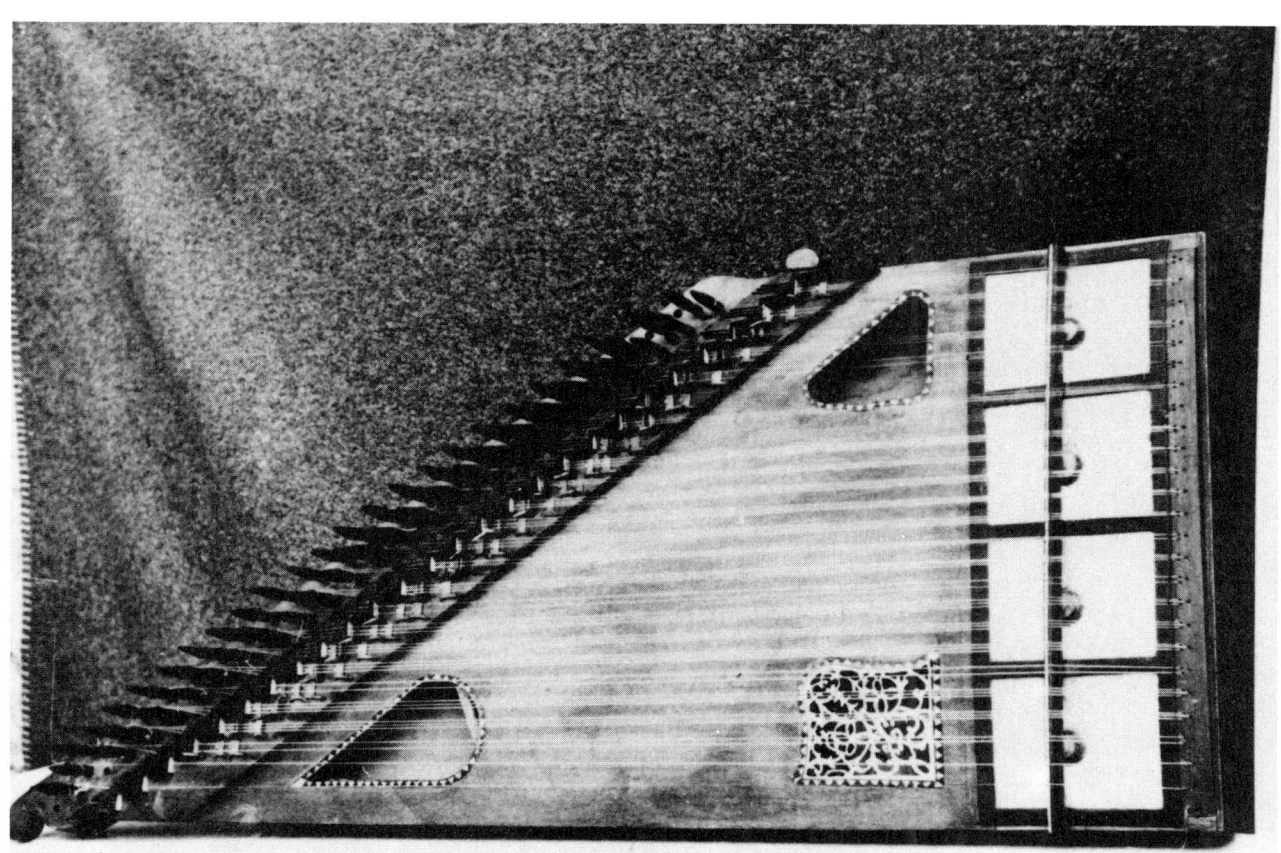

Qanun, an Arab psaltery. Courtesy of Office National du Tourisme Tunisien.

Another chordophone used in Arab culture is the *qanun*, a psaltery. The psaltery is cited in the Old Testament as a musical instrument of the Middle East. This instrument is a zither, using several strings, as many as a hundred tuned in triple courses, to provide melodic elaboration in an instrumental ensemble. The ancient qanun, known as the *nuzha* as well, had numerous strings, thirty-two on some instrument and as many as 105 on larger ones, usually arranged in triple courses. The modern qanun is shaped like a trapezoid, with tuning pegs on the diagonal side. The performer plucks the strings with picks attached to the right hand, occasionally using the left hand to bend and alter pitches. The instrument is either held against one's chest when standing or rested on the knees when seated. Since it has a range in excess of three octaves, its function in performance is to elaborate the melody, often in a higher octave, thus lending a heterophonic texture to the basic musical ensemble.

As with the ud, the qanun became known in Western Europe during the Crusades, where it was called the *psaltery*. It was depicted in medieval paintings and illuminated manuscripts as an instrument to accompany the chanting of psalms. It generally faded in importance during the Ars Nova as multi-stringed instruments were adapted with mechanical devices to pluck or strike the strings from levers attached to keys, ultimately leading to the development of the harpsichord and clavichord in the Western world. It is interesting, however, that the trapezoidal configuration was preserved in the arrangement of strings even with these instruments.

The *kamanja* is a spike-fiddle with four metal strings, often tuned a-e'-a'-e", that is, in both fourths and fifths. The resonating body of the instrument, which may be cylindrical or globular, is covered with animal skin. The instrument is played with a bow, tensioned by the performer's hand, and the spike on the bottom of the resonator allows the instrument to be rotated slightly in performance in conjunction with bowing. More of a Persian than a strictly Arab instrument, it is the only bowed instrument used in much of the Middle East. It is more important in Central Asian music. The bowing technique allows more subtlety of expression than is possible on other chordophones and it is therefore suitable for playing both as a solo or ensemble instrument.

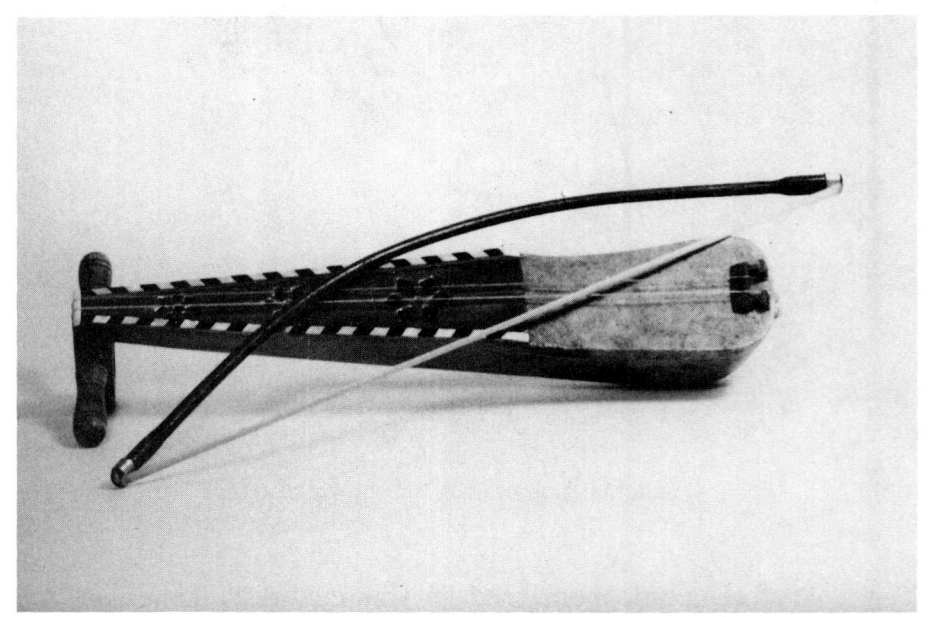

A two-string rabab with bow. Courtesy of Office National du Tourisme Tunisien.

The *rabab* is more like a Western violin in some cases, similar to the kamanja in others. The term, rabab, appears as early as the tenth century, where it referred to both types of fiddles, wooden bodied as well as parchment covered, regardless whether or not the spike is present. The body is sometimes pear-shaped, other times, quadrangular or even circular. It is generally played on the knee, like a small cello, rather than under the performer's chin. (When the Western violin is used in Arab music, this position is observed.) The rabab, like other Arab instruments, has traveled far, indigenous now to north African music as well as Indonesian, where it is known as the *rebab*.

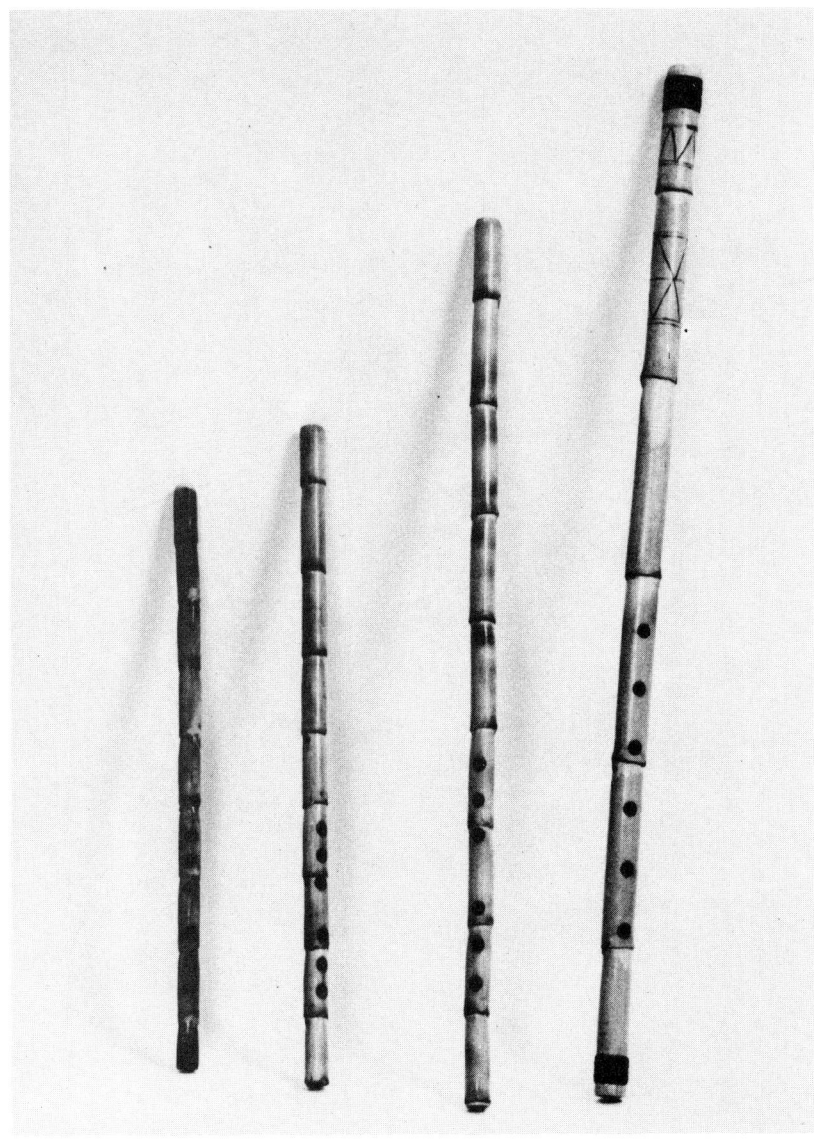

Several versions of the nay, Arabian end-blown flute. Courtesy of Office National du Tourisme Tunisien.

In addition to these chordophones, there is an end-blown aerophone used in most Middle Eastern regions called the *nay*. It is made in various lengths, which determine its fundamental pitch. Thus, *nay mahur* is pitched in C, *nay dukah* in D, and so on. Nays, which either use an open, bevelled mouthpiece or a capped top with a metal mouthpiece, are made of either wood or metal. Their playing range is about three octaves, with pitches being produced by overblowing as well as finger position. Depending on the region, some have as few as three, others as many as ten finger-holes plus a thumb-hole. The instrument is somewhat generic, being named differently in various regions, including *qasaba* in North Africa, *shabbaba* in Iraq, and *suffara* or *gasba* in Egypt. In Iran, Turkey, and Azerbaijan, it is called *ney*, and has folk counterparts throughout the area, such as the Kurdish *shimshal*.

Tuvin (Tashkent) zurna player. Photo by Bolojinsky. Courtesy of the University Museum, University of Pennsylvania, Neg. No. S4-140736.

A general term that refers both to single or double reed wind instruments as well as their performance in Arab culture is *mizmar*. Mizmar includes the *mijwiz*, a single reed, and *zurna*, a double reed. Although mizmar originally meant either the playing of a wind instrument or beautiful singing, it generally refers only to the former now. However, when a flute player sings and plays, this is still termed a mizmar.

Zurna, known as the zokra in Tunisia. Courtesy of Office National du Tourisme Tunisien.

In addition to string and wind instruments, there are percussion instruments indigenous to Arab culture. The *darabukka* is a single-headed drum with a frame shaped like a goblet. The frame is wood, metal, or even pottery, with the bottom side open, which allows for resonance in performance. The instrument is often held under the performer's arm or rested on the leg. "Darba" in Arabic means "to strike" and may be the derivative root of the word, darabukka, which is also called *derbocka* (Morocco and Algeria), *dumbelek* (Turkey), and *dombek* or *zarb* in Iran. As with many Arab instruments, the basic drum is found throughout much of North Africa, Indonesia, and Malaysia as well as the Balkans, where, for example, in Albania, it is called the *darabuke*.

Frame drum, known as bendir in Tunisia. Courtesy of Office National du Tourisme Tunisien.

Another drum, characterized as a frame-, rather than a vessel-drum, with a single head is the *duff* (also *daff*), which frequently has rattles around its frame much like a tambourine. This simple instrument was mentioned in the sayings of the Prophet Muhammad, and has been associated with mizmar, even though it is not an aerophone. It appears to have had religious significance throughout the history of Islam, but is also used in folk music. Its shape, often round, can also be hexagonal, octagonal, or even square, with or without rattles. It is occasionally double-headed.

Tunisian tar (left) and tabla (right), which is also known as the duff. Courtesy of Office National du Tourisme Tunisien.

Although this brief discussion hardly exhausts the possibility of Arab and Middle Eastern instruments, it does provide prototypical models of basic instruments used throughout this vast region. In summary, categories and alternative nomenclature will be provided to assist students in sorting out various names which describe the same type of instruments.

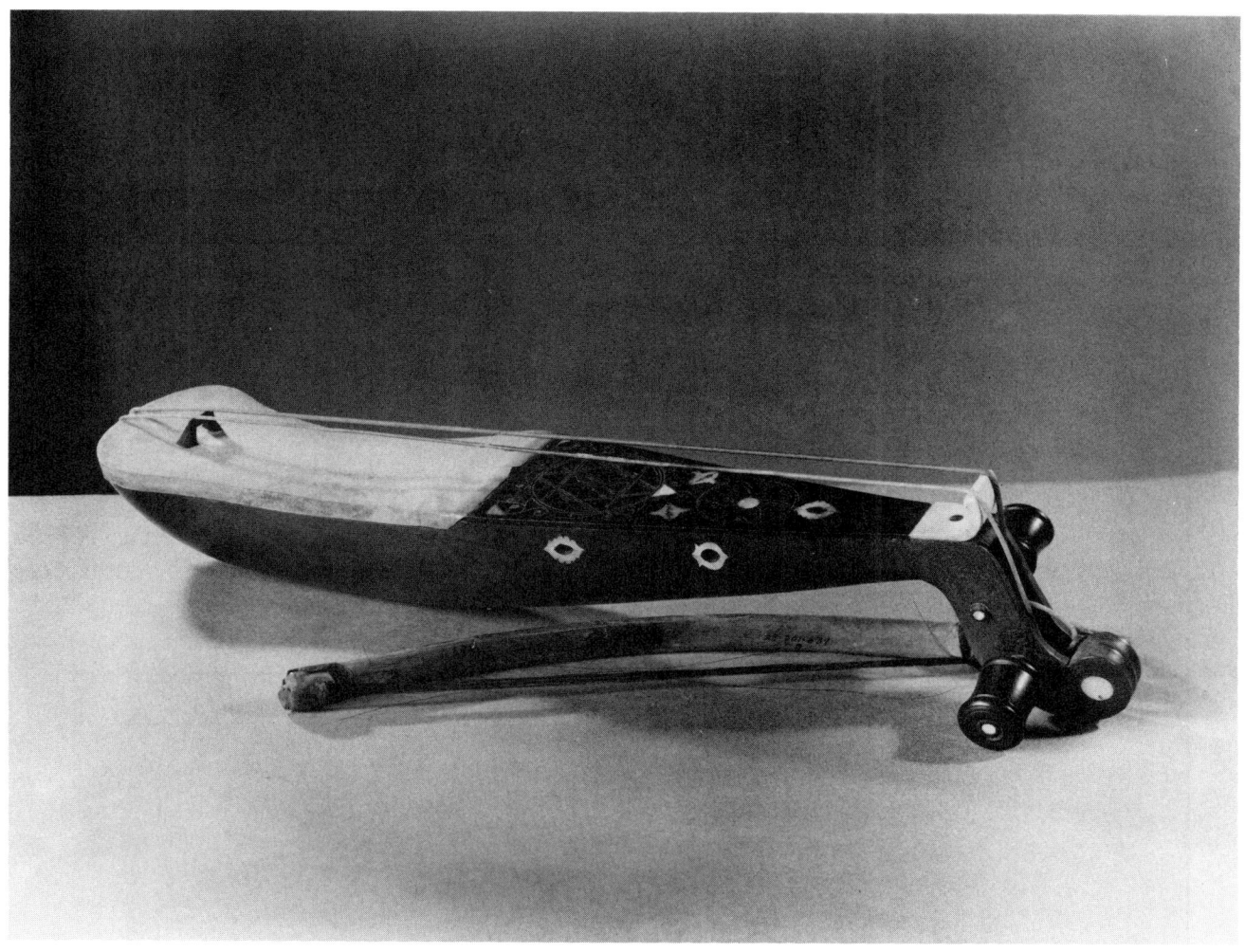

Moroccan rabab with bow (c. 1897-88), also known as kemence, rubab, and rebab in other countries.
Courtesy of the University Museum, University of Pennsylvania,
Neg. No. S8-41053, Object #29-201-639.

CHORDOPHONES	AEROPHONES
Kamanja	*Nay*
Ghichak (Central Asia)	Gasba and Qawwal (Egypt)
Joze (Iraq and Afghanistan)	Juwak and Fhal (North Africa)
K'amancha (Armenia)	Ney (Iran, Turkey, and Azerbaijan)
Kemanche (Azerbaijan and Georgia)	Qasba (Yemen)
	Pik and Munjeira (Syria and Lebanon)
Qanun	Shabbaba, Blur, and Bluir (Iraq)
Psaltery (Western Europe)	Zumbara (Sudan)
Rabab	*Zurna*
Kemence (Turkey)	Abuba (Armenia)
Rebab (Indonesia)	Ghayta (Egypt)
Rubab (India)	Kaba and Jifti (Turkey)
	Tazamar (Algeria)
Ud	Zamr (Morocco and Tunisia)
Lute (Western Europe)	Zumare (Albania)
	Zumbara (Sudan)
	Zammara (Iraq and Egypt)

MEMBRANOPHONES
Duff (daff)
Daf (Iran)
Daff (Iraq)
Dap (Armenia)
Deff and Diaff (Azerbaijan)
Darabukka
Darbuke (Albania)
Derbocka (Algeria and Morocco)
Dombek and Zarb (Iran)
Dumbelek (Turkey)

Other instruments of the region include:

CHORDOPHONES	AEROPHONES
Santur (dulcimer)	Jirba or Hibban (bagpipes)
Sehtar (long-necked lute)	Karna (trumpet)
Simsimiyya (lyre)	Shawm (oboe)
Tar (long-necked lute)	**MEMBRANOPHONES**
IDIOPHONES	Tabl (cylindrical drum)
Kaset (cymbals)	Tar (frame drum)
Qaraqeb (metal castanets)	Tbilat or Naqqarat (kettledrums)
Sunuf or Sajat (finger cymbals)	Zarb (single-headed drum)

Moroccan double-head drums, known as the tbel. Marrakesh, Morocco.
Courtesy of © David Burckhalter (1982).

Tunisian tabla. Courtesy of Office National du Tourisme Tunisien.

Singing in Arab Culture

Singing has already been discussed in connection with the nawba, the multimovement form which combines both instrumental and vocal music. Additional genres of vocal music will be discussed here. In general, a great deal of Arab vocal music follows the rhythm and rhyme of the poetry used as text.

Ataba is a form of sung poetry in four-line stanzas, that is, *quatrains*. Although the term ataba is used in Jordon, Lebanon, Syria, and Palestine, it is called *'ubudhiyya* (that which gives pain) in Iraq. The first three lines of each share similar word sounds, such as a repeated consonant within a series of words, known as an *assonance*. It is typical for each quatrain to have an aaab scheme, that is, the first three lines end with a syllable that rhymes. This may be extended for subsequent stanzas as cccb, dddb, and so forth, resulting in overall strophic form. Ataba and 'ubudhiyya are performed as improvised solo songs, often by two musicians in call-response fashion. The singing is accompanied by hand clapping, resulting in a song with much rhythmic vitality. The audience may respond on the final line of each stanza or even insert a refrain of its own. Since an ataba has a love topic, whether desire for one's chosen mate or sorrow for his/her absence or death, the overall mood is melancholic if not sad. It is almost always accompanied by the rabab.

Closely related to the ataba is the *mawal*, which may have either five, six, or seven line stanzas. There is typically a rhyme scheme of some fashion. The Egyptian mawal uses an aaaba scheme, the Iraqi, aaabbba. Mawal derives from the lament, "O my masters", and is sad, alluding to the text: "I try to smile, but my heart is crying."

Although both ataba and mawal are strophic, the classical *qasida*, discussed as part of nawba, is the most ancient of sung poetic forms. Qasida may have over 100 lines, each with a set number of poetic feet as well as the same rhyme scheme, that is, aaaaaaaa. . . . Each line presents a self-contained image or thought, with the song unified by a standard tune or variations on it. Although the form of the poetry is set, each performer varies the ordering of lines and melodic interpretation, which makes the performance "new." The singer of the qasida accompanies him/herself on ud, using the instrument to provide interludes between lines and sections. As with ataba and mawal, it is presented during social gatherings, usually by male singers and performers. Its unity, as with other Arab songs, is less through content than poetic structure, including word sounds, rhyme schemes, and number of lines. .

This is true for the *ghazal*, a short poem on love themes or camaraderie, often quite erotic. The ghazal is arranged in couplets, five to fifteen in total, using a rhyme scheme of aa, ba, ca, and so forth. In the final couplet, the poet gives his/her signature as "leave-taking" from the audience, a poetic/musical structure that seems to be used in many cultures, including, as we shall see, the Mexican corrido.

Tashkent nakars. Photo by Bolojinsky. Courtesy of the University Museum, University of Pennsylvania, Neg. No. S4-140737.

The *layali* is based on the words: "Leli ya leli ya ayni" ("Beauty of the night! Light of my eyes!") rather than a set poem. The melodic improvisations, which characterize all of the above genres, are simply based on these words, which function like nonsensical syllables in layali. This practice, however, is not unique to layali, but can be added as a refrain or extra line to almost any group singing of a secular nature. The words "Halali ya mali" ("the girl or the money"), for example, is used as a refrain to many songs in Lebanon and Syria.

Although the above genres are secular songs presented by singers in social settings, their textual references frequently allude to Islam and the faith which has united the Arab world for over a millennium. Just as references to the "Almighty" are found in Western art and folk music, so do allusions to Allah, Muhammad, religious tales, and morality permeate Arab vocal music. There is, however, some music which is purely reserved for religious utterances. *Adhan* (*azan* in Iran) is a sung call to prayer, given by the *muezzin* from a minaret or even the street five times a day. Its words begin with:

Allah akbar   God is most great

Tunisian nakars. Courtesy of Office National du Tourisme Tunisien.

This call to prayer is still a way to punctuate the passage of the day in many Arab countries. Other strictly religious chants and songs include the *tejwid*, a vocal recitation of the Koran, which may be performed at any time, any place. It is said to bring blessing on the singer as well as those who hear it. In addition, an *anashid*, a hymn, glorifies Allah, sung by laymen called *munshids* (as opposed to the professional muezzin) attached to a mosque. Muwashshah and qasida can be used in worship, too, particularly among the numerous brotherhoods that exist in the Arab world.

Key Terms and Concepts

Abbasid
Adhan (azan)
Ajinas (jins)
Ajza
Anashid
Assonance
Ataba
Bamm
Bardasht
Bu'd tanee ny
Conjunct
Darabukka
Dastgah-ha (dastgah)
Dawr
Disjunct
Duff (daff)
Dum
Durub
Fasil
Ghammaz
Gusheh-ha (gusheh)
Huda
Iqa'at (iqa)
Kamanja
Khafif
Layali
Mabda
Magamat (maqam)
Makam
Mawal
Mizmar
Muezzin
Mugam
Muganeb kabeer
Muganeb sagheer
Munshid
Muwashshahat
Nagarat
Nagham
Nagrah
Nawba
Nay
Psaltery
Qanun

Qarar
Qasida
Quatrain
Rabab
Rebab
Reng
Shudad
Taba
Tahmila
Tak
Taqm
Taqsim
Tejwid
Thaqil
'Ubudhiyya
Ud
Umayyad
Uzal
Wasle
Zahir
Zir
Zurna

Self-Checking Chapter Review

Match Column II to Column I	
Column I	Column II
1. darabukka	A. end-blown flute
2. iqa'at	B. joining rhythmic cycles so there is a rest between
3. maqam	C. recitation of a classical poem
4. nawba	D. multimovement cantata
5. ud	E. Arabic time cycles
6. qanun	F. Arabic lute
7. nay	G. Arabic melodic system
8. mizmar	H. joining rhythmic cycles so there is no rest between
9. huda	I. goblet-framed drum
10. jins	J. spike-fiddle
11. duff	K. Arabic psaltery
12. kamanja	L. caravan song
13. disjunct	M. single-headed frame drum
14. conjunct	N. unit of maqam
15. qasida	O. wind instruments

Answers			
1.	I	9.	L
2.	E	10.	N
3.	G	11.	M
4.	D	12.	J
5.	F	13.	B
6.	K	14.	H
7.	A	15.	C
8.	O		

Selected Bibliography

Bishai, Wilson B. (1973). *Humanities in the Arabic-Islamic World.* Dubuque, Iowa: Wm. C. Brown Company, Publishers.

Browning, Robert (ed.) (1984). *Music of the Islamic World and Its Influences.* New York: Athens Printing Company.

Goldron, Romain (1968). *Ancient and Oriental Music.* New York: Doubleday & Company, Inc.

Jargy, Simon (1971). *La musique arabe.* Paris: Presses Universitaires de France.

Jenkins, Jean and Poul Rovsing Olsen (1976). *Music and Musical Instruments in the World of Islam.* London: World of Islam Festival Publishing Company.

Malm, William P. (1977). *Music Cultures of the Pacific, The Near East, and Asia* (2nd edition). Englewood Cliffs, New Jersey: Prentice-Hall, Inc.

Picken, Laurence (1975). *Folk Musical Instruments of Turkey.* London: Oxford University Press.

Ribera, Julian (1929). *Music in Ancient Arabia and Spain.* (Translated and Abridged by Eleanor Hague and Marion Leffingwell.) Palo Alto, California: Stanford University Press.

Sachs, Curt (1943). *The Rise of Music in the Ancient World.* New York: W. W. Norton & Company, Inc.

Salvador-Daniel, Francesco (nineteenth century) (Henry George Farmer, ed.). *The Music and Musical Instruments of the Arab.* London: William Reeves.

Sawa, George Dimitri (1989). *Music Performance Practice in the Early Abbasid Era.* (132-320 AD/750-932 AD). Toronto: Pontifical Institute of Medieval Studies.

Strunk, Oliver (1977). *Essays on Music in the Byzantine World.* (Foreword by Kenneth Levy). New York: W.W. Norton & Company, Inc.

Wright, Owen (1978). *The Modal System of Arab and Persian Music: A.D. 1250-1400.* Oxford: Oxford University Press.

Zonis, Ella (1973). *Classical Persian Music: An Introduction.* Cambridge: Harvard University Press.

Selected Discography

Algeria
Sahara: Music Gourara
Unesco Collection: Musical Atlas
Odeon (EMI) C064-18079

Ali Hassan Kuban: From Nubia to Cairo
Shanachie Records Corp. 64036

An Introduction to Music of the Near East
Musical Heritage Society Inc. MHS 1803

Arabian Music: Maqam
Unesco Collection: Modal Music and Improvisations, VI-3
Musical Sources
Philips 6586 006

Arabic and Druse Music
Ethnic Folkways Library FE 4480

Arabic Songs and Dances
Folkways Records FW 8763
(Also Albatros VPA 8263)

Around the World: Near East
Lyrichord Discs LLST 7288

Azerbaijani Mugam
Unesco Collection: Modal Music and Improvisations, VI-9
Philips 6586 027

Bukhara: Musical Crossroads of Asia
Smithsonian Folkways CD SF 40050

Classical Music of Iran: The Dastgah Systems
Smithsonian Folkways CD SF 40039

Fantastic Arabe: Oud and Harp Music
Lyrichord Discs LLST 7318

Folk Music of Palestine
Ethnic Folkways Library FE 4408

Iran I
Unesco Collection: A Musical Anthology of the Orient
Barenreiter-Musicaphon BM 30 L 2004

Iranian Dastgah
Unesco Collection: Modal Music and Improvisations, VI-1
Musical Sources
Philips 6586 005

Iraq: Makamat
Ocora 79

Lebanon I
Unesco Collection: A Musical Anthology of the Orient
Barenreiter-Musicaphon BM 30 SL 2030

Master Musicians of Jajouka
(Music of Morocco)
Musical Heritage Society Inc. MHS 3292/3

Music for the Classical Oud
Folkways Records FW 8761

Music of Azerbaijan, The
Unesco Collection: A Musical Anthology of the Orient
Barenreiter-Musicaphon BM 30 L 2024

Music of Islam and Sufism in Morocco, The
Unesco Collection: A Musical Anthology of the Orient
Barenreiter-Musicaphon BM 30 SL 2027

Music of South Arabia
Ethnic Folkways Library P 421

Music of the Near and Middle East
Lyrichord Discs LL 160

Oriental Nights
Monitor Records MSF 766

Oud, The
Lyrichord Discs LLST 7160

Sung Poetry of the Middle East
Unesco Collection: Sung Poetry (Secular and Mystic) Vii-1
Philips 6586 024

Syria: Sunnite Islam
Unesco Collection: Musical Atlas
Odeon (EMI) C064-17885

Taqasim and Layali: Cairo Tradition
Unesco Collection: Modal Music and Improvisations, VI-5
Musical Sources
Philips 6586 0192

Endnotes

1. Bishai, Wilson B. (1973). *Humanities in the Arabic-Islamic World.* Dubuque, Iowa: Wm C. Brown Company Publishers, page 20.

CHAPTER FOUR

MUSIC OF THE CHINESE CULTURE

Chinese culture includes numerous ethnic groupings. Manchu performers at Tucson Meet Yourself.
Photo © David Burckhalter (1989).
Courtesy of Jim Griffith and the Southwest Folklore Center, Tucson, Arizona.

China, as a culture, is a large and diverse group of people which presently includes inhabitants of the East Asian mainland country known as the People's Republic of China as well as Hong Kong and Taiwan (Republic of China). The cultural group now exceeds one billion persons.

In addition, the Chinese culture may be considered to extend far beyond these borders to residents of numerous countries around the world, including the United States, Canada, Thailand, Singapore, and Indonesia, where perhaps another twelve million Chinese have emigrated. These groups have often been the more conservative element of Chinese culture, striving to keep musical traditions alive, traditions that date back several centuries, to the time of Confucius.

A twenty-one hundred year-old tomb was recently discovered and explored by archaeologists in the People's Republic of China. This tomb, which dated from the Han Dynasty (206 B.C.--A.D. 221) contained not only a corpse, but many artifacts, including three musical instruments, from the period, thus showing how important music must have been to the immanent personage who was buried in the tomb. In addition to the twenty-five string wooden zither (*se*) and twenty-two-pipe mouth organ (*sheng*), the twelve pitch pipes used to establish tuning for the entire empire were found. There were also numerous figurines representing a banquet scene, including several musicians with their instruments. Music was apparently integral to Chinese society 2500 years ago.

"Realms of the Immortals." (showing Chinese chordophones)
China, Sung dynasty, 13th Century.
Courtesy of the Freer Gallery of Art,
Smithsonian Institution, Neg. No. 5381B:18.13.

Probably no major state throughout history has applied the fine arts to everyday living as rigorously as has China. Throughout their long history, when an ordinary Chinese person appreciated music, he/she was happier and therefore easier to govern. Confucius, who lived hundreds of years before Christ, equated music with joy. Music, dancing, and ceremony, he believed, were primarily designed to lead people in the proper direction, society's correct path. This not only created a happier, more productive society, but, according to the wishes of their rulers, a stable political situation.

All of the arts are in time with the universe in China. This is the essence of Chinese music and philosophy. Arts must be in rhythm with the entire universe, used neither for their own sake nor for sheer entertainment, but as social binder. If a scale were found to be out of tune, it was believed, there was danger that the social order, including government and state, might collapse.

> . . .the true basis of expression was not individualism and the exhibition of a fundamentally almost tragic confrontation with oneself and the facts of existence; on the contrary, expression, which was achieved with complete naturalness, resulted from obedience to certain universal laws that lie behind artistic creation as behind everything else.[1]

The major religions in China are Confucianism, Buddhism, and Taoism. Confucius, who lived in the late fifth and early fourth century B.C., was a private tutor. Legends about him provided inspiration for future generations of artists. Since he was a literary man, the Chinese have always honored writers. Most emperors since his time have been involved with the arts, whether through poetry, painting or music.

Chinese Dragon Dancer at Tucson Meet Yourself. Photo © David Burckhalter (1989). Courtesy of Jim Griffith and the Southwest Folklore Center, Tucson, Arizona.

Confucius said that the universe is a closed system into which all creatures must articulate. This is the only means for survival of all. There are therefore sacred rituals and rules of conduct which are essential to observe if a harmonious relationship is to be maintained between the universe and its inhabitants. Humans must strive to maintain the natural order through observing social patterns and adhering to basic structures. All beliefs which subsequently were to come to China proved to be compatible with this philosophy, including Taoism, founded by Lao-tzu, and Buddhism, which manifested itself in both the Little Vehicle (Hinayana) and Great Vehicle (Mayayana).

Since the time of Confucius, Chinese music (yueh) has been considered one of the six important arts, which include li (conduct), she (athletics, particularly archery,) yu (athletics, particularly charioteering), shu (writing and history) and shu (mathematics).

Music in the Chinese courts throughout history was thus rigidly organized and controlled. Each dynasty had a Bureau of Music. Specialists were used to establish basic pitches and keep music in tune with the universe. Music was used for palace feasts, festivals, and military occasions and was therefore classified as ritual music (*ya-yueh*), ceremonial entertainment (*yan-yueh*), and processional (marching) music. The greatest reigns and dynasties were characterized by equally great music. Music was important for leading a moral life, at least for Chinese rulers. Music was believed to bring virtue to their souls, but this was neither possible nor necessary for commoners and animals. Confucius, it was said, was mistakenly imprisoned at one time in his life. He was released, however, when he displayed skill on the *qin*, a string instrument. No one, it was believed, who played an instrument so beautifully, could be a criminal. Those who performed well must not only be rulers, they must be virtuous.

The Chinese have always believed the harmony of the universe results from the merging of two forces, one positive and one negative. These are called, respectively, *yang* (+) and *yin* (-). These opposing but complimentary forces permeate not only their beliefs concerning the universe, but of music as well.

> The Yin and Yang were like the warp and woof in the fibre of Chinese life. They are discernible very early in two main aspects of ancient Chinese society, ritual and divination--the one concerned with the performance of rites on earth, the other seeking to understand the ways of nature and Heaven.[2]

Chinese culture has always been rich in symbols, as exemplified in their calligraphy. It also permeates religion, art, poetry, and dress. This symbolism is seen through numbers, including the number five. The cosmos includes five elements--time, space, matter, energy, and sound. There are five branches of government: *gong*, the ruler; *shang*, the ministers; *jue*, the people; *zhe*, affairs; and *yu*, things (affairs). (These same terms are used to name the five pitches of the Chinese scale!) In astronomy, five points divide heaven into one central polar region and four peripheral areas. Five sacred mountains are recognized, one each in the provinces of Shantung, Hunan, Shensi, Hopei, and Honan. North, South, East, West and a Zenith point represent five directions. Five planets, five virtues, five flavors, and five colors (red, yellow, blue or green, white, and black) are all part of the Chinese system.

The five pitches of the Chinese scale were thus important symbols of the state, the cosmos, and almost everything else. Each dynasty that came to power in China immediately began the task of redetermining the fundamental tones. Their survival as rulers as well as preservation of the social order depended on music!

Chinese ceremonial bell. Courtesy of the Freer Gallery of Art, Smithsonian Institution, Neg. No. 41.9-1.

Since comprehending Chinese history depends on some understanding of the dynasties (ruling families), the following chronology will be useful throughout this chapter:

Dynasty	Dates
Shang	1700-1050 B.C.
Zhou	1050-221 B.C.
Qin	221-206 B.C.
Han	206 B.C.-A.D. 221
Wei (Three Kingdoms)	221-265
Jin	265-420
Southern and Northern Dynasties	420-589
Sui	581-618
Tang	618-907
Five Dynasties	906-960
Song	960-1279
Yuan	1260-1368

Dynasty	Dates
Ming	1368-1644
Qing (Manchu)	1644-1911
Republic of China	1911-1949 mainland
	1949-present on Taiwan
People's Republic of China	1949-present

Before the Han dynasty, China was a small, feudal state. After many centuries of discord, unification was achieved in 221 B.C. during the Qin dynasty, thus ending centuries of feudal wars. Emperor Shi Huang-ti unified literature, language, and philosophy as well as burned all previous works in government archives, including documents on music. He then named himself the first emperor of China (shi = beginning) and built the Great Wall as a fitting symbol to protect his newly unified country and keep out foreign invaders.

Colossal stone head of a Bodhisattva (c. Sixth century A.D.) from China. Courtesy of the University Museum, University of Pennsylvania, Neg. No. S8-1323, Object #C354.

During the Han dynasty, a Bureau of Music and Musicians (Yueh Fu) was created to place music under government auspices. This was perpetuated under the Wei dynasty as well but was abolished during the Jin dynasty, creating a revolt by musicians which was ultimately suppressed. During the next two hundred years, China became a divided country, the South remaining Chinese, the North falling under the influence of foreigners, particularly Mongols.

The country was reunited under the Sui dynasty. Emperor Wen Ti organized a massive orchestra for ceremonial purposes and, by the end of the Sui dynasty, there were 30,000 musicians and dancers supported by the state.

"A Man Taking His Ease." (showing Chinese lute)
China, Ming dynasty, 15th-16th Centuries. Courtesy of the Freer Gallery
of Art, Smithsonian Institution, Neg. No. 11.232-2.

The Tang dynasty was a golden age for Chinese culture. During this era, three types of music were recognized: *Ya Yueh* (court music); *Su Yueh* (common music); and *Nu Yueh* (foreign music). Opera was also established during this period, exhibiting many of the traits associated with Chinese opera to this day, including the alternation between songs of dialogue (recitative) and of musical merit (aria) as well as singing in head-voice or falsetto. Women's roles were often played by boys. The clown character became established in musical theatre, even being played by the emperor Yuan Hsuan Tsung during his reign. Emperor Ming Huang (713-756) organized the Pear Garden school to train court entertainers.

The Song dynasty was characterized by expanded economic activity and heightened prosperity. There was a corresponding expansion of artistic activities. In music, there were attempts to restore Ya Yueh, appropriate music and dances for the court, as well as to reaffirm the standard pitches. Emperor Huitsung became so involved with the arts, however, that he neglected the more pragmatic concerns of leading his nation and was carried off by barbarians, leading to a dynasty headed by the Mongols, the Yuan. Kublai Khan was the first Yuan emperor, commencing a dynasty dominated by soldiers and horsemen as well as influences from more remote areas of Asia, such as Tibet. New scales and instruments were introduced during the Yuan dynasty, including a 90-pipe mouth organ. For the first time, Buddhism became the principal religion of China, temporarily replacing Confucianism.

The Ming dynasty sought to purge the country of all foreign influences. Emperor Hungwu closed the frontiers. Contact with areas outside of China ceased as the culture attempted to restore the accomplishments of the Tang and Song dynasties. The glories of the past were never truly restored, but new art works and techniques did evolve. Zhu Zaiyu, a prince, developed the principles of equal-temperament during this period, fully a century before it appeared in Europe. Ming isolationism ended when the Portuguese and Spanish Jesuit missionaries arrived. Western ideas began to permeate Chinese culture.

The Qing dynasty was dominated by foreign influence, specifically Manchurian, with the introduction of new instruments. Emperor Ch'ien Lung, greatly interested in music, wrote treatises on and edited dictionaries of music. Since 1912, music has been used to serve the needs of republicanism, particularly by fostering nationalism through patriotic songs and opera. This has been particularly attenuated with the separation of China in 1949 into two countries, the Republic of China (Taiwan) and People's Republic of China (mainland China). In conclusion, it is important to realize the alternation in China between isolationist tendencies and foreign influence. This exemplifies the principle of yang and yin in political, social, and artistic arenas, leading to a broad-based culture characterized by periods in which new ideas were introduced followed by attempts to restore authentic Chinese culture.

Melodic Structure: Lu

Since the Chinese believed that political stability depended upon a rigid ordering of all elements in the universe, including music, how pitches were established was a concern in the culture even before 2000 B.C. Instruments which could maintain a stable pitch over a period of years, such as panpipes, stone chimes, or bronze bells were the preferred models, not chordophones nor the human voice, where pitch might be relative. The exact mathematical relationships were worked out and documented by 239 B.C.

The fundamental tone in China is called *huangzhong* (yellow bell), established by a given length of pipe or by a bell or stone of set dimensions. (We shall use the pipe (tube) system here!) All other pitches were derived from huangzhong, much as, in the metric system, linear measurement is derived from the meter, defined as one ten-millionth (.0000001) of the distance from equator to pole along a meridian. Establishing pitches in the Chinese system was mathematical and precise, based on subtracting as well as adding lengths to generate a cycle of pitches. The second pitch, *linzhong* (forest bell), was established by using a pipe 2/3 the length of huangzhong. It has been discovered that huangzhong was close to the pitch "f" in our system, so linzhong would be a perfect fifth higher (702 cents), close to "c".

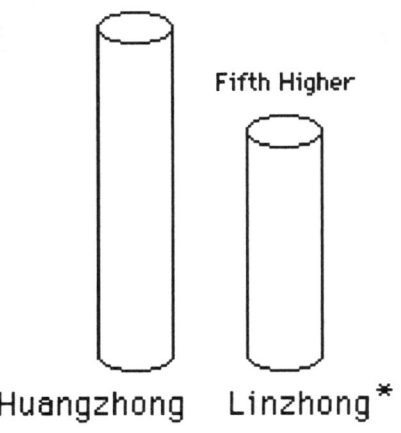

*2/3 length of Huangzhong

Linzhong would now be used to determine a third pitch a fifth yet higher, which would result in "g", *jiazhong* (great frame). However, since subsequent reduction of a wind pipe (bell or stone) would eventually result in infinitesimally smaller objects, in reality, jiazhong was doubled in length (size), lowering the pitch one octave. This is the same thing as using the ratio 4/3 of linzhong, rather than 2/3, resulting in an inversion of the perfect fifth higher to a perfect fourth lower.

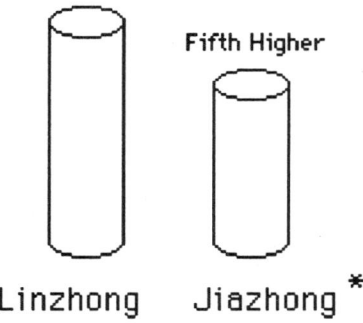

*2/3 length of Linzhong

The pattern of using a 2/3 ratio, followed by 4/3, then 2/3, 4/3, and so on, was used to generate twelve basic pitches or *lus*. Those which were derived from the 2/3 ratio, an ascending fifth, are considered male (yang +), while those derived from the 4/3 ratio, a descending fourth, are female (yin -) pitches:

The lus, twelve in number, correspond to the months of the year as well as hours of the day, and each was used to generate a series of scales for its respective month or hour. However, since perfect fifths and fourths were used to generate this sequence of lus, a discrepancy always resulted on the thirteenth pitch, never allowing the cycle, whether musical or cosmic, to be completed. Although it should have been identical to huangzhong, the thirteenth pitch was actually higher by 25 cents, one-eighth of a pitch. In other words, there was no point of congruence in this theoretical system, that is, a return to the fundamental pitch.

In a society in which music was the basis for political stability, this problem was one which received continual attention. Pythagoras similarly noted this in the Western world around 400 B.C., fully independently of his contemporaries in China, and this discrepancy, in our culture at least, is called the *Pythagorean comma*. Since the lus, much like early Western pitches, were acoustically based, derived from pure intervals based on mathematical proportions applied to vibrating strings and surfaces, there were some musical problems inherent in the system, at least from a contemporary viewpoint. The system, however, worked well for the Chinese for two basic reasons: (1) not all twelve notes were used, at least chromatically; and (2) the system was not used harmonically.

Chinese music is *pentatonic*, that is, it uses scales with five discrete pitches, not twelve. If, in the sequence of the twelve lus shown above, the first *five* are chosen, and then arranged in ascending pitch order, a pentatonic scale is formed, the repetition of the beginning pitch closing the scale within an octave:

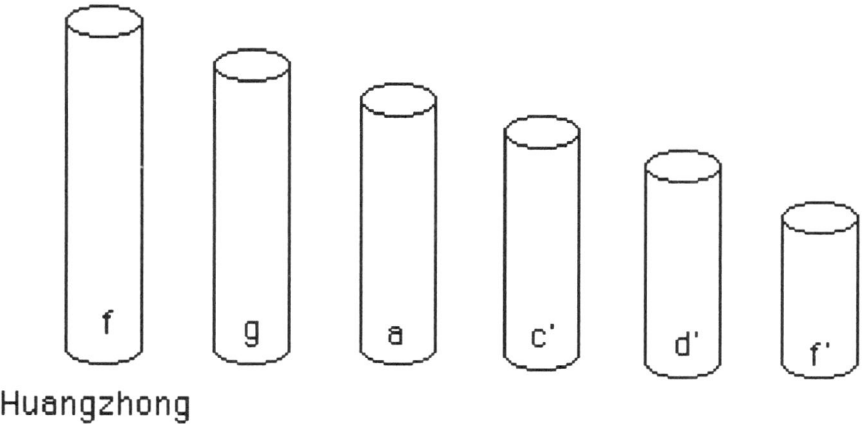

Any five lus in succession will generate the same pentatonic scale transposed. This scale is so important in Chinese music that a type of sol-fa system is used to designate each pitch in position:

gong	shang	jue	zhe	yu	gong
1	2	3	4	5	
200 cents	200 cents	300 cents	200 cents	300 cents	

Between gong, shang, and jue, respectively, there is approximately a whole step (200 cents), as there is between zhe and yu. The only other interval, as between jue and zhe as well as yu and gong (octave higher), is slightly wider. It is a minor third (300 cents). Thus, within the octave, all intervals are either whole-steps or minor thirds, resulting in a scale which has no strong tendency tones, such as half-steps. Since there is no tendency that pulls a melody back to it, this means that gong does not function like a tonic. Therefore, any pitch, gong, shang, jue, zhe, or yu, can be used as a melody's final. A melody that ends on gong is said to be in the *gong-mode*, one that ends on shang, the *shang-mode*, and so on. There are thus *five* different modes, also called *diao*, as well as twelve different positions for each set of five modes, resulting in a total of 60 diao. Since only five successive lus are used in any scale, not distantly related ones, the Pythagorean comma creates no tuning problems in Chinese music.

In practice, beginning with the late Zhou dynasty (sixth century B.C.), two additional pitches were interpolated in the minor thirds as passing tones, creating heptatonic scales. These are called *bian tones*. They form half-step relationships, respectively, with zhe and high gong, but do not really alter the pentatonic quality of the Chinese scale since they are used more as ornaments than structural pitches.

*Bian tones   *   *

Their inclusion did not result in a major scale, however, but was more like an untempered Lydian mode. In the consideration of modes, seven different pitches could result in 84 diao, a figure mentioned throughout a great deal of Chinese music history.

Derivation of the twelve lus has been attributed to the emperor Huang-ti, who sent Ling Lun, a musician, to the Western mountains in 2697 B.C., it was said, to cut twelve bamboo pipes from which all music in China would be tuned. Ling Lun heard the beautiful singing of both male and female phoenixes and cut his bamboo pipes to duplicate their sounds. He returned to China with twelve perfect pitch pipes. These were subsequently lost, thereafter giving rise to each dynasty's preoccupation with recovering the "exact" pitches on which to base their music, as evidenced by the pipes discovered in the Han dynasty tomb.

Over the centuries, the discrepancy of 25 cents, however, was noted in the untempered octave. Four thousand years later, in 1584, Prince Zhu Zaiyu of the Ming Dynasty evolved a method of equal temperament using a tempered fifth of 699.69 cents (c. 700) rather than the pure fifth of 702 cents. This resulted in a return to huangzhong after twelve lus, mitigating the so-called Pythagorean comma. (Each lu was 2 cents smaller, resulting in reduction of the discrepancy by c.2 x 12 or c. 25 cents.) As already noted, this Asian version of equal-temperament occurred some hundred years *before* Werckmeister evolved such technology for the Western world, thus demonstrating the scientific approach the Chinese used in music. Unfortunately, Zhu Zaiyu's system was never officially adopted and equal temperament came to be known throughout the world through the European, not the Chinese, model.

Young boy in Peking opera. Courtesy of National Fu Hsing Dramatic Arts Academy, Taipei, Taiwan, Republic of China.

Melodic variety, the rise and fall of pitches, in Chinese music is closely connected with the spoken language, which is inflected. This means that the meanings of words are determined by how they are pitched. In Chinese, one word can have several meanings, depending how it is inflected, that is, whether its pitch remains static, rises, or falls, as well as whether it is stressed or unstressed. "Chih", when spoken at a level, unstressed pitch means "know." When stressed, it becomes "eyes blurred and irritated." If the pitch ascends and it is unstressed, the word means "happiness," but if it ascends and is stressed, it means "salted beans." If the pitch descends and is unstressed, the word becomes "wisdom." Stressed and descending, it means "wing" or "fin." Chinese words are therefore classified by their tone, which can be "even", "rising", "going", or "entering".

The inflected nature of speech has some impact on the setting of poetry to music, with rising tones often set to ascending melodic lines, lowering tones with descending. Rigid correlation, however, is not always observed, but is used for dramatic punctuation. Chinese is almost a monosyllabic language and, because each word is pitched, the language itself is quite musical.

Pitch, of course, is not used in an absolute sense in speaking, but is a function of the speaker's natural voice, whether male or female. The rising and falling of words as well as melodic lines, however, does reflect the balance of yang and yin, applied yet again to contrasting effects.

Harmonic Structure: Heterophony

Western music almost always includes harmony, typically as background to support a melody or series of melodies. Melody and harmony generally agree in tonality, which means the pitches used in the melody clearly outline what chord should be used. The issue of harmony is somewhat complex in Western music, given that our history has been concerned with the element for over a thousand years.

In Asian cultures, such as Chinese, however, harmony is almost incidental to musical development. It occurs, but is not used to support a well-focused melody in the foreground. It occurs rather as a result of divergent pitches that *might* occur in two or more simultaneous but slightly different versions of the main melody. This is known as *heterophony*, a texture that is largely Asian.

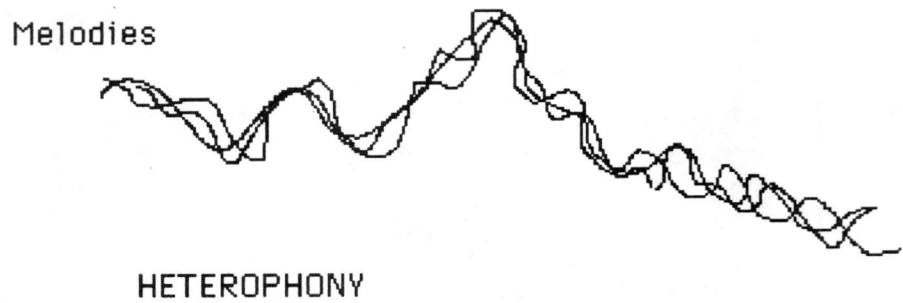

Heterophony is most lucid when there is different timbre on each version of the melodic line, one sustained, another detached, a third, elaborated through ornamentation. When singing is accompanied by instruments, for example, they closely follow the voice, in both rhythm and melodic contour. This texture, foreign to Western thinking, is quite typical of most Asian music, particularly Chinese, Japanese, and Korean.

Instruments of China

It has been traditional throughout Chinese history to classify instruments by the eight materials of which they are constructed, rather than their means of sound production, such as strings or wind. This is called the *bayin* system and the eight materials are metal, stone, silk, bamboo, gourd, earth (pottery), skin, and wood.

Since pitch stability in instruments was important throughout history, enabling the lus to be used as the basis for all pitch determination, metal has always been an important material for making instruments. Similarly, stone instruments, known generically as *lithophones*, were important. Jade chimes were as common in China as bronze chimes and gongs. Other materials, particularly silk (strings) or skin (drums), were much more mercurial in their production of pitches, being subject to changes in temperature and humidity. Although these eight materials provide historical interest, demonstrating a Chinese penchant for classification schemes, whether five pitches, twelve lus, or eight materials, we will examine several Chinese instruments, as we have others throughout this text, through their sound production means, beginning with several chordophones.

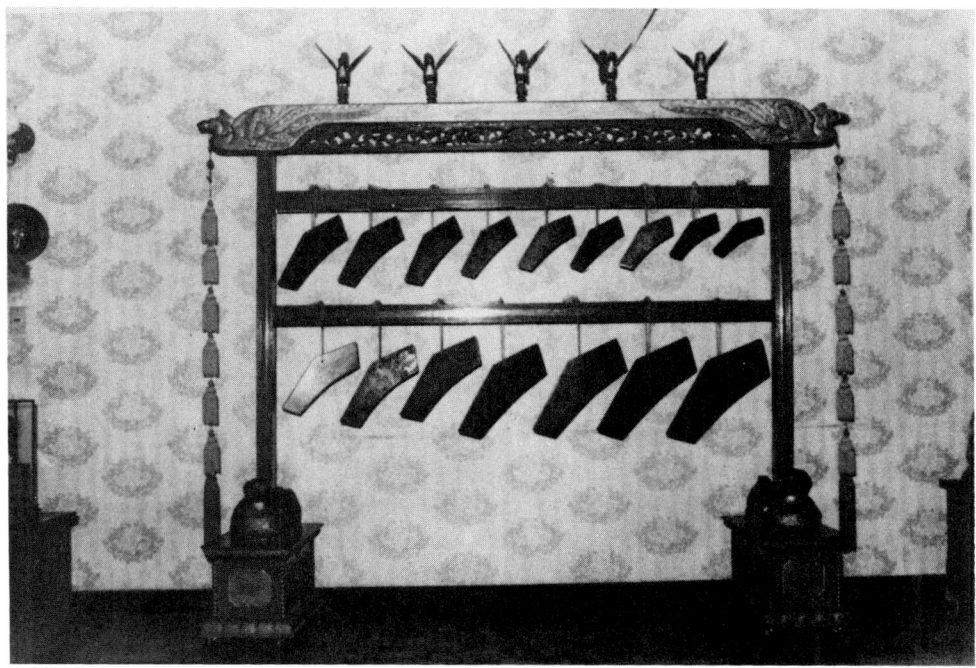

Bianjing, Chinese stone chimes, an example of a lithophone. Constructed and photographed by Chuang Pen-li. Courtesy of K. H. Han, Northern Illinois University.

The *qin*, a zither-like chordophone, dates from 700 B.C. It has at least five strings (silk) which cross its entire long, flat sounding board. It is usually positioned during performance on a table in front of the performer. Since the qin has always been associated with Confucianism, it is therefore considered an instrument of intellectuals. Scholars and monks, who had the time to master it, often hung the qin on the walls of their houses to link symbolically the past with the present. It is a difficult instrument to master and has never been considered an instrument of the common folk, only of privileged intellectual classes.

Before the time of Confucius, five strings were typical. Two more were later added, each made of twisted silk. In performance, the player's right hand actually plucks the strings, while the left moves along the unfretted sound board, stopping pitches relative to thirteen positioned dots of mother-of-pearl. Unlike many Asian zithers, however, the qin does not use bridges to elevate the strings from the body of the instrument. Because of the general looseness of the silk strings, the sound produced is not loud. Subtle effects can be produced, including harmonics or "floating" tones.

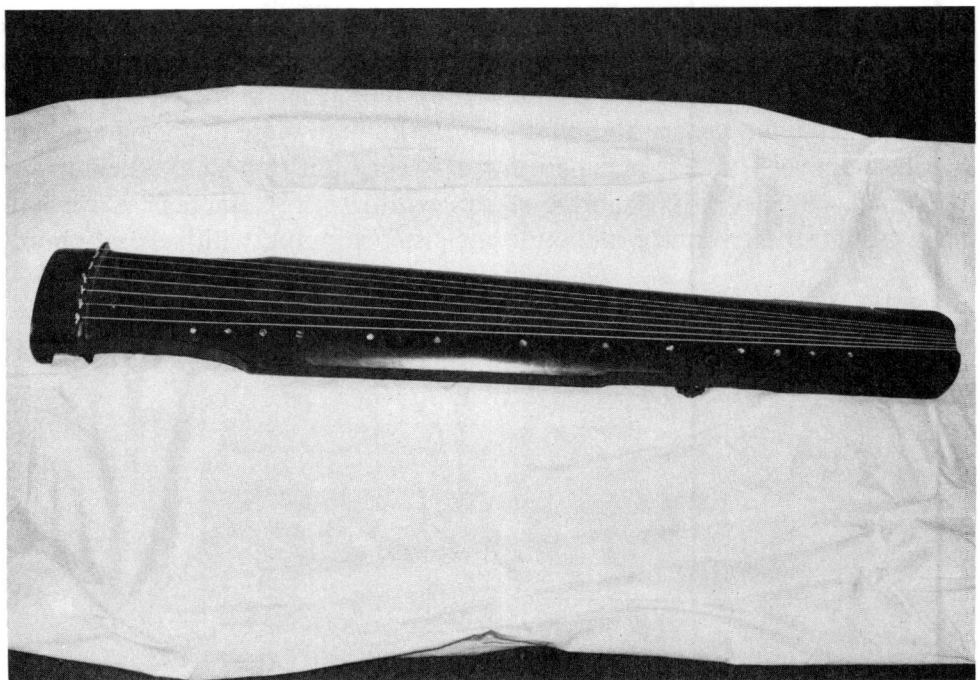

Ming dynasty qin with seven strings and thirteen positioned dots. Courtesy of K. H. Han, Northern Illinois University.

The qin is considered an allegory of the universe since its top is rounded like the arch of heaven. The flatness of its bottom represents the earth. It is only logical that its music became a symbol for harmony between heaven and earth. Famous qins throughout history have been anointed with proper names, including "Pine Fairy" or "Echo of a Goose Cry", and the most appropriate place for playing one, it was said, was in the mountains or at least in front of a scroll depicting mountains. Since the instrument had divine connotations and performing on it was tantamount to a religious experience, there were certain conditions under which it simply could not be played, including rainy weather, in the presence of rude or coarse people, after drinking or sex, when sweating, or while wearing soiled clothes.

Qins are art objects in their own right, often finished with a coat of black, red, and green lacquer or with a mottled effect. They are used both for solo playing and in ensembles, especially in court ceremonies. They are also used to accompany the player's singing, much as we use a guitar. The greatest period of solo playing was during the Ming dynasty when twenty-four touches (playing techniques) were developed and codified. In recent years, there has been renewed interest in the qin. New compositions have been written for it as well as older works transcribed into Western notation.

The *zheng* is also a zither, but, unlike the qin, uses bridges to elevate the strings away from the body of the instrument. The zheng has been used less for ceremonials and rituals but more for personal entertainment. It has been associated more with nature and romance than intellectualism. Although the zheng cannot be traced back as far as the qin, it was known in Chinese literature by the time of the Qin dynasty (c.220 B.C.) In antiquity, zhengs sometimes had twelve, other times, thirteen strings. Since the Qing dynasty (eighteenth century), sixteen strings have been standard, each with a moveable bridge shaped like an upside-down "Y" used for tuning. The tuning is basically pentatonic and the sixteen strings therefore allow a three-octave range. Strings originally were silk, but steel is now generally used.

Zheng, 16-string zither with moveable bridges.
Courtesy of K. H. Han, Northern Illinois University.

In performance, the player plucks the right segment of the string (right of the bridge) with fingernail or pick, while the left hand is used to manipulate the left segment, producing ornaments, including pitch deflection and vibrato. Although zheng music is occasionally notated on the Western staff, *cipher notation*, using relative pitch with numbers representing the strings, rather than fixed staff notation, is still preferred.

For the past one-hundred years, solo performance on zheng has been more important than ensemble work. Solo pieces are typically programmatic, describing the tranquillity of nature or a romantic subject.

Professor Tsai-ping Liang performing on zheng.
Photo by George Tarbay. Courtesy of K. H. Han, Northern Illinois University.

The *sanxian* is a simpler chordophone than either qin or zheng, classified as a lute rather than zither since it has a long neck attached to a resonating body at its lower end, much like an American banjo. It dates from the Yuan dynasty (thirteenth century) but may actually be much older. The sanxian has been used both in regional opera as well as folk music because of its inherent simplicity.

The sanxian has three strings, tuned in fifths and fourths, such as D-A-d or G-d-g. The pitch, however, is not fixed, but is set relative to the singer's range, since it is an accompanying instrument, or to conform to other instruments when used in ensemble. Its neck has no frets and the strings, which may be used to play either melodies or chordal combinations, are plucked with a large ivory pick. It has a range of two to three octaves. The box resonator at the base of the instrument is hollow but covered with animal parchment, such as snake skin.

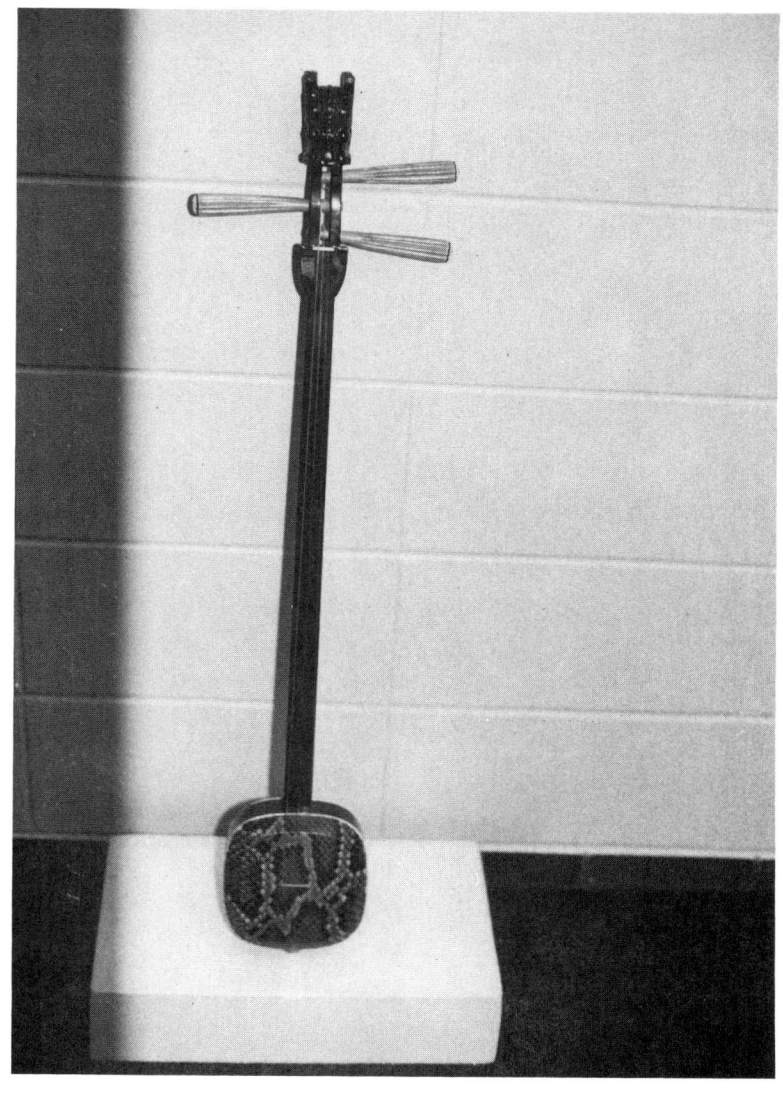

Sanxian, 3-string chordophone with snake skin-covered resonator. Courtesy of K. H. Han, Northern Illinois University.

The forerunner of the *piba* has been traced to the Han dynasty, but the type with pear-shaped resonator probably dates from the Wei dynasty. This chordophone is characterized as a short-necked lute with raised ivory or wood frets, sixteen, seventeen, or twenty-four in number, depending on which version. It has four silk or nylon strings, tuned in fourths, fifths, or octaves (A D E a). The pear-shaped body which so readily distinguishes the instrument is made of teak wood. It is common for the flat, front part of the body to be inlaid with beautiful wood patterns or stone.

The piba has a three to four octave range. The frets produce half-steps in succession, but microtones can be produced by slightly pulling a string sideways within a fret. Cipher notation is used, Arabic numerals indicating the main octave, a dot under a number indicating the octave below, a dot above, the higher octave.

Piba, a 4-string lute.
Courtesy of K. H. Han, Northern Illinois University.

Pibas were used to provide entertainment at banquets, eventually developing into a solo instrument for virtuoso display, playing programmatic depicting nature or battle scenes. They are also used in ensembles and to accompany singing. A closely related chordophone is the *yueqin*, "moon-zither", with a circular resonator and four fretted strings, which is used in similar ways.

The *erhu* is a bowed-lute made in various sizes and known by a variety of names, including *nanhu* in Southern China or the more generic *huqin*. ("Er" means "two" and "hu" means barbarian, suggesting its derivation from Mongolia.) The erhu has two strings, tuned in fifths, with a bow permanently attached between the strings. The neck is long and unfretted, the resonator covered by skin. It has not been found in artifacts of early dynasties, probably because of its rather lowly, folk-like status, or, perhaps, assimilation more recently during the Yuan dynasty. It is therefore a recent additional to the list of Chinese instruments and has apparently found its greatest use in theatre, especially Peking opera. It is also used to accompany folk singing.

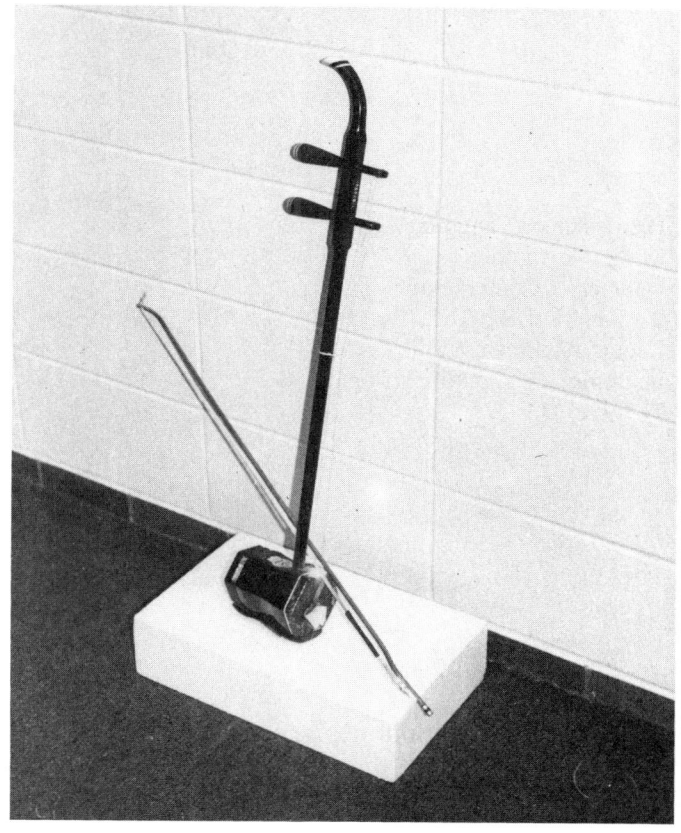

Erhu, 2-string fiddle with attached bow. Courtesy of K. H. Han, Northern Illinois University.

The *yangqin* ("foreign" qin), a recent instrument in China (fifteenth century), is a hammer dulcimer (psaltery) played with two bamboo hammers held in the performer's hands. Much like the Persian santur, it is an instrument which lends itself to virtuoso, solo performance.

Yangqin, hammer dulcimer. Courtesy of K. H. Han, Northern Illinois University.

Performer on yangqin, using two wooden hammers. Courtesy of the American Folklife Center, Smithsonian Institution, Photo No. 87-9952-33.

Chinese idiophones represent the most stable pitch producers in the culture. They were therefore used in religious ceremonies as well as the source for determining and maintaining the official lus of the kingdom. Although a chordophone can scarcely maintain its tuning through one performance, an idiophone stays in tune for centuries. The *bianzhong* is a set of tuned bronze bells, hung on a framework in two rows of eight bells each, creating a diatonic scale. It is played by one person using two mallets. Similarly, the *bianjing* uses sixteen tuned jade or limestone pieces, each

Bianzhong, set of tuned bells. Constructed and photographed by Chuang Pen-li. Courtesy of K. H. Han, Northern Illinois University.

shaped like a carpenter's square and suspended from the frame. The bianjing was often used to signal the beginning and ending of musical events in temple ceremonies. Lithophones such as this may represent the oldest extant instruments of China, having been used c. 1800 B.C.

Bells and gongs have always been part of Chinese culture. A single gong (*luo*) is struck by a beater while pairs of gongs are struck together. Small sets of gongs (*yunluo*) are suspended in a frame and played with mallets. All are used in theatre, worship, and folk music.

Yunluo, a series of suspended gongs.
Courtesy of K. H. Han, Northern Illinois University.

In addition to metal, wood has been used for idiophones, including the *zhu*, a wooden box, sounded to commence religious ceremonies, and the *yu*, a hollow wooden animal with a spiny back. Its head is struck and back scraped in Confucian ceremonies. Other wooden idiophones include *shuangmu*, castanets, and *ban*, clappers, used in theatre. The *muqin*, a xylophone, is a recent addition to the Chinese pantheon of musical instruments.

Among membranophones, the *taogu*, an hour-glass drum, is used, as well as the *jiangu*, a single-headed drum, and *dagu*, kettledrums.

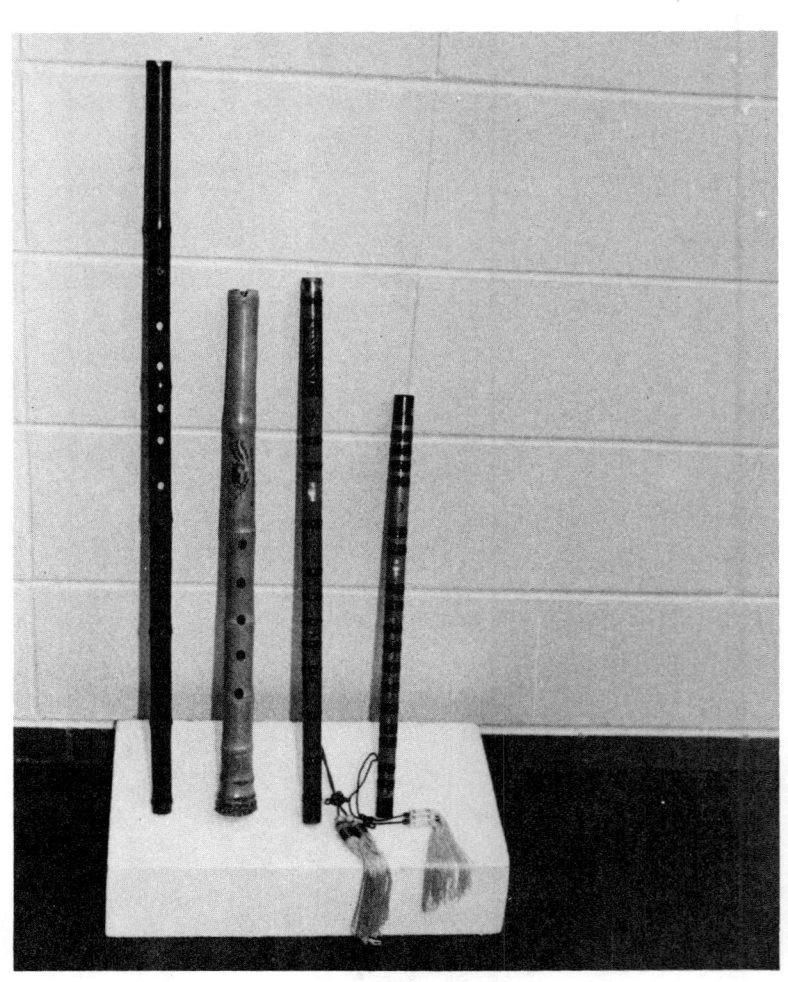

Chinese aerophones. Xiao, vertical flute, (two on left) and di, transverse flute (two on right). Courtesy of K. H. Han, Northern Illinois University.

There are a variety of aerophones in the culture, too, including the *di*, a transverse flute, and *xiao*, a vertical flute, and *suona*, an oboe-like instrument. The following chart lists the common instruments used in Chinese music. The only noticeable absence is any type of cup-shaped mouthpiece aerophones.

CHORDOPHONES	IDIOPHONES
Plucked Chordophones	Ban (clappers)
Kunghou	Bianjing (stone chimes)
Piba	Bianzhong
Qin	Diaopo (cymbals)
Sanxian	Fangxiang (brass chimes)
Se (Se-an)	Luo
Yueqin	Muqin
Zheng	Paiban (clappers)
	Shizhan (water bowls)
Bowed Chordophones	Shuangmu
Gehu	Yinjing (single bells)
Huqin (Erhu)	Yunluo
	AEROPHONES
Hammered Chordophones	Bangdi (piccolo)
Yangqin	Di
MEMBRANOPHONES	Guan (oboe)
Dagu	Sheng (harmonica)
Jiangu	Suona
Taogu	Xiao
	Xuan (ocarina)

In recent years, there has been an attempt to improve and provide more bass resonance in Chinese instrumental music, especially in large ensembles, including the orchestra. This has resulted in the enlargement of the erhu into the *zhonghu*, *dahu*, and *dihu* as well as development of a four-stringed cello-like instrument, the *gehu*. In addition, the Western cello and bass have also been added. Fretted string instruments, too, have been modified to allow tempered and chromatic tunings, which has been accompanied by a tendency to build aerophones, such as flutes, out of better wood than bamboo as well as to make them in two sections to facilitate tuning.

Sheng, a Chinese mouth organ.
The performer cups the base of the instrument in his hands as he draws air in to produce sound.
Courtesy of K. H. Han, Northern Illinois University.

The gourd in this sheng has been replaced with a metal air reservoir. Courtesy of K. H. Han, Northern Illinois University.

Xuan, Chinese ocarinas made of fired clay (pottery). Courtesy of K. H. Han, Northern Illinois University.

Singing in China: Opera and Vocal Music

Chinese culture has long been rich in theatre productions of opera-like stories. During the Yuan dynasty, opera-drama was popular among common people since it told stories of heroes, lovers, bravery, and valor, incorporating Chinese folk songs. Much as our own medieval miracle plays were instructive as well as entertaining to an illiterate population, musical theatre has been a vehicle to embody culture, aesthetics, and morality around the world for whomever watched it. Chinese opera included a small orchestra of on-stage musicians, eventually developing into Northern and Southern styles which differed in dialect as well as stories portrayed and instruments used.

Kunqu was a later development of regional opera, combining both Northern and Southern styles into one. In these works, folk material and literary texts were blended into a written libretto, resulting in slow, melismatic arias in four-four time, accompanied by di, xiao, or piba. The plots were often complex and some dialogue, between arias, was spoken in a style described as heightened speech.

Scene from Peking opera showing dan and jing.
Courtesy of the American Folklife Center, Smithsonian Institution,
Photo No. 88-15041.

Peking opera, the best known musical theatre presentation of China, dates from c. 1790. It is still popular in the People's Republic. Peking opera may best be described as a blend of musical arias, spoken dialogue, acrobatics and dancing, as well as mime. It has become known as national drama, a culmination and refinement of all regional opera.

In Peking opera, props and staging are minimal, but characters and gestures are highly stylized. There are basic types of actors, characterized not by vocal range, as in Western opera, but by this scheme:

Dan	Female roles, such as:	
	Huatan	coquette (flower dan)
	Ch'ing-i	faithful wife
Sheng	Male roles, such as:	
	Wusheng	warrior
	Xiaosheng	scholar-lover
	Laosheng	older man
Jing	Statesman, god, but possibly warrior or bandit. These actors use painted faces to indicate their character:	
	Scarlet face = dignity White face = treachery Black face = strength	
Zhou	Clown and jester	

Virtuous female character. Courtesy of National Fu Hsing Dramatic Arts Academy, Taipei, Taiwan, Republic of China.

During the nineteenth century, opera companies were all male or female, but mixed companies became common by the 1930's. Many of the traditional classifications became obsolete. Gestures, movements, and make-up have remained highly stylized and easily recognizable to Chinese audiences. Military characters must be competent in acrobatics for the battle scenes they play. Huatan walks and gestures differently than ch'ing-i to convey her flirtatious manner. Laosheng is bearded and has a resonant, low voice while xiaosheng uses a nasal, high-pitched voice in falsetto.

The stories of Peking opera are derived from legends taken from former dynasties as well as novels. They include stories of intrigue, bravery, and war, often with a strongly moralistic message. The contemporary versions are based on political themes. Arias are derived from about thirty stock melodies, well-known to Chinese audiences, but adapted to the libretto and context of each new opera. Most result in melismatic vocal lines in varying tempo, but usually duple meter. There is little or no harmony since the accompanying instruments merely duplicate the singing line or provide a slight variation on it, as described in the discussion above on heterophony. The main accompanying instruments are erhu, piba, sanxian, and yueqin as well as a variety of percussion instruments, drums, clappers, cymbals, and gongs, which highlight and punctuate stage action. Although the di and suona are used, they are not as important as string and percussion instruments.

Old man fighting with young boy. Courtesy of National Fu Hsing Dramatic Arts Academy, Taipei, Taiwan, Republic of China.

Peking opera is rarely the work of one composer now, but, rather, arranged by a committee of artists. Since the melodies of the arias are multi-purpose, observing the inflections of the language through parallel melodic movement is not strictly observed.

Peking opera was performed originally by touring groups of actors who were considered low-class and common. It was performed in teahouse-theatres throughout China, with audiences regarding it more as a social rather than an aesthetic event. When the emperors of China began to favor it in the late nineteenth century as a unifying form of social entertainment, it began to be performed in guildhouses, private residences, and restaurant-theatres. Women gradually took over the dan roles as it was assimilated into the mainstream of Chinese culture.

Understatement is an abiding quality of Peking opera as well as much of China's music. Nowhere is suggestion more apparent than in Peking opera where sets are minimal, portrayal a matter of inference and mime, except in the bold acrobatic, militaristic scenes. To a certain extent, this understatement applies to a great deal of instrumental music as well, so typically programmatic and evocative of a mood or setting. The aesthetic throughout the culture is intellectually based, not goal-oriented like much Western art music. The underlying principle is one of control, restraint, and balance.

Key Terms and Concepts

Ban
Bayin
Bianjing
Bian tone
Bianzhong
Cipher notation
Dagu
Dan
Di
Diao
Dynasty
Erhu
Gehu
Gong
Heterophony
Huangzhong
Huqin
Jiangu
Jing
Kunqu
Linzhong
Lithophone
Lu
Luo
Muqin
Nanhu
Peking Opera
Pentatonic
Piba
Pythagorean comma
Qin
Sanxian
Se
Sheng
Shuangmu
Suona
Taogu
Xiao
Yangqin
Yang/yin
Yu
Yueqin
Yunluo
Zheng
Zhou
Zhu

Self-checking Chapter Review

Match Column II to Column I	
Column I	**Column II**
1. pentatonic	A. gong, shang, jue, zhe, yu
2. qin	B. vertical flute
3. sheng	C. three-string lute
4. tones of scale	D. yang and yin
5. sanxian	E. zither with thirteen strings and moveable bridges
6. erhu	F. five-tone scale
7. Confucius	G. Chinese philosopher
8. Yellow Bell	H. bowed lute
9. piba	I. clown role
10. Tang	J. Chinese dynasty
11. plus and minus forces	K. huangzhong
12 dan	L. female role
13. bian	M. ornamental pitch
14. xiao	N. four-string lute
15. zheng	O. zither with five strings
16. zhou	P. male role

Answers			
1.	F	9.	N
2.	O	10.	J
3.	P	11.	D
4.	A	12.	L
5.	C	13.	M
6.	H	14.	B
7.	G	15.	E
8.	K	16.	I

Selected Bibliography

Alley, Rewi and Eva Siao (1957). *Peking Opera: An Introduction Through Pictures*. Peking: New World Press.

Bodman, Helene (1988). *Chinese Musical Iconography: A History of Musical Instruments Depicted in Chinese Art*. Taipei: Asian-Pacific Cultural Center.

Broderick, Alan Houghton (1949). *An Outline of Chinese Painting*. Cambridge: Harvard University Press.

DeWoskin, Kenneth J. (1982). *A Song for One or Two: Music and the Concept of Art in Early China*. Ann Arbor: Center for Chinese Studies, University of Michigan.

Geopper, Roger (1963). *The Essence of Chinese Painting*. London: Lund Humphries and Co., Ltd.

Gulik, Van Robert (1968). *The Lore of the Chinese Lute*. Tokyo: Sophia University.

Halson, Elizabeth (1966). *Peking Opera*. London: Oxford University Press.

Heren, Louis, C.P. Fitzgerald, Michael Freeberne, Brian Hook, and David Bonavia (1974). *China's Three Thousand Years: The Story of a Great Civilization*. New York: Macmillan Publishing Co. Inc.

Hsu, Wen-ying (1972). *Origin of Music in China*. (Reprinted from *Chinese Culture*, Vol. XIII, No. 3 (Sept. 1972), a paper delivered at the 1970 Annual Meeting of the Society of Ethnomusicology, Seattle, Washington, October 29, 1970.)

Kaplan, Fredric M. and Arne J. deKeijzer (1982). *The China Guidebook*. New York: Eurasia Press.

Kaufmann, Walter (1976). *Musical References in the Chinese Classics*. Detroit: Information Coordinators.

Kraus, Richard Curt (1989). *Pianos and Politics in China: Middle-Class Ambitions and the Struggle over Western Music*. New York: Oxford University Press.

Liang, David Ming-Yueh (1972). *The Chinese Chin: Its History and Music*. San Francisco: Chinese National Music Association, The San Francisco Conservatory of Music.

_____ (1985). *Music of a Billion: An Introduction to Chinese Musical Culture*. New York: Heinrichshofen.

Lieberman, Fredric (1979). *Chinese Music: An Annotated Bibliography*. New York: Garland Publishing Co.

Levis, John Hazedel (1963). *Foundations of Chinese Musical Art* (Second edition). New York: Paragon Book Reprint Corp. (First edition, 1936, Peking).

Malm, William P (1967). *Music Cultures of the Pacific, the Near East, and Asia.* Englewood Cliffs, New Jersey: Prentice-Hall, Inc.

Purcell, William L. (1966). *An Introduction to Asian Music.* New York: The Asia Society.

Scott, A.C. (1957). *The Classical Theatre of China.* London: Allen & Unwin.

Wiant, Bliss (1965). *The Music of China.* Hong Kong: Chung Chi Publications (The Chinese University of Hong Kong).

Selected Discography

Ambush from All Sides
China Record Company M-2037

Beating the Dragon Robe
Folkways Records FW 8883

China I
Anthology AST 4000

China: Shantung Folk Music (Traditional Instrumental Pieces)
Nonesuch Records H-72051

China's Instrumental Heritage
Lyrichord Discs LL 92

China's Treasures
Lyrichord Discs LLST 7227

Chinese Classical Instrumental Music
Folkways Records FW 6812

Chinese Classical Masterpieces for the Pipa and Ch'in
Lyrichord Discs LL 82

Chinese Classical Music
Lyrichord Discs LL 72

Chinese Drums and Gongs
Lyrichord Discs LL 102

Chinese Folk and Art Songs
Spoken Arts Record #205

Chinese Folk Opera
Bruno Hi-Fi Records BR-50157

Chinese Masterpieces for the Erh-Hu
Lyrichord Discs LL 132 and LLST 7132

Chinese Music (Excerpts from Cantonese Music Drama)
Folkways Records FW 8880

Chinese Opera: Songs of Music
Cantonese Music Drama
Folkways Records FW 8880

Eleven Centuries of Chinese Classical Music
(Music from the Tang, Song, Yuan, and Ming Dynasties, 600-1600)
Everest Records #3427

Ellie Mao: An Anthology of Chinese Folk Songs
Folkways Records FW 8877

Exotic Music of Ancient China
Lyrichord Discs LL 122

Hong Kong
Musical Atlas
EMI (Odeon) C064-17968

Imperial Bells of China, The
Fortuna Records 17075-2

Masterpieces for the Cheng
Lyrichord Discs LL 142 and LLST 7142

Music from the People's Republic of China
Rounder Records Corp. CD 4008

Music of Asia: Japan/China/Okinawa
Folkways Records FW 8745

On the Docks
(Peking Opera)
China Record Company M-841-844

Peking Opera
Seraphim 60201

Raid on the White Tiger Regiment
(Peking Opera)
China Record Company M-824-27

Red Lantern, The
(Peking Opera)
China Record Company DM-6157-60

Ruse of the Empty City, The
(Peking Opera)
Folkways Records FW 8882

Shachapang
(Peking Opera)
China Record Company DM 6161-64

Shantung: Music of Confucious' Homeland
Lyrichord Discs LL 112

Spring Comes Early to the Commune
(Peking Opera)
China Record Company M-972

West Meets East
Folkways Records FSS 37455

White-Haired Girl, The
Excerpts from Ballet Music
China Record Company DM 6151, 6152, 6153

Endnotes

1. Geopper, Roger (1963). *The Essence of Chinese Painting.* London: Lund Humphries and Co., Ltd., page 11.

2. Mai-Mai, Sze (1959). *The Way of Chinese Painting: Its Ideas and Techniques.* New York: Random House, page 44.

CHAPTER FIVE

MUSIC OF JAPAN

Bugaku mask used in dances of gagaku.
Courtesy of the Library of Congress Collections LCUSZ62:90995.

Although the setting for Japanese music could be a concert hall, more typically, one hears Japanese music in an out-of-doors setting, such as a temple compound or an imperial courtyard with gardens and ponds nearby. Since the Japanese link much of their existence and art with the environment, when music is performed indoors, painted screens may be placed behind the musicians to give the illusion of nature. Japanese music incorporates more than the purely aural and musicians often wear elaborate and beautiful costumes made of the finest silk. Movements may also be stylized, including their approach to the stage as well as playing technique. Even preparation for a concert is important. The koto performer considers the beginning of the concert not when he/she walks on the stage, but, rather, when the traditional kimono is donned in the dressing room.

Japan is an Asian country consisting of four main islands: Honshu, Kyushu, Hokkaido, and Shikoku.

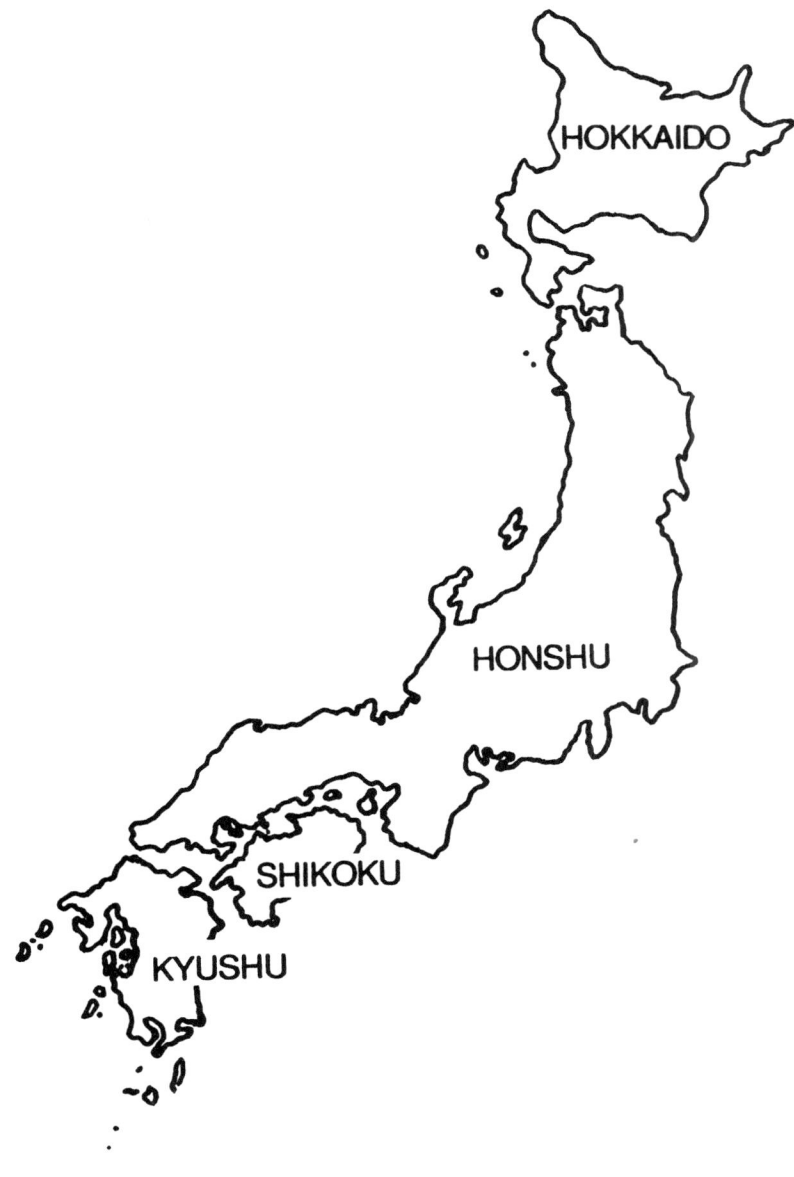

Its importance in world music, much like its economic importance throughout the world, far outweighs its minimal land mass of 370,000 square kilometers. Like the Chinese, Japanese who live as expatriates in other countries throughout the globe have helped to disseminate and preserve many aspects of the culture, including its diverse types of music.

Two of the Four Accomplishments: Music and Games.
Koto, Japanese zither, is seen in lower right. Edo Period, Utagawa Toyohiro (1773-1828). Courtesy of the Freer Gallery of Art, Smithsonian Institution, Neg. No. 03.58-1.

Japanese music includes theatre forms, such as *noh drama* and *kabuki*, court traditions, such as *gagaku*, folk idioms, Buddhist chanting (*shomyo*), as well as purely instrumental idioms which have developed in the last two-hundred years. As with China, the musical traditions of Japan span several hundred years. Although Western music appears to be eclipsing traditional genres, in reality, the ancient practices are fostered and preserved through a guild system. The importance of music in Japan can be documented throughout its history, which, like the Chinese dynasties, can be arranged chronologically as:

Political period	Dates
Asuka	552-645 A.D.
Nara	710-794
Early Heian	794-897
Later Heian	897-1192
Kamakura	1192-1333
Muromachi	1333-1573
Momoyama	1573-1603
Edo	1603-1868
Meiji	1868-1912
Modern state	1912-

Chinese Buddhism was introduced into Japan during the Asuka period and Chinese culture continued to be assimilated throughout the Nara period, when the government was centered in the city of the same name. During the Heian periods, the capital became Kyoto and culture was supported by aristocrats and bureaucrats until the feudal warriors, *samurai*, began to dominate. The Kamakura period was centered in a city of that name while Muromachi refers to the shogunate which dominated during that period. The Ashikaga family dominated the period called Muromachi, as did other feudal shogunates during the Momoyama and Edo periods, when Tokyo became the capital. Japan was opened to the world during the Meiji restoration following 1868.

Some of Japan's musical instruments are thought to have been used in the earliest periods and are therefore indigenous. During the Asuka through Early Heian periods, Chinese culture was imported into Japan, often via Korea, and adapted into island traditions. This was particularly true for court music and dance, which became known as gagaku during the Nara period. Music often followed class lines, some considered appropriate only for rulers, others for warriors, and some for peasants.

Dotaku, ceremonial bell. Courtesy of the Freer Gallery of Art, Smithsonian Institution, Neg. No. 68.73-2.

Music was often part of Buddhist and Shinto ritual as well. In both beliefs, it is essential that humanity live harmoniously with nature. This is particularly important in a land with limited area and scarce resources and, as a result, diversity and adaptation have been acceptable to the culture throughout history. Japan has been somewhat of an artistic cul-de-sac, continually absorbing and refining all significant aspects of other cultures with which it has been in contact.

The only abiding principle which seems to link most music is a three-part division, known as *jo*, *ha*, and *kyu*, (*johakyu*) which is expressed through tempo. Jo is a slow introduction, ha, the exposition or breaking apart, and kyu, the denouement or rush to the finish. Thus, in Japanese music, slow works (jo) generally precede faster ones (kyu). The tripartite concept can be applied to tempo within a single movement, to three movements in succession, or even to larger cycles of musical activity, such as gagaku or noh drama. Japanese music is especially difficult to characterize since it is an ancient art form which has evolved over centuries. The remainder of this chapter will examine commonalities in musical structure, as well as some of the actual traditions and practices themselves.

Korean drummers playing chwago, suspended drum of court orchestra. The playing side is struck with a soft-headed stick. Many Korean and Japanese instruments are derived from China. Courtesy of the American Folklife Center, Smithsonian Institution, Photo No. 89-17083-9.

Melodic Structure: Ritsu and Ryo Scales

There are twelve tones in the Japanese pitch system. These were derived from China during the Heian period and are similarly based on the Pythagorean cycle. Music adapted by Japan from China during its T'ang dynasty is referred to as *togaku* (Tang music) while music derived from Korea is known as *komagaku* (Korean music), reflecting the Japanese penchant for documenting the source of ideas it has borrowed.

In practice, these twelve tones have become associated with Western pitches, designated by letter names:

E	hyojo
F	shosetsu
F♯	shimomu
G	sojo
G♯	fusho
A	oshiki
A♯	rankei
B	banshiki
C	shinsen
C♯	kamimu
D	ichikotsu
D♯	tangin

Since scales and tunings are often derived from the actual instruments used, particularly string instruments, there were a variety of scales and modes that were used during the Heian periods and earlier. By the Kamakura period, however, scales, modes, and pitch designation became more standardized, with two main categories of scales, *ritsu* and *ryo*. These categories were both basically pentatonic, five-toned, with two additional pitches used ornamentally, much like bian-tones in China. Modes in which a major third occurs between the first and third pitches are ryo, a minor third, ritsu. In addition, togaku repertory identified three modes, called *choshi*, within each category by the pitch name on which each was based.

Except for mode six, the name of each reflects the tonal center designated above under the twelve tones. (There were also three modes derived from komagaku based on these scales.) In addition to the absolute pitches of each mode, a sol-fa system was used, allowing transposition of any choshi to other pitch degrees:

Scale degree	1	2	3	4*	5	6	7*
Name	kyu	sho	kaku	henchi	chi	u	henkyu

*ornamental pitches

During the Edo period, two additional scales evolved, both pentatonic, using half-steps. These are *yosen* and *insen*, which are, respectively, ryo and ritsu:

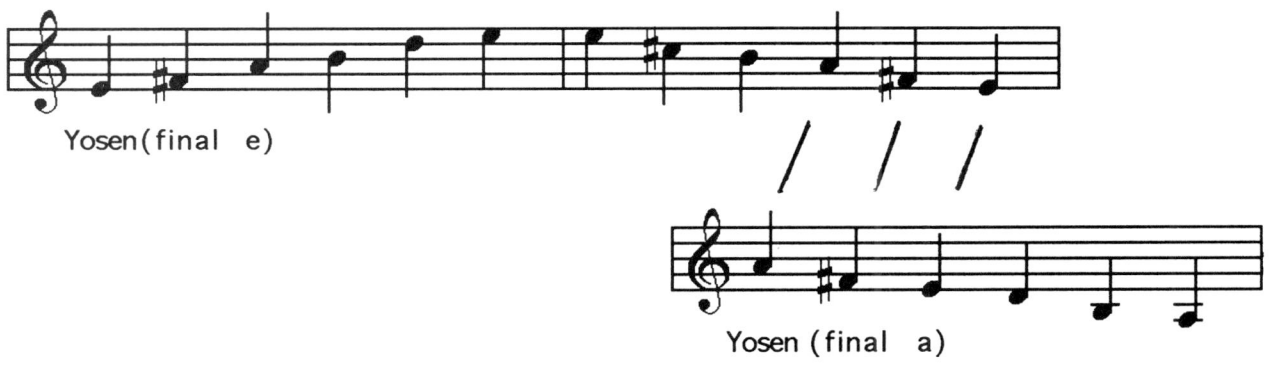

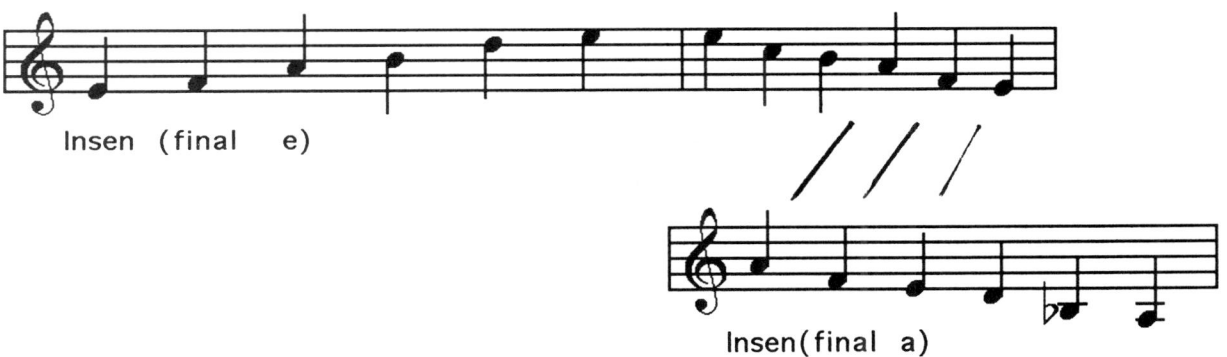

These scales, which slightly vary between ascending and descending version, allowed for transposition within a composition to a scale on a different tonal center. What characterizes most Japanese music, however, is its general pentatonic arrangement *with* half-steps, which provide tendencies within melodic lines.

"The Visit of Genji to Utsusemi," from the *Tale of Genji*. Japan, Edo Period, Tosa School, 18th Century. Courtesy of the Freer Gallery of Art, Smithsonian Institution, Neg. No. 04.117.

Genres of Japanese Music and Theatre

Many genres of Japanese music originated in other countries and were carefully adapted to fit the island culture. *Gagaku*, meaning "elegant music", is one such genre. It is defined as a blend of dance, theatre, costuming, masking, music, and visual effects resulting in a total theatrical experience. Gagaku originated during the T'ang dynasty of China, where it was called *yen yueh*, and was introduced into Japan in the eighth century. With the decline of the T'ang kingdom, the genre failed to survive in China. By contrast, due to the relative isolation of Japan during the same time, the Heian era, gagaku flourished and developed into a full Japanese art form. At the beginning of Japan's Golden Age (c. A.D. 710), Temmu, the emperor, found it necessary to appoint a director of court music to train musicians, who numbered over 250, for gagaku, as well as teachers and pupils from China and Korea. By the ninth century, in a return to isolationism, however, attempts were made to eliminate foreign influences from court music. Foreign teachers and performers were expelled and the profession of music became reserved for select families. From its inception in China, it was a form reserved for royal personages, not common folk. The instruments, props, and even the musicians of gagaku were considered property of the emperor.

Gagaku has four main categories:

Kangen — Instrumental music
Bugaku — Dance and music
Saibara and Roei — Non-religious songs
Shinto vocal music.

In kangen, over thirty instruments may be used. Generally, music of gagaku has been divided into *togaku*, music of the Left, and *komagaku*, music of the Right, depending on its origin. Left, a superior position, means the music and dances are derived from China while Right refers to Korea and Manchuria. As we have seen, this means the scales and modes used as well as instruments. (These instruments will be discussed below.)

Bugaku, the dance portion of gagaku, is similarly divided into music of the Left and Right, depending on its derivation. All dances are highly stylized and slow with few tempo changes. Dances of both sides are evenly divided, which creates an alternation of color as well as sound since dances of the Left wear red robes, the Right, green. Symmetry is continually emphasized in bugaku, between and within dances, both by body movements and dancers' positions. Balance and proportion is continually emphasized in all dances with masks helping to characterize each dance and mood. Bugaku begins with the *embu*, which presents one dancer of the Left and one of the Right. There is then an alternation and equal number of dances presented by both sides, the more solemn pieces occurring at the beginning, but becoming lighter as events progress. In general, dances are accompanied by instruments associated with the country from which the dances are derived. There are no string instruments used in togaku as in bugaku, only winds. This is not true for kangen, however. Since modes are alternated as well in kangen and bugaku, the first piece in each mode is preceded by a little prelude in which the new tonic is established. Presented by the mouth organ, this prelude is called *netori*, which is in free style with slow tempo.

The third category of gagaku is non-religious songs. *Saibara* are songs of pack-horse drivers, six pieces of which are extant, but have really been elevated to the status of art song. *Roei* are chants, based on Chinese-style poems.

Boy with a Flute. Edo Period, Katsushika Hokusai (1760-1849). Courtesy of the Freer Gallery of Art, Smithsonian Institution, Neg. No. 04.254.

Shinto ceremonial music is the fourth component of gagaku in which dancing and instrumental music are included. *Torimono* are those songs which praise the gods or petition them for special help. Since religious music was really the province of common people, not the court, its role in gagaku is somewhat minimal. Saibara are included to provide entertainment for the gods.

Singing in gagaku is not usually measured by a metric beat, but, rather, is somewhat elastic, which means the beat lasts for the duration of a long breath, taken in, held, and gently expelled. This requires the musicians to have empathy with one another in order to feel and coordinate the progression of musical events, rather than being ruled by a steady beat.

Gagaku has always been music of the imperial household, not available to the common citizen. In recent times, however, public presentations have been held for tourists as well as scholars. Since its roots are so firmly from antiquity, it does not have the mass appeal of other types of Japanese musical theatre.

Scene from a Kabuki play. Edo Period, Torii Kiyonobu I (1664-1729).
Courtesy of the Freer Gallery of Art, Smithsonian Institution, Neg. No. 98.14-1.

Noh drama began in the early middle ages of Japan, the fourteenth century, and prospered outside of the imperial court. Established by Kannami Kiyotsugu (1333-84) and his son, Zeami Motokiyo (1363-1443), under the sponsorship of Ashikaga Yoshimitsu, a feudal lord, it derives in part from gagaku as well as older forms of entertainment, such as masked renditions of ancient myths, as well as Buddhist chanting. It was created as a diversion for feudal masters and was presented in temples so commoners could see it as well. It is therefore not as elegant and lavish as gagaku, relying less on scenery and gestures, more on elaborate costumes and masks. The two founders and their successors created over 2,000 dramas between the fourteenth and sixteenth centuries, 200 of which are still performed today. Zeami, himself, created over 100 of these.

In noh, several short plays or acts of a single play are linked together by comic scenes. Both monologue and dialogue occur, as well as singing, which is called *utai*. Accompaniment is provided by four instruments, a flute and three drums, collectively called *hayashi*. The libretto for singing is derived from Japanese poetry, arranged in two lines, the first in seven syllables, the second in five. These are performed against eight beats, elastic in nature, particularly beats 2, 4, or 8, that are counted by two of the drums in hayashi, usually audibly. The words are thus delivered through song in rather stereotypical melodic units, much like recitative.

Noh mask. Courtesy of the Library of Congress Collections LCUSZ62:90993.

The main actor of noh, who assumes a different role and mask throughout the spectacle, is called the *shite*. He might portray a stately woman in one act, but become the ghost of a shogun in the second. His costumes will be elegant and colorful while those of other actors and musicians will be somber. The second principal actor, *waki*, does not wear a mask. The comic actor, *kyogen*, appears between acts, while the main actor is changing costumes in preparation for his next portrayal. Kyogen wear masks, portraying animals, gods, humans, or demons. Performers do not alternate between parts, that is, shite represents one class of actors, waki another. This is rigidly controlled by guilds.

Noh begins with a dance that functions both as introduction and prayer, the *okina*, followed by solo and chorus chanting, instrumental sections, dialogue, and more dancing. The repertory consists of five types of plays, usually presented in this order: *shin* (about gods); *nan* (about men); *nyo* (about women); *kyo* (about mentally deranged persons); and *ki* (about demons). In a complete noh performance, five plays, dealing with these subjects in this order, are presented, punctuated by comic scenes between each. This could result in a series of plays that might last eight or more hours.

Everything in noh is highly stylized, including dialogue and singing, from entrance to exit. Singing is accompanied by the orchestra of four. Both orchestra and noh chorus consisting of eight singers, are seated on the stage, which is thrust-like with a passage-way leading to it:

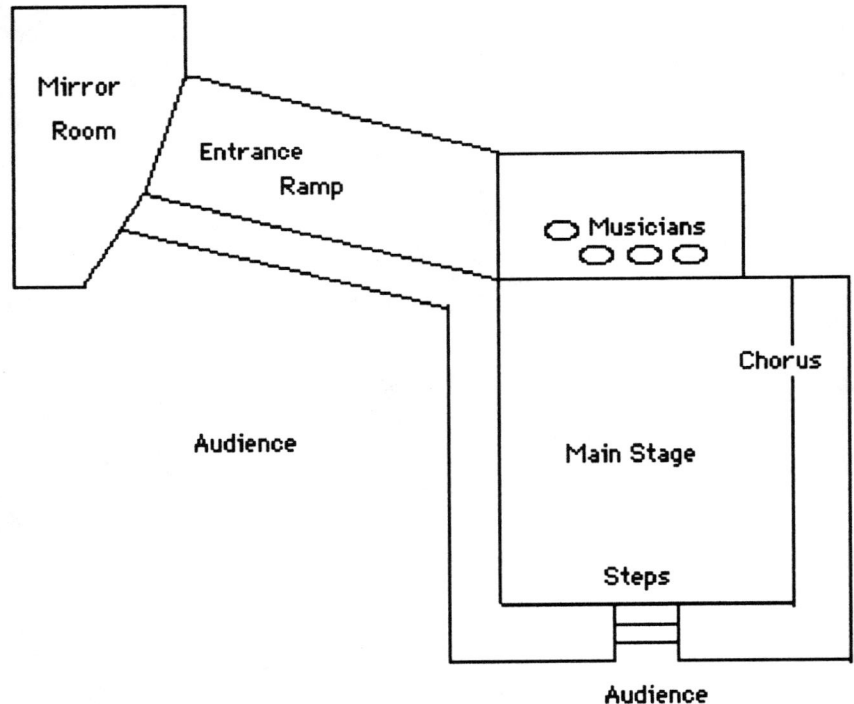

This allows the audience to view the action from two sides. Clay vases placed under the stage echo and amplify the voices of actors so they can project to a large audience in an open-air environment. The long walkway on the left of the stage leads to the dressing room for the actors, known as the mirror-room.

Since each play in a series consists of two parts, the first act presents the shite in one form after his death, the second act as he was before death, allowing viewers to consider conditions that led to the reincarnated form, since time is developed backwards.

Singing in noh is considered soft or strong, depending upon intervals and range used. Soft singing, *yowagin*, centers around three nuclear pitches, a high, middle, and low, usually separated by the interval of a perfect fourth:

Nuclear pitch *   *   *

Higher and lower pitches are used, as well as secondary pitches between, but the former end phrases and entire songs, with the exception of the middle pitch. Strong singing, *tsuyogin*, uses two nuclear pitches, separated by a minor third, in the same way:

Nuclear pitch *   *

Compared to yowagin, tsuyogin has much less melodic movement, often appearing monotonic. Singers are accompanied by the flute, which provides neither unison melody nor counterpoint, but, rather, a slightly altered version of the melodic formula being sung, thus a heterophonic texture.

During the Edo period (sixteenth century), *kabuki* developed, based in part on noh. Okuni, a woman who danced in temples, allegedly invented kabuki. Her dances became so popular that she left the temple to perform on a stage in Kyoto, often portraying both men and women on stage. Gradually, these presentations were expanded and became true theatre pieces which appealed to common people because of the erotic realism. Since kabuki became associated with both female and male prostitution, the Japanese government stepped in to control such productions during the seventeenth century, ruling that all characters henceforth had to be played by men. Even now, men portray all characters in kabuki, both male and female roles, the latter which are referred to as *onnagata*. Members of contemporary kabuki companies belong to one of only eight families which perpetuate the tradition, tracing their roots throughout the 300-year-old history of this type of theatre. About twenty plays form the standard repertory for a kabuki company.

Scene from *Kagami-Jishi*, one of the famous classic dramas of the kabuki repertoire. Kabuki chorus and drummers are seen at rear of stage. Courtesy of the Embassy of Japan.

Two types of stories are portrayed in kabuki. *Jidaimono* (period plays) present tales of the Edo period, stories of intrigue, treason, and action. *Sewamono* (genre plays), by contrast, deal with romantic subjects. Each has several sections, called *dan*, five in the former, three in the latter. Each play will demonstrate the *johakyu* principle, beginning slowly, developing, and then rushing to conclusion. The conclusion is called the *kiri*.

The stage in kabuki is approached through an elevated bridge that leads through the viewers, much like the walkway used in fashion shows. This allows for dramatic entrances and exits throughout the plays, which tend to be fast paced and exiting, using language that was typical during the Edo period.

Singing in kabuki is at times lyric, other times, more like recitative, delineating singing prowess from mere declamation, somewhat like Western opera. This is also a rather intermediary type of parlando singing as well. The general term used to refer to music of kabuki is *gidayu*, which includes singing as well as instrumental sections, whether used as interlude or to accompany singing and dancing.

Scene from *Musume Dojoji*, one of the famous classic dramas of the kabuki repertoire. Onnagata is seen stage right, orchestra upstage, including performers on shamisen, taiko, o-tsuzumi, and ko-tsuzumi. Courtesy of the Embassy of Japan.

There are two groups of instrumentalists used in kabuki, one on stage, one off. The on-stage group, termed *debayashi*, sits on an elevated platform up-stage. The off-stage group, termed *geza*, sits in a room to the right of the stage. Debayashi accompanies dance and narration, geza, lyric songs. Geza groups also provide mood and set the scene for the entire production, much like any pit orchestra.

Private bunraku, puppet show. Edo period, Ukiyo-e school, Okumura Masanobu. Courtesy of the Freer Gallery of Art, Smithsonian Institution, Neg. No. 02.250.

Another theatre genre of the Edo period, *bunraku*, uses similar repertory. Bunraku is puppet theatre, a genre which dates from the seventeenth century. Originally centered in Edo (Tokyo), the tradition moved to Osaka in 1657 because of the great fire in Edo. Although puppetry dates from the twelfth century in Japan, during the Edo period, the genre assumed standard procedures and arrangements of music and musicians. The puppets, who are adorned in lavish costumes, are about half the size of humans and they are manipulated by three puppeteers on stage, dressed in black, head to toe. One manipulates puppets' feet, the second, the left arms, and the third, right arms and heads, a procedure standard since 1734.

In bunraku, there is a narrator (*tayu*) who sits on a platform at one side of the stage accompanied by an instrumentalist on the *shamisen*, a three-string chordophone. It is common for tayu and shamisen player to be replaced during a single performance since the demands upon their talents are so intense.

The music of bunraku is called *gidayu-bushi*, named after a famous tayu, Gidayu Takemoto, who lived between 1651-1714. Tayu sing, comment, narrate, and also provide all dialogue for the puppets, including roles of hero, heroine, villain, and demons. There are four styles of gidayu in both bunraku and kabuki, which share similar repertoire and traits. The musical sections of declamation, much like recitative, are called *kotoba* while lyrical singing, much like arias, is called *fushi* (or *ji*). Parlando singing is called *iro* while the purely instrumental sections are called *ai*. All four types are an on-going part of both bunraku and kabuki. Although instrumentalists were once confined to off-stage positions or concealment behind a bamboo screen, since 1734, they, too, have been positioned on-stage.

Girl Manipulating a Puppet. Edo period, Tsukioka Settei (1710-86). Courtesy of the Freer Gallery of Art, Smithsonian Institution, Neg. No. 5350B:61.25.

Instrumental Genres

A third type of musical genre which developed during the Edo period is not part of musical theatre, but, rather, is purely instrumental, including both solo and chamber music. The most typical instruments used are the shamisen, *shakuhachi*, an aerophone, and *koto*, another chordophone. Each instrument will be discussed in detail in the following section, but a brief description of forms will be given here. When these three instruments are heard as a trio, it is known as *sankyoku*.

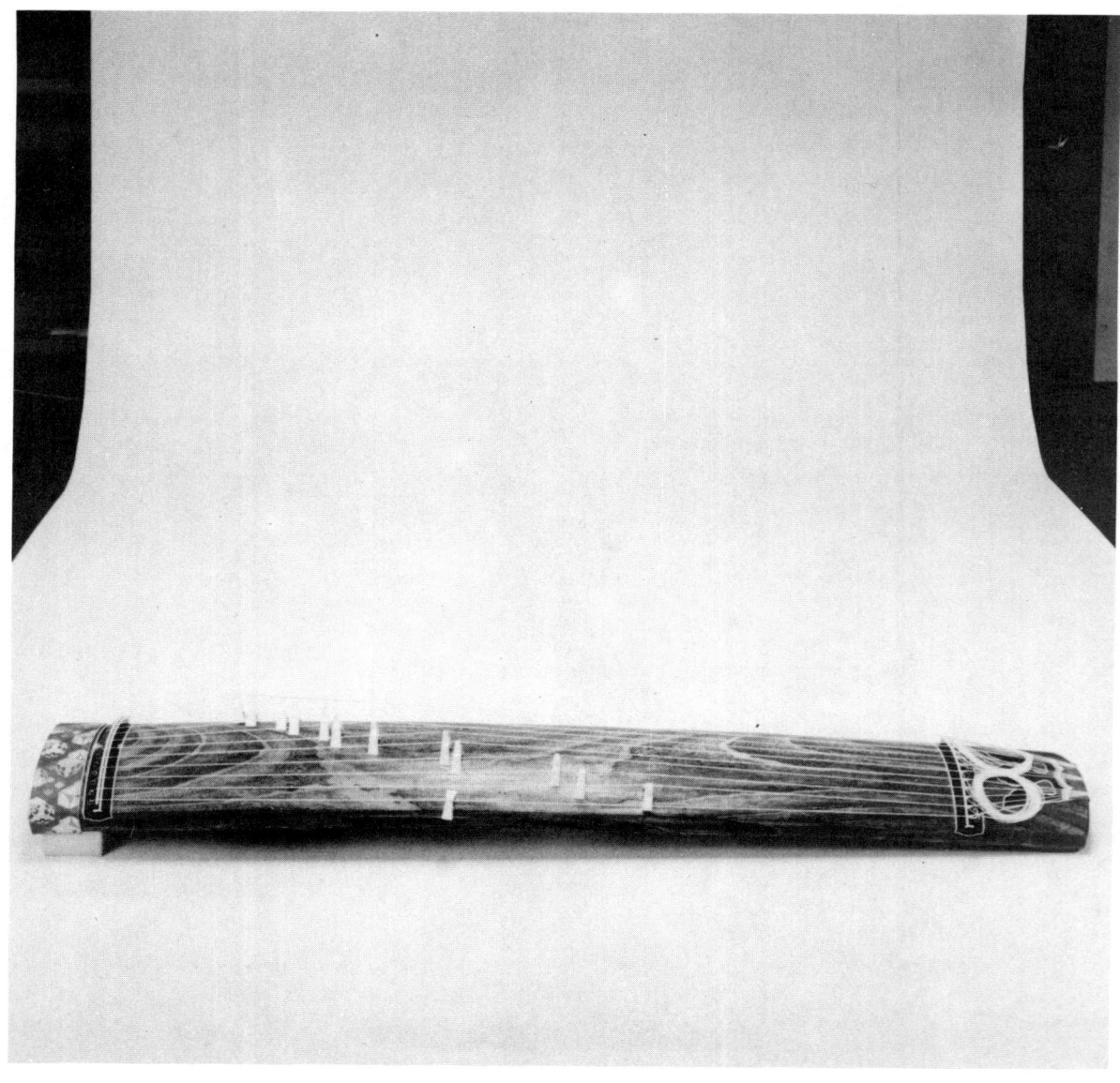

Koto, 13-string zither with moveable bridges.
Courtesy of Scienceland, Inc., Shashinka Photo Library, New York, New York

Since so much instrumental music was connected with theatre, it is not surprising to find literary connections, at least in length of phrases and sections, in it. Two types of compositions existed during the Edo period. *Danmono* is basically theme and variations. Except for the theme, each section, *dan*, consists of 104 beats, which is twenty-six measures in common time. The theme is slightly longer by four or eight beats. A composition is usually named by the number of sections which occur, including the theme. *Godan* has five sections, *rokudan*, six. Since *shirabe* is a term denoting an instrumental piece, *rokudan-no-shirabe* means an instrumental theme with five continuous variations. In keeping with the johakyu sectioning, which is a recurrent idea in all music and art, variations tend to begin slowly, gradually speeding up as well as adding notes in the melody, much like Western divisions. The solo variation, danmono, is attributed to Yatsuhashi Kengyo, a blind koto player who lived during the seventeenth century. He undoubtedly derived this instrumental form from the singing of *kumi*, lyric poetry set in strophes and accompanied by koto. In performance, it was expected that the instrumentalist slightly vary the accompaniment for each strophe, which, when poetry is eliminated, results in danmono. It is interesting to note that variations in European music resulted from much the same practice, accompanying dance. When instrumentalists slightly varied each verse or stanza, regular in number of beats, phrases, and sections because of the dance-based rhythms, theme and variations (divisions) resulted in our own music as well. How interesting it is that this can occur in unrelated cultures without contact but for the same reasons and about the same time in history!

In addition to danmono, *kimiuta* is a set of continuous songs (*uta*) (often six in number), sung and accompanied by the same person on koto. Each uta typically consisted of eight phrases (one for each line of poetry, which had either five or seven syllables), set in four measures of common time. Voice and koto maintained the same melody, at least a version of it, resulting in heterophony. When singing was no longer included, the koto was left performing an instrumental composition of the same length and structure.

In later periods, additional instrumental genres evolved, often similarly based on poetic structures. *Jiuta* are lyric songs accompanied by shamisen or koto, These were interwoven in a new musical form in the eighteenth century, *tegotomono*, in which songs and instrumental interludes alternate.

Instruments of Japan

Many of the instruments of Japan appear to be similar to those of China. This is a reasonable observation since Japan, throughout its long history, has had considerable contact with China, borrowing and adapting much of Chinese culture, including its musical practice and instruments.

We will begin with a discussion of Japanese chordophones, generically called *nigin*. Among these is the koto, which is an adaptation of the Chinese qin. It is much like the contemporary zheng as well. Symbolically, the koto represents a dragon, with each part of the instrument corresponding to the animal's anatomy. The upper surface is the dragon's back, the lower, the belly. The long bridge at the right end is the dragon's horn, the left end, the tail. The angular projection at the right end of the instrument, as the player faces it, represents a forked tongue. The wooden instrument is a little less than six feet long and quite narrow, less than one foot, in proportion to its length. In performance, it is either placed flat on the floor with the performer kneeling over it or on a stand, in which case the player sits in a chair.

Koto performer plucking and depressing strings. Courtesy of Scienceland, Inc., Shashinka Photo Library, New York, New York

There are thirteen strings on the modern koto, all of the same thickness, length, and material. Tuning is therefore accomplished by placing small, moveable bridges in the shape of an upside-down "Y" under each string at a given position. These bridges are made of ivory, wood, or even plastic. They divide the string into two segments, often leaving as much as 2/3 of some strings unplayable, since only the segment to the right of the bridge is actually plucked. The performer plucks the strings with picks, known as *tsumes*, placed on thumb, index, and middle fingers. These picks also vary in thickness, shape, and material, depending on tradition. Since each of the thirteen strings has a set length for each tuning, it does not require stopping (shortening) in performance, like a guitar or violin. The performer thus is free to create ornaments with the left portion of the string, which means the string may be depressed after it is struck.

The koto is one of the oldest instruments of Japan. The Chinese qin, from which it is derived, had only five strings and was seven feet long. It originated in China during Emperor Fukki's reign, which was two thousand years B.C. Two additional strings were eventually added, but the instrument did not have moveable bridges. The *chiku-no-koto* was the first zither with thirteen strings and the *so-no-koto*, which came much later, used low bridges to elevate the strings slightly away from the body of the instrument. Performers also used tsumes made of thick paper. These two instruments were the prototype for the modern Japanese koto. The Japanese, however, began to use higher bridges made of ivory, which placed more tension on the strings and made the sound louder and clearer, as well as tightly twisted strings of silk, coated with wax. These earliest kotos, dating from the Nara period, were known as *yamato-kotos* or *wagons*. They varied regionally by number of strings, height of bridges, shape of tsumes, and tuning.

There are presenting two schools of koto playing in Japan, the *Ikuta-koto* and *Yamada-koto*. The basic difference is in use of picks, the Ikuta using square-ended tsumes, the Yamada, elliptical ivory tsumes.

In addition, the instruments of the Yamada tradition tend to be slightly bigger with higher and stouter bridges. This results in a difference in sound. The Ikuta sound is delicate, Yamada, bold and virtuosic. The two types of kotos even differ in surface decoration as well, Ikuta using inlays of ivory or tortoise shell while Yamada instruments are relatively free of ornamentation. The Ikuta tradition dates from the early 1700's, the Yamada, about a century later.

Tuning for the koto vary, but there are three common systems, each showing the pentatonic predilection. These are *Kumoi*, *Hira-joshi*, and *Iwato*:

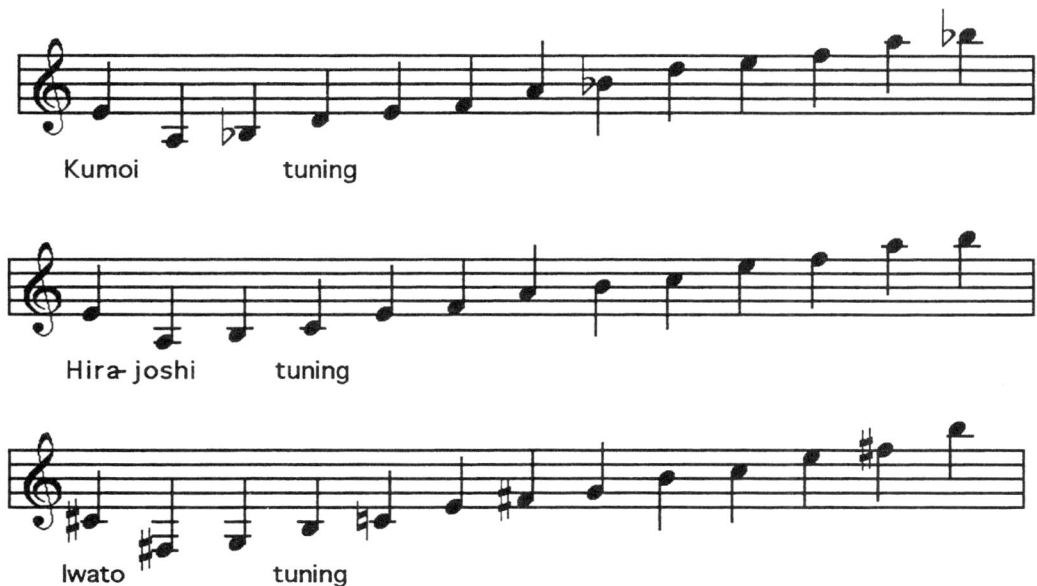

Koto ornaments, like gamakas of Indian music and *agrements* of the French Baroque era, are stylized, providing subtle and tasteful deviations in the melodic line. The *osu* is an effect made when the left hand slightly depresses the string to the left of the bridge (on the non-playing side). It may occur as the string is plucked or slightly afterwards, resulting in pitch bending effect. *Niju oshi* is similar, but alters the pitch within a wider interval, more of a whole-step than merely a half-step, which is true for osu. *Kaki* is an ornament made by slightly striking an adjacent string (either side) as one approaches a given string. *Nagaski* is a type of glissando while *shu* means the tsume is scrapped along one string. *Uchi* is an ornament created by beating the strings to the left of the bridges with the left hand, particularly during melodic pauses. All of this demonstrates the intricacies involved in koto playing.

In ancient gagaku, the koto, also called *so* or *gakuso* in this ensemble, was used as an instrument of the Left, reflecting its roots in Chinese culture. The generic term for koto music, whether solo or to accompany singing, is *sokyoku*. Presently, the koto is used to accompany singing, particularly in the genre referred to as *utamono*, which functions much like lieder. A form of solo koto playing is *danmono*, theme and variations.

The koto has always been considered an instrument of the home, predominantly played by women, rather than as an instrument of the stage. It was also played throughout history by blind men to accompany kumi, lyric poetry, which accounts for the derivation of danmono. Learning to play the koto was basically a rote process, which enabled blind musicians to excel on it. There is notation which is read in columns downward, right to left. Strings are indicated by number, one to thirteen, while another set of symbols represents playing style, accidentals, and ornaments. Time division is by circles, some with double lines to indicate time units like our bar lines, other circles simply to indicate the beat. When words occur, they are on the left side of each column. This type of notation is a tablature. Although most koto melodies can be indicated with Western staff notation, indication of ornaments is difficult.

KOTO TABLATURE

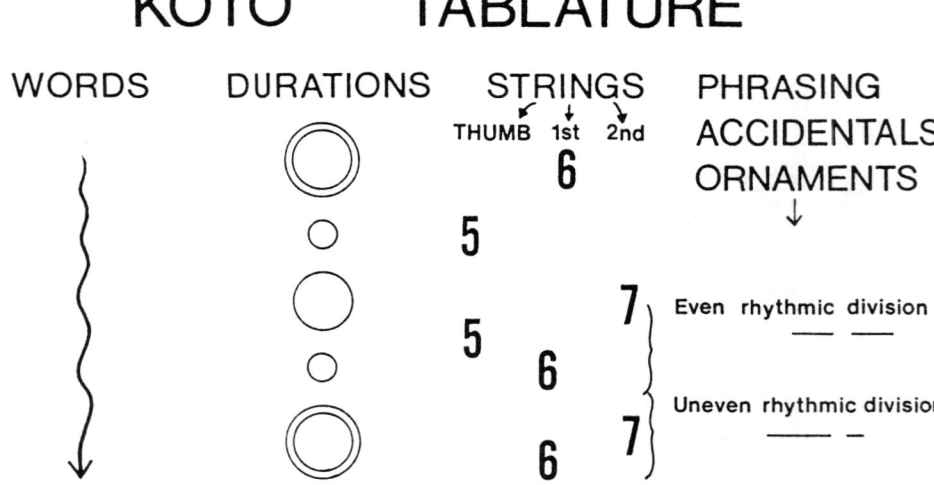

Another popular chordophone of Japan is the shamisen, introduced earlier in this chapter. It, too, is derived from a Chinese counterpart, the sanxian, which existed in China during the Yuan dynasty (thirteenth century). First the instrument was adopted on the island of Loo Choo (Ryukyu Islands), from which it was later imported into Japan about 400 years ago.

Female Impersonator Tuning a Shamisen.
Edo period, Toriyama Sekien (1713-88).
Courtesy of the Freer Gallery of Art,
Smithsonian Institution Neg. No. 02.230.

The shamisan is a Japanese version of the banjo in some ways. It is a lute-like instrument, with a long neck. Its overall length is 2 1/2 feet, with a hollow, square resonating chamber at its base. In China, this hollow chamber was covered with snakeskin. Since there was a paucity of large snakes in Japan, domestic animals often contributed parchment to the shamisen, particularly cats. The value of the instrument in the past was measured by the number of nipple marks that showed on the resonator.

The shamisen has three strings, each with the same length but different thickness. In performance, the instrument is held much like a guitar or banjo, with the performer stopping these strings along the neck, which has no frets. In addition, the performer's right hand strums the strings across the covered belly of the instrument with a *bachi*, a large pick. The pick hits the parchment at the same time it strikes the string, creating a percussive and often raucous effect. Unlike the koto, the shamisen has always been an instrument associated with theatre, entertainers, and even amateurs. Its simple structure and technique are undoubtedly responsible for its popularity and it has been used to accompany just about everything except prayer, where it might be too boisterous. The tunings are equally straight forward, including *Honchosi*, the standard tuning, as well as *Niagari* and *Sansagari*.

All three tunings are compatible with hirajoshi tuning on koto, which must be used whenever the instruments play together. All pitches, however, are relative, not absolute.

The shamisen is used in kabuki ensembles, both geza and debayashi. In kabuki derived from bunraku, the narrator is accompanied by shamisen. When the shamisen accompanies singing, the vocal line is typically duplicated on the strings, slightly anticipating or being behind the singer. This, of course, results in heterophony. In addition, the click of the bachi on the resonator creates a rhythmic accompaniment.

Another Japanese chordophone, used in kangen as well as bugaku (danced portion) of gagaku as an instrument of the Left is the *biwa*, an adaptation of the Chinese piba. Like the piba, the biwa has four strings, tuned variously as:

In gagaku, the performer sits so the gourd end of the instrument rests on the floor with the neck rising perpendicular. (The instrument is also held horizontally in other uses.) The strings are more widely spaced on the resonator end. Unlike the shamisen, also a lute-configured instrument, the biwa has frets, four or five, on the neck, which do not allow for high pitches on any one string, but, rather, the majority of the string length to vibrate. This results in great resonance and volume from the small instrument. Strumming is done with a bachi, often across all strings, with the fourth string playing melodies. This results in more of a homophonic texture than many Japanese instruments, since the melody is somewhat supported by open chords strummed across the lower three strings. The harmonic support is more in the nature of chordal drones than harmonic progression in the Western sense.

Japanese dinner scene, including taiko and shamisen.
Courtesy of the American Folklife Center, Smithsonian Institution,
Photo No. 85-0289-18.

The biwa, imported during the T'ang dynasty, gained great popularity during the samurai reigns in later centuries. It is an instrument which has often been used to accompany narratives of military glories. It has also been used by Buddhist priests to accompany chants. As a solo instrument, it is capable of a variety of dynamic levels, lending to virtuoso treatment and therefore great popularity as a solo instrument.

The final chordophone, the four-string *kokyu*, is a spiked-fiddle, shaped somewhat like the shamisen. Unlike the shamisen, it is bowed, not plucked. Used in chamber music as well as tragic stories in puppet plays, it is a recent addition to Japan, having been imported only within the last two hundred years.

There are several aerophones, classified as *sankan*, that are used in Japanese music, particularly to accompany singing and dancing in gagaku and noh. The *sho*, a mouth-organ which derives from the Chinese sheng, is used in gagaku as a Left instrument, both in kangen and bugaku. It consists of a small wooden wind chest with 17 bamboo pipes protruding. These are arranged from the shortest on either side to a long one in the middle. Like the sheng, the pipes sound only when the player draws air in and covers the finger holes, allowing the reed inside to vibrate. The effect is chordal, that is, a series of parallel chords are produced, supporting a melody on the bottom, much like medieval fauxbourdon. In togaku, the sho typically performs a series of chords with six pitches, each added to the cluster from the bottom up as the performer crescendos. The sho is used almost exclusively in court music.

Shakuhachi, traditional Japanese aerophone played in vertical position. Courtesy of the Embassy of Japan.

By contrast, there are aerophones which are configured much like Western woodwinds, some played vertically, others, transversely. The *shakuhachi*, a vertical bamboo flute about twenty inches long, is derived from the Chinese xiao. (Shaku = foot, hachi = eight, thus 1 foot, 8 inches = 20 inches.) It first appeared in Japan during the fourteenth century and was used by wandering Buddhist priests, known as *komuso*, as a solo instrument. It has thus always been an instrument associated with men and priesthood. During the fourteenth century, when the samurai gave up their land to enter the priesthood, they frequently wandered the countryside. Since they were not allowed to carry weapons, the shakuhachi was a suitable substitute since it would be used as a billy club for defense.

Shakuhachis naturally sound a pitch close to an open D, with the finger holes producing f, g, a, c, and octave d, showing a clear pentatonic arrangement. Half-holing allows both diatonic and chromatic pitches to be sounded:

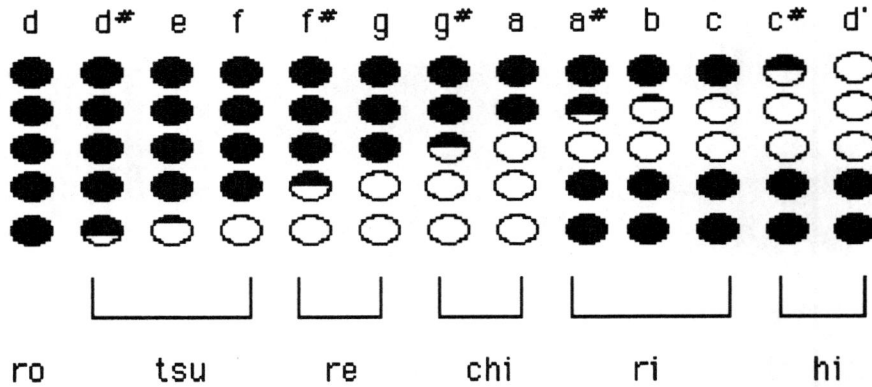

Ornaments are produced by the performer slightly shaking the head.

The shakuhachi has not been associated with theatre, but, rather, as part of Buddhist ritual. In more recent centuries, the chamber group, *sankyoku*, has brought shakuhachi, koto, and shamisen together purely as an instrumental trio. In this ensemble, each plays a version of the same melody, resulting in heterophonic texture. This combination works well because of the sustaining power of the shakuhachi, carrying the main melody as the two chordophones either abbreviate or elaborate their melodic version simultaneously.

The aerophones associated with theatre include the *ryuteki*, a transverse flute with seven fingerholes, and the *hichiriki*, a small double-reed flute with nine fingerholes, which often is the leader in court music because of its penetrating quality. In gagaku, both are used in music of the Left, but the ryuteki is exchanged for a smaller transverse flute, the *komabue*, an instrument with six fingerholes, in music of the Right. In purely instrumental sections, kangen, one wind will carry the melody while the second adds counterpoint. When accompanying singing, they duplicate the melody in heterophonic texture. Colored brocade is usually attached to the closed end of a flute, red for the ryuteki, green for the komabue, reflecting their origin.

In noh drama, a transverse flute (*fue*), *nokan*, is used. It is similar to the ryuteki and is also used in the hayashi group in kabuki.

Percussion instruments are known as *sanko*, which includes membranophones and idiophones. The membranophones of Japan are often the ceremonial instruments of stage orchestra, counting beats but also symbolically representing the past. Some are hour-glass shaped drums, some have vessel frames, and others are simple cylinders. They are both single- and double-headed.

Traditional Japanese percussion instruments. Left to right, ko-tsuzumi (shoulder drum), o-tsuzumi (hip drum), and taiko. The surface of the taiko is covered with cow hide, except for the small area in the center where deer skin is used. The o-tsuzumi has head of cow hide, the ko-tsuzumi, horse hide. The tone of all three drums is adjusted by the tension of the linen cords. Courtesy of the Embassy of Japan.

The noh orchestra, which consists of four performers on stage, has only four instruments. In addition to the nokan, three percussion instruments are used. The *ko-tsuzumi*, a double-headed hourglass, is held on the right shoulder and played with the right hand. The *o-tsuzumi*, a larger hourglass drum, is held on the left hip and struck with the fingers of the right hand. These two drums are used to mark the four-beat phrase, calling out to each other as part of the performance. Each traditionally plays basic patterns, five for the former, three for the latter. The *taiko*, used in gagaku as well, is a flat, double-headed frame drum played with sticks. It is positioned in a red, wooden stand so it slants upward towards the percussionist. The left hand hits the drum head with light strokes called *mebachi* while the right hand produces louder strokes called *obachi*. The right hand must hit in the center of the head (c. 20" in diameter) while the left hand hits slightly off-center.

The largest drum, often used in pairs, one on each side of the stage, is the *dadaiko*, which has heads tacked to frame. Other bass drums include the smaller *tsuri-daiko*, suspended in a frame. The *kakko* is a barrow drum positioned in a stand and hit on both sides with unpadded mallets. The kakko performer uses eight traditional rhythmic patterns, including *sei*, which is a single, sharp blow with the right hand stick, and *katarai*, repeated left-hand beats in accelerando. The *san-no-tsuzumi*, an hour-glassed drum larger than its noh counterparts, is hit with a single mallet. All hour-glass drums have tensioned strings between the heads which may be pressed or squeezed to alter the pitch of the drum head. The color of the strings indicates the competency of the performer. Orange-red indicates an ordinary performer, but light blue a higher rank, with lilac reserved for the most competent. In gagaku, the san-no-tsuzumi is used in music of the Right.

Hayashi, a small Japanese musical ensemble. This group consists of (left to right) taiko, o-tsuzumi, ko-tsuzumi, and shamisen, which has a resonator covered with cat skin. Courtesy of the Embassy of Japan.

A variety of idiophones compliment all of the above instruments in ensembles, including the *shoko*, a large metal gong, used in both court music and Buddhist ritual. There are also *rei* (bells), *chappa* (cymbals), *hyoshigi* (wood blocks), and *sasara* (rattles). These are particularly important in kabuki, where they enhance the excitement and drama much as in Peking opera.

The following provides a summary of Japanese instruments.

CHORDOPHONES	AEROPHONES
Biwa	Fue (noh-kan)
Kokyu (bowed lute with 3-4 strings)	Hichiriki
Koto	Komabue
Shamisen	Ryuteki
Wagon (zither)	Shakuhachi
Yamato-koto (two-string zither)	Shinobue (transverse flute)
Yakumo-koto (zither with no bridges)	Sho
IDIOPHONES	**MEMBRANOPHONES**
Binzasara (clapper)	Dadaiko
Chappa (cymbals)	Kakko
Dora (gong)	Keiroko (hand drum)
Rei (bells)	Ko-tsuzumi
Shoko	O-tsuzumi
Toko Dobatsu (cymbal)	San-no-tsuzumi
	Taiko

Singing in Japan

Vocal music has been discussed throughout this chapter in relationship to court and theatre music. Most vocal music is part of larger genres involving stage presentation and instrumental music. However, a few vocal genres may be considered independently. *Kimiuta*, which emerged during the seventeenth century in Japan, is a group of poems that are set to music and sung as a cycle. They are accompanied by koto. Shorter songs which emerged during the Edo period include the *kouta* and *hauta*, both of which are accompanied by shamisen. A longer genre called *nagauta* (love song) developed in the early eighteenth century. It is used in kabuki as well as strictly vocal concerts. Nagauta is much like a cantata since it includes vocal sections with shamisen accompaniment as well as instrumental sections using the nokan, shinobue, and the three noh drums, ko-tsuzumi, o-tsuzumi, and taiko. There are also sections in which voice and all instruments participate.

Key Terms and Concepts

Ai
Bachi
Biwa
Bugaku
Bunraku
Chappa
Choshi
Dadaiko
Danmono
Debayashi
Embu
Fue
Fushi
Gagaku
Gakuso
Geza
Gidayu
Godan
Hayashi
Hichiriki
Hira-joshi
Honchosi
Hyoshigi
Ikuda
Insen
Iro
Iwato
Jidaimono
Jiuta
Johakyu
Kabuki
Kaki
Kakko
Kangen
Katarai
Kimiuta
Kiri
Kokyu
Komabue
Komagaku
Komuso
Koto
Kotoba
Ko-tsuzumi

Kumi
Kumoi
Kyogen
Mebachi
Nagauta
Nagaski
Netori
Niagari
Nigin
Niji Oshi
Noh drama
Nokan
Obachi
Okina
Onnagata
Osu
O-tsuzumi
Rei
Ritsu
Roei
Rokudan
Ryo
Ryuteki
Saibara
Samurai
Sankan
Sanko
Sankyoku
San-no-tsuzumi
Sansagari
Sasara
Sei
Sewamono
Shakuhachi
Shamisen
Shirabe
Shite
Sho
Shoko
Shomyo
Shu
So
Sokyoku
Taiko

Tayu
Tegotomono
Togaku
Torimono
Tsumes
Tsuri-daiko
Tsuyogin
Uchi
Uta
Utai
Utamono
Wagon
Waki
Yamada
Yamato-koto
Yen Yueh
Yosen
Yowagin

Self-Checking Chapter Review

| Match Column II to Column I ||
Column I	Column II
1. bachi	A. principal actor in noh drama
2. sankyoku	B. vertical aerophone used by priests
3. koto	C. music for koto
4. shamisen	D. Japanese oboe
5. kabuki	E. uses orchestra of 1 flute, 3 drums
6. shite	F. trio of shakuhachi, koto, shamisen
7. rokudan	G. court music
8. shakuhachi	H. shoulder drum
9. noh	I. shamisen pick
10. hichiriki	J. largest drum
11. sokyoku	K. theatre piece using all-male cast
12. ko-tsuzumi	L. koto tradition
13. yamada	M. zither with thirteen strings
14. dadaiko	N. theme and five variations
15. gagaku	O. three-stringed lute

Answers			
1.	I	9.	E
2.	F	10.	D
3.	M	11.	C
4.	O	12.	H
5.	K	13.	L
6.	A	14.	J
7.	N	15.	G
8.	B		

Selected Bibliography

Adriaansz, Willem (1973). *The Kumiuta and Danmono Traditions of Japanese Koto Music.* Los Angeles: University of California Press.

Blades, James (1975). *Percussion Instruments and Their History.* London: Faber and Faber Ltd.

Ernst, Earle (1956). *The Kabuki Theatre.* Grove Press.

Garfias, Robert (1959). *Gagaku.* New York: Theatre Arts Books.

_____ (1959). *Gagaku: The Music and Dance of the Japanese Imperial Household.* (Ed. by Lincoln Kirstein). New York: Theatre Arts Books.

Harich-Schneider, Eta (1954). *The Rhythmical Patterns in Gagaku and Bugaku.* Leiden: E.J. Brill.

Kishibe, Shigeo (1969). *The Traditional Music of Japan.* Tokyo: Kokusai Bunka Shinkokai (Japan Cultural Society).

Malm, William P. (1967). *Music Cultures of the Pacific, the Near East, and Asia.* Englewood Cliffs, NJ: Prentice-Hall, Inc.

_____ (1963). *Nagauta the Heart of Kabuki Music.* Rutland, Vermont: Charles E. Tuttle.

_____ (1986). *Six Hidden Views of Japanese Music.* Los Angeles: University of California Press.

Piggott, Sir Francis (1971). *The Music and Musical Instruments of Japan* (Second edition). New York: Da Capo Press.

Purcell, William L. (1966). *An Introduction to Asian Music.* New York: The Asia Society.

Sunaga, Katsumi (1936). *Japanese Music.* Tokyo: Japan Tourist Bureau, Maruzen Company Ltd.

Togi, Masataro (1971). *Gagaku: Court Music and Dance.* (Translated by Don Kenny). New York: Walker/Weatherhill, in collaboration with Tankosha, Kyoto.

Wade, Bonnie C. (1976). *Tegotomono: Music for the Japanese Koto.* London: Greenwood Press.

Selected Discography

A Festival of Japanese Music in Hawaii
Folkways Records FE 8885 and 8886

Art of the Japanese Bamboo Flute, The
The Atlas Collection
Olympic Records 6117

Art of the Koto: The Music of Japan
Elektra Records EKS-7234

Bamboo Textures
Toshiba Records TP-72323

Bell Ringing in the Empty Sky, A
Japanese Shakuhachi Music
Nonesuch Records H-72025

Buddhist Chant
Lyrichord Discs LL 118 (2 records)

18th Century Traditional Music of Japan
(Koto Music of the Edo Period)
Everest Records 3306

Columbia World Library of Folk and Primitive Music
V. 11 Folk Music from Japan

Flower Dance: Japanese Folk Melodies
Nonesuch Records H-72020

Folk Music from Japan: The Ryukyus, Formosa, and Korea
Columbia Records 91A 02019

Folk Music of Japan
Folkways Records FE 4429

Gagaku: The Imperial Court Music of Japan
Lyrichords Discs LL 126

Japan
Unesco Collection: Musical Atlas
Odeon (EMI) C-064-17967

Japanese Kabuki Nagauta Music
Lyrichord Discs LLST 7134

Japanese Koto Classics
Nonesuch Records H-72008

Japanese Koto Music with Shamisen and Shakuhachi
Lyrichords Discs LLST 7131

Japanese Musical Atlas
Odeon C 064 17967

Japanese Noh Music
Lyrichord Discs LLST 7137

Japanese Temple Music:
Zen, Nembutsu and Yamabushi Chants
Lyrichord Discs LL 116-118

Koto Music of Japan, The
Nonesuch Records HS 72005

Koto: Music of the One-String Ichigenkin
Folkways Records FW 8746

National Folk Songs of Japan
Folkways Records FE 4524 A/B

Noh Plays of Japan
Cademon TC 2019 (2 records)

Shomyo: Buddhist Ritual for Japan
Unesco Collection: Musical Sources
Philip 6586-021

Takarazuka Dance Theatre
Columbia Records WL 163

Traditional Folk Songs of Japan
Folkways Records FE 4534

UNESCO Collection: A Musical Anthology of the Orient
Barenrieter-Musicaphon BM 30 L-2012--L-2017
- Japan I: Music of Sokyoku
- Japan II: Gagaku
- Japan III: Music of the Edo Period
- Japan IV: Buddhist Music
- Japan V: Shinto Music
- Japan VI: Music of Noh Drama

UNESCO Collection: Musical Sources
　　Shomyo: Buddhist Ritual for Japan
Philips 6586021

Zen, Goeika, and Shomyo Chants
Lyrichord Discs LLST 7116

CHAPTER SIX

MUSIC OF INDONESIA

Kendang player, Sri Djoko Raharjo. University of Wisconsin: Madison Javanese Gamelan Kyai Telaga Rukmi (The Venerable Lake of Gold). Courtesy of K. H. Han, Northern Illinois University.

"Unity in Diversity" (Bhinneka Tunggal Ika) is the motto of Indonesia, a country which includes about 6000 islands, half of which are inhabited, spread over 3,400 miles, east to west, 1,250 miles, north to south. It includes the main islands of Java, Bali, Sumatra, Kalimantan, and Sulawesi as well as hundreds of smaller ones, embracing over 300 distinct cultural groups within its population of 150 million people. The propinquity of this island country, formerly known as the East Indies, to trade routes which connected to India, the Middle East, and Southeast Asia, as well as the West, has resulted in a cultural melting pot which has absorbed Hinduism, Islam, and Western thought.

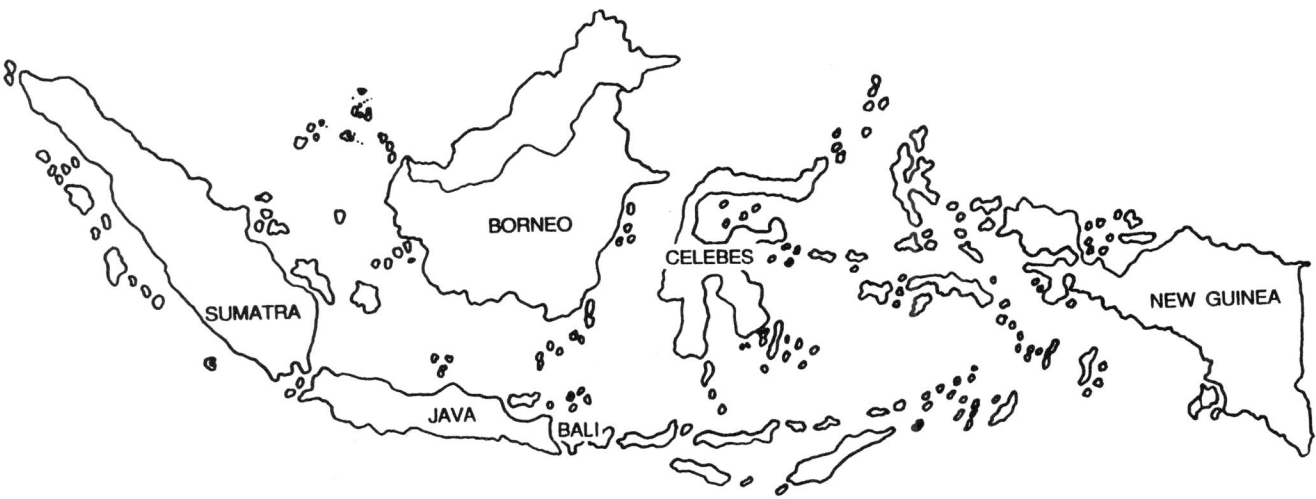

The most densely populated region of this archipelago is known as the Greater Sunda Islands, which includes all of the islands listed above, with the exception of Bali, which is part of the Lesser Sunda group, a chain of small islands stretching from Bali east to Timor. A third group is the Moluccas, which lie north of Lesser Sunda and east of Sulawesi. The last grouping of Indonesia is actually the western portion of New Guinea, which is known as Irian Jaya (West Irian).

The economy of Indonesia is basically agriculture, but it is also a country rich in petroleum. Its people are a blend of many races and traditions, speaking over 250 distinct languages. Its musical traditions, however, are clearly focused and rooted in music of the *gamelan*, an instrumental ensemble consisting of metallophones, gongs, and gong-chimes. Since the ability to forge gongs developed earlier than the seventh century in Java, the gamelan tradition is quite old. The Javanese even exported gongs to other countries of Southeast Asia which used gongs, including Thailand, Burma, and Malaysia.

Although the gamelan tradition is largely centered in the islands of Java and Bali, there is commonality in all gamelans throughout Indonesia, particularly in tuning, construction, musical structure, and performance practice. These commonalities will be examined in this chapter.

Marching gamelan, including suspended gong ageng. Ubud, Bali.
Courtesy © David Burckhalter (1992).

The gamelan ("gamel" = to handle, "gangsa" = bronze) is a metallic-sounding ensemble, consisting of keyed *metallophones* (metal xylophones) which busily sound simultaneously, as well as suspended gongs of varying sizes that clang at regular intervals. Bronze forging was brought from Southeast Asia during the third century B.C. By the second or first century B.C., the gamelan had evolved into existence. Compared to instrumental groups of China, Japan, India, or Arabia, this is a much larger ensemble. The gamelan, meaning "orchestra", sometimes has as many as seventy-five performers, including instrumentalists and singers. Next to the European symphony orchestra, it represents one of the largest ensembles of performers in the world. Gamelans, however, can also be small. Some chamber groups have three or four instrumentalists. There is no conductor. The entire ensemble is triggered by a lead drummer who sits in front, giving visual signals with hand and aural cues on the drum.

Gamelan in temple pavilion, Batubulan, Bali.
Suspended gong can be seen in left, as well as two genders, kendang (center), and rebab (right).
Courtesy © David Burckhalter (1992).

All gamelans have similar instruments, structures, and traditions, yet each is unique. A palace gamelan might have seventy performers, consisting of instruments with bronze keys that are ornate and richly decorated. A village gamelan might be much older, consisting of fifteen performers, with unpretentious instruments made with brass or iron keys. Even the tuning is different between gamelans since the instrument maker tunes the entire set of instruments to give it a unique sound. This is no standard pitch in Indonesia. Although the government attempted to standardize pitch in 1961 by establishing an Indonesian equivalent of $a=440$, it never caught on. Instrument makers have their own way of tuning. Even parallel instruments in the same ensemble are constructed to be slightly out of tune with one another, creating beats when the corresponding metal key on each is struck. This produces a shimmering effect which is indigenous to gamelan music. Precise tuning would obviate this sound.

Kendang player (left) leads the ensemble.
Courtesy © David Burckhalter (1992).

In Bali, which is predominantly Hindu, gamelans are used for celebrations in temple celebrations. In special open pavilions, called *taring*, gamelans play as an offering to Hindu gods. These festivals are held frequently, every seven months during a full moon. The music, dance, and drama are all consecrated as appeasement to the gods, not unlike the daily rice offerings that are left in corners and nooks to court good gods and ward off bad ones. Animistic beliefs, which permeate all Balinese society, make participation in musical ensembles a special type of individual offering to the gods. In Java, the gamelan is used in puppet plays, called *wayang kulit*, as well as to accompany dancing.

The gamelan is frequently an amateur group in Indonesia. In Bali, participants undoubtedly earn their living in rice paddies or town markets during the day. In the evening, they come to the *seka* (clubhouse) to rehearse music. There are numerous clubs in Bali, including music clubs. Most are male dominated and have established rules governing participation and attendance. The music clubs are rigidly organized and fines are levied when performers miss a rehearsal. The instruments of the gamelan, which are owned by the club or town, are a source of civic pride, requiring several thousands of dollars to purchase. Any money earned by the group is used to maintain old or purchase new instruments. Most gamelans are known by a proper title, such as *The Venerable Dark Cloud*, rather than by name of village. Although each has its own unique sound and repertoire, common references and uses unite all gamelans. The closeness of the arts to all Indonesians is part of this. Indonesians understand literature, drama, and music because it has been part of their acculturation since early childhood. Art and music serve as unifier, socializer, and entertainer, all at the same time, thus justifying the motto: "Unity in Diversity."

South Sulawesi gamelan.
Courtesy of the American Folklife Center, Smithsonian Institution,
Photo No. 91-15074-1.

Structure of Gamelan Music

Gamelan music is built in layers of sound. As many as thirty layers can operate in an ensemble simultaneously, yet each functions within a strict domain and requires group empathy. There is little random improvisation, although casual observers often think this is so. The unifying structure for most gamelan compositions is a slow moving melody in long note values, a *cantus firmus*, or fixed melody. It is not heard above harmony, which is often true of Western music, but, rather, is buried somewhere in the middle of the ensemble, providing the foundation for melodies which occur both above or below it.

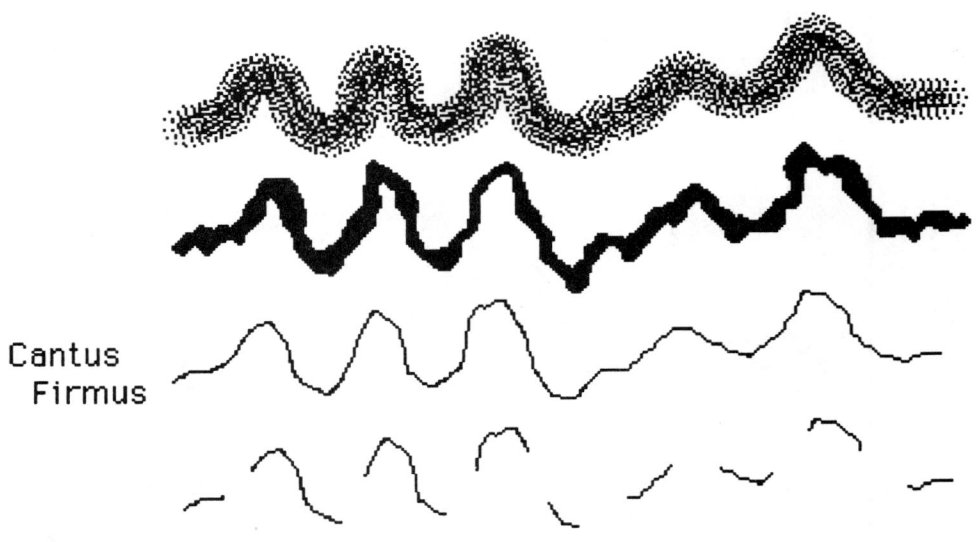

This core melody is elaborated by instruments which are higher in the pitch spectrum much like a division (doubling or tripling of note values). In general, the higher the instrument, the more notes it plays relative to the core melody. There may be rapid alteration of pitches between two or more instruments in upper parts, resulting in hocket-like effects. Instruments which lie under the cantus firmus, however, generally play an abbreviated version of it. The entire musical structure results in heterophony. Each layer of sound is thus differentiated by register as well as complexity of melody. Each repetition of the cantus firmus provides an opportunity to add timbres or elaborations, allowing a composition to grow and intensify.

In addition to the melodic instruments of the gamelan, which are predominant, several gongs and drums are used as time keepers. They are referred to as the *colotomic* group, providing punctuation to a rhythmic cycle that has been predetermined. This cycle, based on the original length of the cantus firmus, becomes audible to other performers and listeners through rhythmic punctuation. The largest gong generally sounds the *last* beat of each cycle, while smaller gongs and kettles provide smaller division within the cycle. This is largely determined by size of the instrument, the smallest one usually sounding each beat.

Both cantus firmus and colotomic structure are created by the conductor in many cases. He teaches it by rote to each performer during rehearsal and then directs it from front of the gamelan during performance by arm gestures and drumming patterns. In this way, each gamelan develops its unique repertoire.

Dissonance in gamelan compositions occurs between structural points. Consonance reappears when the instruments strike a unison at each repetition of the cantus firmus. The larger gamelans may add a soloist, whether vocalist, flutist, or string player, who improvises above the many strata. This part may become the most noticeable, but is still governed by the structure of the cantus firmus and colotomic structure. Since no other instrument doubles this added soloist, he/she is somewhat free to wander melodically. The nature of the voice, flute, or string instrument will also allow narrower pitch intervals to be used than can be accomplished on the keyed metallophones which adhere to one of two predominate scales.

Three colotomic instruments in Northern Illinois University Balinese Gamelan Angklung. Kempur (center), medium gong, rincik (left), 8-disc cymbals on back of a turtle, and kelenang (right), small time-beating kettle. Courtesy of K. H. Han, Northern Illinois University.

The gamelan is thus a multilayered musical medium that varies in density by the number of strata. It is still remarkably homogeneous. As Hood, who coined the word "stratification" to refer to this structure, said: "Each stratum has a characteristic and predictable density or number of musical events that occur in a given span of time."[1] The importance of each layer of sound is even reflected in the pay scale of professional gamelans. Those who have the most important parts receive higher wages, not unlike practice in the Western symphony orchestra.

Melodic Structure: Slendro and Pelog Scales

In all of cultures examined in this text so far, tuning is an important concern for the performer. The Indian sitarist must adjust both frets and strings to match the raga presented. In Japan and China, strings on zithers are tuned by moveable bridges placed under the strings. In Indonesia, however, almost all instruments are tuned during construction, since the instruments are keyed metallophones. Most are built in pairs and quartets. Although tuned to the same scale, one member is tuned slightly lower, deviating by a few cents. The difference in beats that occurs when the same key of each instrument is struck produces the shimmering effect so typical of the gamelan. This is the sound the instrument maker strives to obtain and it is not based on theoretical considerations so much as aesthetics. Attempts to standardize pitch have failed because instrument builders have preferred to keep what was beautiful, not what was mathematically correct. Discussion of the two Indonesian scales, then, cannot describe all practice, but, rather, merely allude to basic structure.

There are two tuning systems or *laras* used in Javanese gamelan music, *slendro*, which is pentatonic, and *pelog*, which is heptatonic. The former came into use as early as the sixth century A.D. while the latter developed by the twelfth century. Slendro is bound by an octave, 1200 cents, but there is no set pitch for "1" of the scale across gamelans. "One", which we would translate as tonic, is set by the instrument maker. Obviously, all instruments of the same gamelan must use the same tonic, but it does not necessarily correlate with the tonic in any other gamelan.

Slendro divides the octave into five intervals of 240 cents each, which is slightly wider than a whole-step (200 cents).

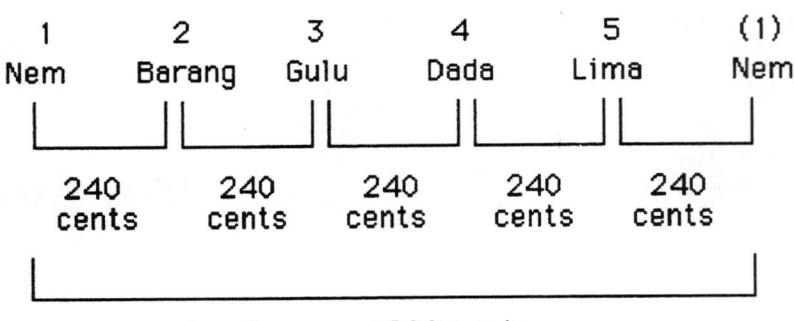

Compared with a Western keyboard with "c" used as tonic for slendro, it is easy to see these pitches do not articulate with our system.

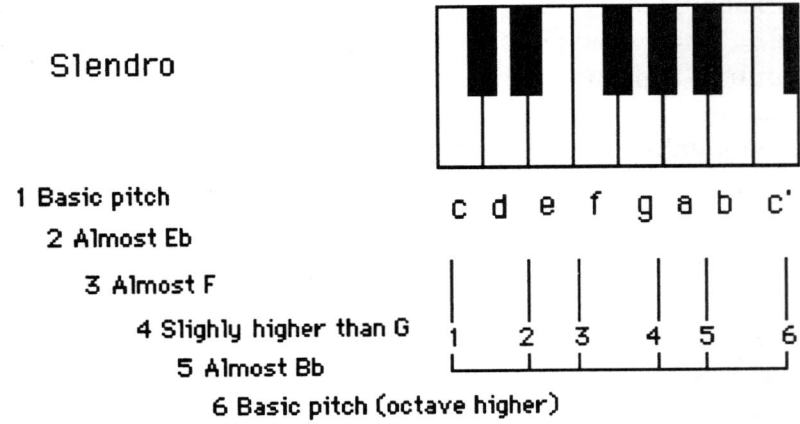

In reality, the 240 cent norm is not strictly applied but is close. Nem to barang might be 263 cents, barang to gulu, 223, and so on. This demonstrates an aesthetic, not scientific, approach to tuning in Indonesia.

Pelog is much less standardized than slendro, but generally consists of two larger intervals and five smaller.

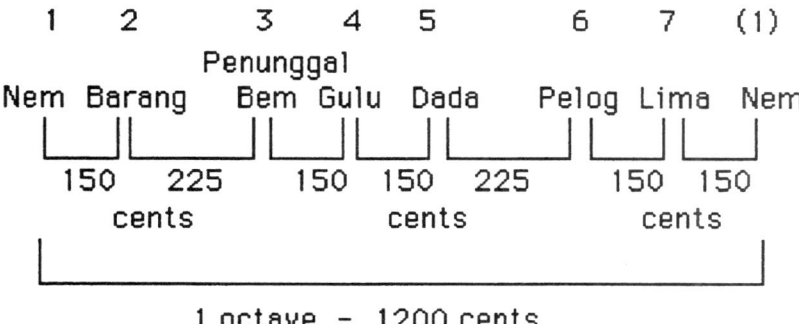

Although these are not precise, the smaller intervals are c. 150 cents, the larger, c. 225, neither of which articulates with our half-steps (100 cents) or whole-steps (200 cents). The smaller intervals are much like the three-quarters tone found in Arab music, being a quarter-tone larger than a half-step. Pelog, nonetheless, has a pentatonic quality. Much like Chinese music with its bian-tones, two of the scale tones function as ornaments rather than as structural pitches.

Compared with the keyboard, again, using "c" as tonic, there is no articulation with Western temperament.

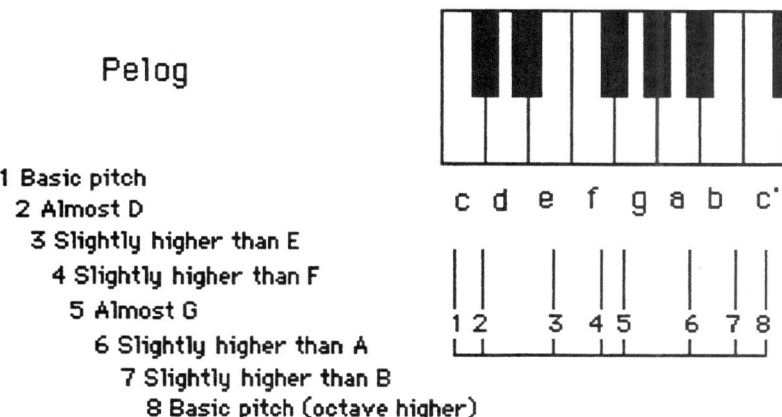

In addition, there is no articulation *between* slendro and pelog. Their notes do not correspond, even when they have the same name in the lara. Gamelans are built to play in one or the other system. Large gamelans have double instruments in each category, one for playing pelog, the other for slendro, which are never played at the same time. They are arranged at 90 degrees to one another, so the performer can turn and begin playing on the twin instrument in a new composition. The only exception in the largest gong, *gong ageng*, which has a low but indeterminate pitch, making it appropriate in either lara. In effect, a large gamelan is two orchestras, but only half are used in any one composition.

Each tuning system is arranged into three modes called *patets*, depending on the pitch which is used as tonic. Modes create different feelings. The three patets of slendro, for example, correspond, respectively, to feelings of happiness, anger, and sadness, somewhat like Indian ragas. They are appropriate at different times of day or night. They are also associated with characters or puppets in theatre performances which incorporate music, dance, and drama.

In slendro, the successive tones of the scale are then indicated as *dong, deng, dung, dang,* and *ding*. Placing a dong on a different pitch or metal key changes the basic mode, but certain relationships are important in patets. Thus, not any pitch may be chosen as dong since there must be a perfect fifth between dong and the lower dung as well as perfect fifth between dong and the higher dang. Dong functions like tonic, dung like subdominant, and dang as dominant. The three patets which result are *patet manyura, patet nem,* and *papet sanga*, using, respectively, nem, gulu, and lima as dong:

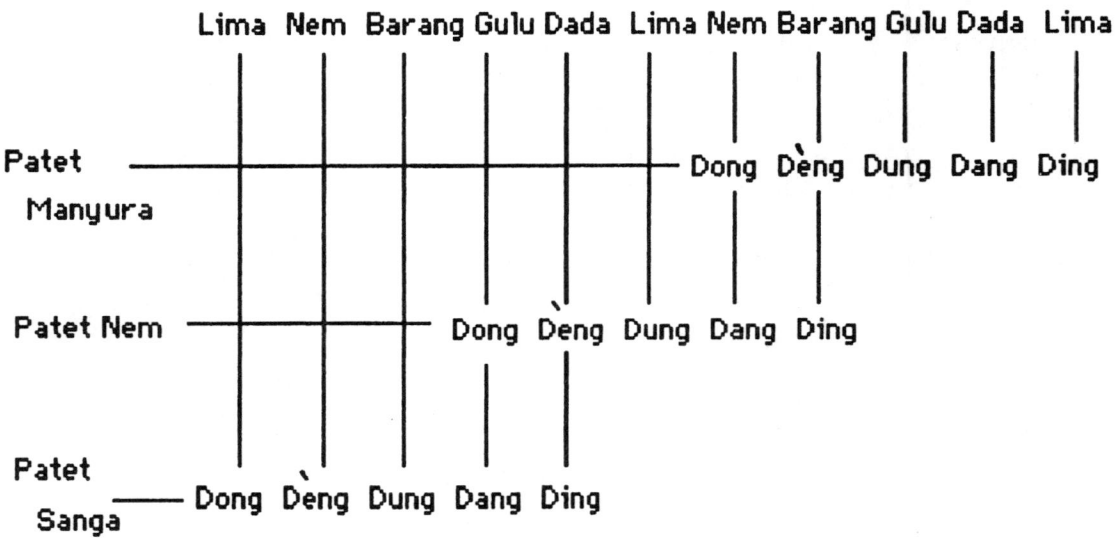

Pelog also has three main patets determined in a similar manner. These are *patet lima*, *patet nem*, and *patet barang*.

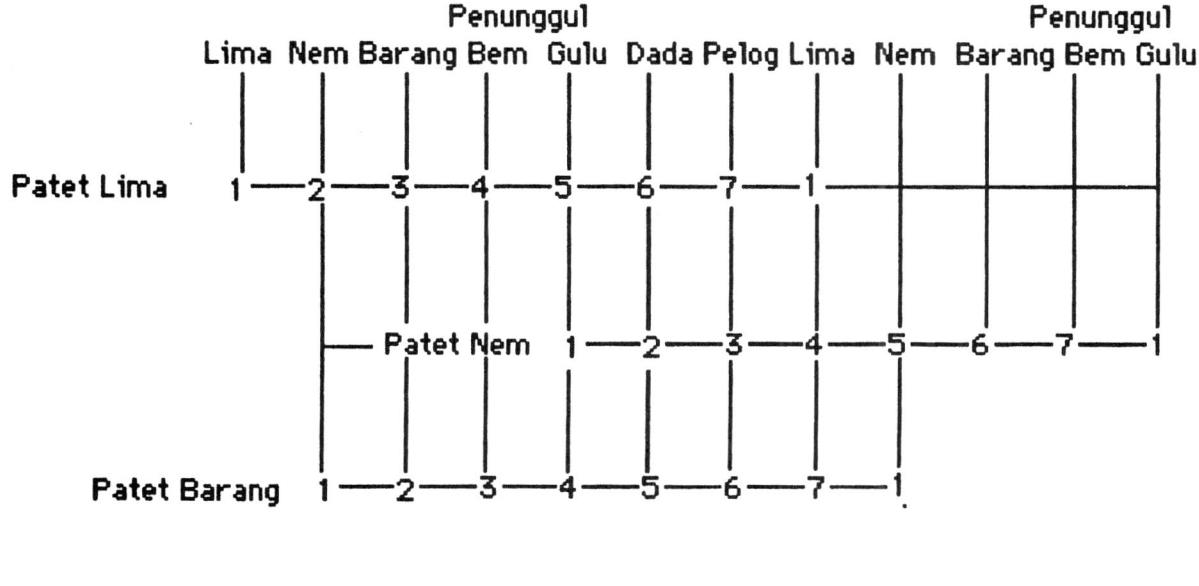

1 = Dong

In addition, there are two secondary patets which function similarly.

Although it would seem that changing tonal centers, as occurs in patets, would do little to change the feeling, it does. The change of tonic changes the general register of pitches used. In addition, each patet is associated with typical melodic and cadential patterns.

Although the discussion here describes mid-Javanese practice, in Eastern Java, slightly different terminology is used for these patets. In slendro, nem, sanga, and manjura, respectively, are known as sepuluh, wolu, and sanga. In pelog, nem, lima, and barang, respectively, are nem, wolu, and sanga. Terminology varies depending on the region of Indonesia.

In Bali, the lara related to the Javanese slendro is called *saih gender wayang*. It is used in orchestras which accompany Balinese shadow puppet plays. There is variation on it, the *saih angklung*, which has only four pitches, and is used with the bamboo anglung. The seven-toned tuning is called *saih pitu*, which has five main pitches and two auxiliary ones. There is also a pentatonic scale used with popular ensembles which is called *selisir*. As with Javanese tuning, there are many variations in register, mood, and function within the two broad categories of pentatonic and heptatonic scales.

Since gamelan music is ancient, tuning systems do not have to be left in written theoretical treatises. They are always present in the extant instruments which, unlike chordophones and aerophones, deteriorate little over time. These instruments provide clear documentation of past practice and its connection to the present. In addition, music of this culture has been notated with a *cipher system*, simply using numbers to indicate the pitches of the patet. This has largely been preserved in manuscripts of the *kraton* or palace in Jogjakarta, a city in mid-Java. Cipher notation is known as *kepatihan*.

Musical Structure: Texture, Melody, and Rhythm

As we have observed, the texture of gamelan music is basically heterophonic, with varying layers, each playing a variation on the basic melody or cantus firmus. The number of layers depends on the number of instruments used. The largest gamelans, such as *gamelan gong kebyar* in Bali, have the greatest complexity. This is known as *stratification*, with each version of the melody somewhat differentiated by register. Those instruments which play the cantus firmus, usually no more than an octave in range, are mid-range instruments. Those which play elaborated versions, one or two octaves above, are higher in range, those which play simpler versions in the octaves under, lower. Melody does not sit on top of the ensemble in the foreground, but, rather, is buried in the middle. Nonetheless, this cantus firmus is the melodic material which unites every composition. In Java, it is called *balungan* ("skeleton"), in Bali, *pokok* ("nuclear"). The balungan or pokok is usually identified by a proper name, which, in turn, becomes the name for the composition (*gending*) on which it is based. The title will also reflect the scale, mode, and rhythmic cycle. In Java, there are over 4000 such melodies, but only about 1000 are regularly used as the basis of a composition. Balungan and pokok are both taken from a repertoire of melodies by conductors or are freely created.

In gamelan music, a composition is frequently created by repetition of the cantus firmus, much like an ostinato, with intensification occurring through the addition of instruments and a corresponding increase in the level of dynamics. The rhythmic cycle which governs these ostinatos is played by a group of drums and gongs known collectively as the colotomic group. As we have seen, the largest gong, gong ageng, sounds the last beat of each cycle. Intermediary portions of the cycle are maintained by smaller gongs and drums, usually onomatopoeically named, that is, by the sound each makes. A small hanging drum, called *kempul*, sounds half-way through the cycle. Other kettle-like gongs, called *kenong*, *ketuk*, and *kempyang*, sound smaller divisions of the cycle. Collectively, this group of instruments maintains the beat structure and the general tempo, following this type of organization:

```
Kempyang    * * * * * * * * * * * * * * * *

Ketuk         *   *   *   *   *   *   *   *

Kenong            *       *       *       *

Kempul                        *           *

Gong Ageng                                *
```

Although this example shows a rhythmic cycle of 16 beats, called *ketawang*, additional cycles are:

Lancaran	8 beats
Ladrang	32 beats
Ketawang Gending Ketuk	32 beats
Gending Ketuk	64 beats

Cycles are usually in 4, 8, 16, or 32 beats and each is also associated with a set tempo. To maintain the rhythmic cycle throughout a composition, three double-headed hand drums are used, one played by the leader of the gamelan. He indicates the basic tempo as well as deviations within it. He also cues entrances and changes in dynamic levels.

Instruments of Indonesia

There are two groups of instruments in Indonesia. Instruments of the "soft" ensemble include a xylophone, flute, zither, and fiddle, while instruments of the "loud" style are keyed-metallophones, gongs, and gong-chimes. The entire range of the gamelan, low to high, encompasses over seven octaves, much like the Western symphony orchestra. The gong ageng sounds a pitch in the area of 35-45 hertz while the highest instruments, both metallophones and fiddle, produce pitches in the range of 2000 hertz. The gamelan is one of the few non-European musical ensembles in the world that has such a wide pitch range, approaching the extreme of the audible frequency spectrum (16-20 hertz) at its lowest level.

We will discuss these instruments in both Java and Bali in the same order used throughout this text: chordophones; aerophones; membranophones; and idiophones. The latter category, unlike many cultures, will be the most extensive.

The *rebab* is a two-stringed lute related to the Arab rabab, a spike-fiddle. It is played with a bow, much like a small cello, and the tension of the bow hair is controlled by the pressure of the performer's finger against them. Its two strings are tuned to gulu and mem, a fifth apart, of the chosen patet and its function is twofold: (1) to open the gending of each composition, presenting a short *buka* or prelude; and (2) to provide counterpoint throughout the composition, slightly anticipating in a rubato style the structural notes of the cantus firmus. Since it is easy to re-tune between compositions, it can be used in either slendro or pelog compositions. Because it plays variable pitch, it usually fills in main notes of the balungen with smaller pitch intervals.

The *celempung* is a zither with 26 or 28 strings in double courses arranged in a case. A similar instrument is the smaller and higher *siter*. Both instruments are plucked with thumbnails and play elaborated versions of the basic melody.

Javanese dancer with accompanying gamelan, including sarons (right), rebab and kendang (right) (c. 1897). Courtesy of The University Museum, University of Pennsylvania, Neg. No. S4-140743

The main aerophone, the *suling*, is an end-blown flute made of bamboo. It similarly elaborates the melody with additional pitches and figurations.

Pakarena (similar to kendang) players from Sulawesi. Courtesy of the American Folklife Center, Smithsonian Institution, Photo No. 91-0163-11.

Membranophones used in gamelan music are the *kendang gending*, a two-sided drum with either a conical or rounded cylindrical shell. Both sides are played, either with hands or wooden mallets as the drum rests in a slightly pitched tray. A smaller version of this drum is called *kendang ketipung*. Whomever plays this drum is the conductor of the ensemble, directing tempo and dynamic changes and cuing main musical events, as well as coordinating the music to the movement of dancers or puppets. A medium-sized drum called *ciblon* or *batangan* is used when the gamelan accompanies dancing. The *bedug* is a larger drum with barrel frame. It is also beaten with a wooden mallet.

Saron in double-headed tiger trough resonator. Field Museum of Natural History, Chicago, Illinois. Courtesy of K. H. Han, Northern Illinois University.

All of these instruments are really support and elaboration to the keyed-metallophones, instruments which are predominant in the ensemble, both in number and effect. The *saron* is a family of such instruments, each consisting of six or seven metal keys on top of a wooden box resonator. In Bali, they are called *gangsa* but function similarly. *Saron barung* is the main instrument of the family, sounding in the range of 586 (octave beginning with d", octave plus second above middle c [c']) to 1014 hertz. The smaller *saron panerus* or *saron peking* is an octave higher while the larger *saron demung* is an octave lower. Most gamelans have at least four sarons, two barungs, one peking, and one demung. Saron barung carries the balungen while its lower counterpart sounds structural pitches of the melody. The higher saron simply doubles the pitches of the barung, much like a division, usually in a syncopated interpretation. A single mallet, often made from the horn of a water buffalo, for striking is held by the right hand while the left immediately dampens the key to prevent overtone buildup. A large gamelan might use four demungs, eight barungs, and two pekings.

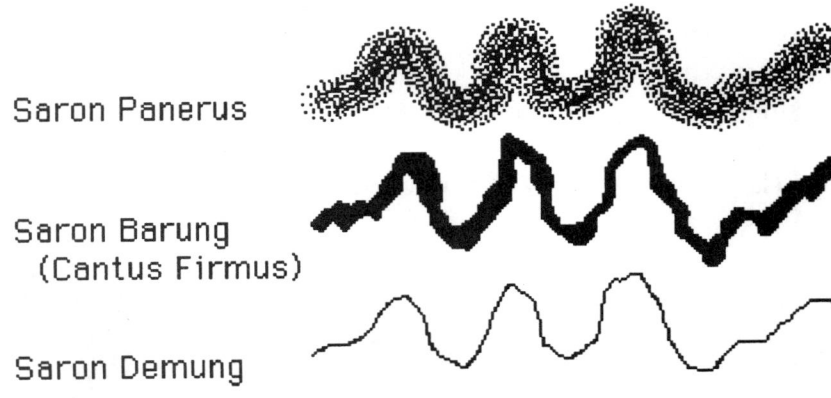

Gender, with individual tube resonator for each key. Field Museum of Natural History, Chicago, Illinois. Courtesy of K. H. Han, Northern Illinois University.

Although similar to the saron, the *gender* family has a different timbre. This is due to the individual tube resonator for each key as well as mallets which are padded. The *gender barung* is the core instrument, playing in the range of 127 (octave beginning with c, octave below middle c [c']) to 684 hertz, and extending two and a half octaves above. The *gender panerus* sounds an octave higher while the *gender panembung*, also called *slentem*, duplicates the lowest octave of the gender barung. It thus has only a one-octave range and is played with a single stick. The other genders are played with two mallets, one in each hand. Since each key, like the saron, must be dampened, the playing technique requires utmost coordination and technique. The function of the gender family is similar to that of the saron, but its gentler timbre, a result of padded mallets, creates subtle contrast.

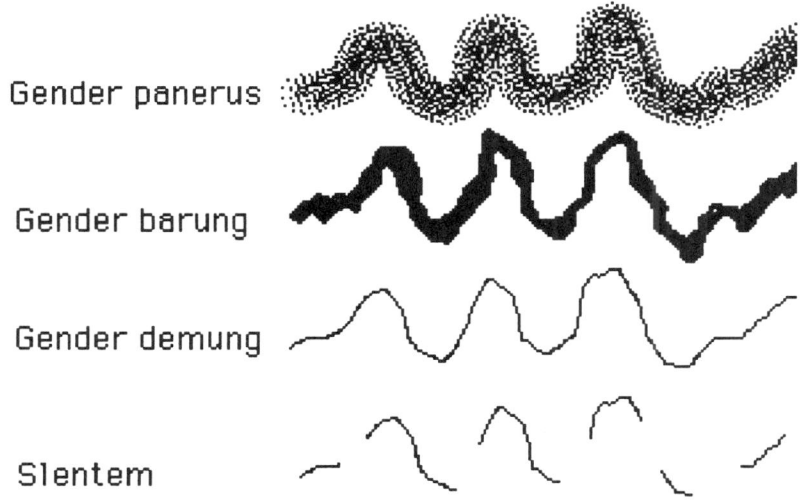

Bonang with beaters. Field Museum of Natural History, Chicago, Illinois.
Courtesy of K. H. Han, Northern Illinois University.

The third class of main instruments is the *bonang* family, described as instruments with gong-chimes resting in a wooden frame. They are placed in the frame on cords, to allow free vibration, and are arranged in a double row. The main *bonang barung* has 14 kettles and its pitch range is c. 295 (c. d', d above middle c [c']) to 1014 hertz. The higher *bonang panerus* overlaps barung by one octave, but sounds an octave higher. The lower *bonang penembung* also overlaps by one octave, but also goes an octave below. Each instrument is played with two mallets. In Bali, a collective version of the bonang, usually played by four persons when there are twelve kettles, is called the *reyong*. A solo instrument similar to the bonang is called *trompong*. The bonang family functions similarly, bonang barung sounding the nuclear theme, while the higher instrument elaborates, syncopates, and anticipates, the lower instrument sounds structural pitches.

The *gambang* is the only idiophone of the gamelan with keys made of wood. It has twenty or twenty-one keys arranged in a wooden trough resonator. Its lowest octave is the same as gender panembung. Its entire range includes at least three higher octaves.

Balinese gong player playing at dance, south-central Bali. Photo by Baron Rodolphe Meyer de Schauensee (c. 1930). Courtesy of The University Museum, University of Pennsylvania, Neg. No. S4-140738.

The colotomic group of instruments used in the gamelan have been discussed above. The vertically suspended gongs include the single gong ageng, which is about a yard in diameter, as well as the kempul, a smaller size gong. Kempul are actually arranged in sets, with a single gong for each pitch of both slendro and pelog, resulting in eleven different gongs. (One pitch is common to both systems, thus there are not twelve (5 + 7) kempul.) The horizontally suspended gong-chimes or kettles include the kenong, ketuk, and kempyang. The kenong is the largest of these and a gamelan might have one for each note of the scale. The ketuk and kempyang are smaller versions of the kenong, the former being low, the latter, higher pitched with more resonance.

Although these instruments are known by slightly different names throughout Indonesia, they function similarly. The main metallophones are called variously *jegogan*, *calung*, and *gangsa*. The Balinese instrument which corresponds to the bonang, we have seen, is known as the *reyong*. If it has four kettles, it is usually played by two performers, if as many as twelve kettles, four performers. Reyong players arrange their gong-chimes in a manner which allows them to play the necessary pitches effectively and quickly, often placing structural tones in corners of the frame.

Octaves placed behind one another in the next row are usually avoided, since these are frequently sounded and such placement would inhibit correct striking. Cymbals are called *ceng-ceng* and *rincik*. Rincik consist of two pairs, one mounted on a small stand and struck by the other pair held in the performer's two hands. They provide rhythmic accent to the Balinese ensemble.

Gong ageng. Field Museum of Natural History, Chicago, Illinois. Courtesy of K. H. Han, Northern Illinois University.

The following provides summary to the discussion of instruments of Indonesia:

CHORDOPHONES	IDIOPHONES
Celempung	Angklung
Rebab	Bonang
Siter	Gambang
AEROPHONES	Gender
Suling	Gong Ageng
MEMBRANOPHONES	Gong Suwukan Kempul
Bedug	Kempyang
Ciblon (Batangan)	Kenong
Kendang Ketipung	Ketuk
Kendang Gending	Saron
	Slentem (Gender Panembung)

It would be a misconception to suggest that all timbres of the gamelan are instrumental. In practice, at least with larger gamelans, a single female vocal line may be added, known as *pesinden*. This voice is free to roam above the heterophonic complex, adding pitches which elaborate the balungen. There may also be a male chorus, called *gerongan*, consisting of as many of fifteen voices. Instruments and voices are added to the heterophonic complex without any dynamic concession. They are free to add tones that deviate from the tuning system. These are called *plesedan*, which translates as "tones that have slid down."[2]

It should be recalled that instruments, in Bali at least, are built in pairs, one tuned slightly higher than its twin. The higher instrument is called *pengisep*, the lower, *pengumbang*. The slight difference between each corresponding metal key creates reverberation and a shimmering sound between the instruments. This is generally typical of Balinese gamelans.

The gamelan stays together because it is motivated by a common pokok or balungen, clearly punctuated by colotomic instruments. Most of the melodic instruments play rote melodies. Only winds, strings, and vocalists improvise. The structure is also held together by much practice and discipline, guided by the conductor. In "soft" playing, he may lead on the rebab. In "strong" playing, he will sit in front of the ensemble with a kendang, directing tempo, and transitions with his head, hand, and drum patterns. The Javanese conductor, *niyaga*, has mastered most of the instruments and is aptly qualified to lead the gamelan. His training might have begun in the colotomic section, advancing to melodic instruments, such as saron, bonang, or gender, and finally refined through improvisation on rebab or suling. These skills are imperative since he must teach each player the appropriate part by rote for each new composition that is created. This tuition occurs from the back side of the instrument, so the conductor must literally know the elaborate stratification forward and backward.

Utility of Gamelan Music

Unlike Europe, India, China, the Arab world, and Japan, there is really no gulf between music of the common and cultured people in Indonesia. The gamelan is known and loved by all levels of society in Java and Bali. One is apt to hear gamelan music in hotels, tourist centers, festivals, and concerts as well as on radio. Performances of *wayang*, dramatic plays depicting stories and myths from the Mahabharata and Ramayana are popular throughout Indonesia. Through these plays, Indonesians learn history and culture as well as societal norms and values. Many have allusions to current events, so there is a communication aspect to them.

Wayang kulit is a play using shadow-puppets. The puppets are made from water-buffalo hide, which is perforated, colored, and placed on a stick. The puppeteer, the *dalang*, holds each puppet against a white screen behind which there is an oil or electric lamp. Since the light shines through the translucent puppet, the image is projected on the screen. The audience, sitting on the opposite side, sees only the shadow, articulated and decorated from the outline as well as the perforations which allow light to shine through. The dalang is responsible for creating all voices of the puppets, including singing and special sound effects, an awesome task given there may be over 250 puppets in a single show.

Shadow puppet of wayang kulit. Courtesy of The University Museum, University of Pennsylvania, Neg. No. S8-40904, Object #29-91-108.

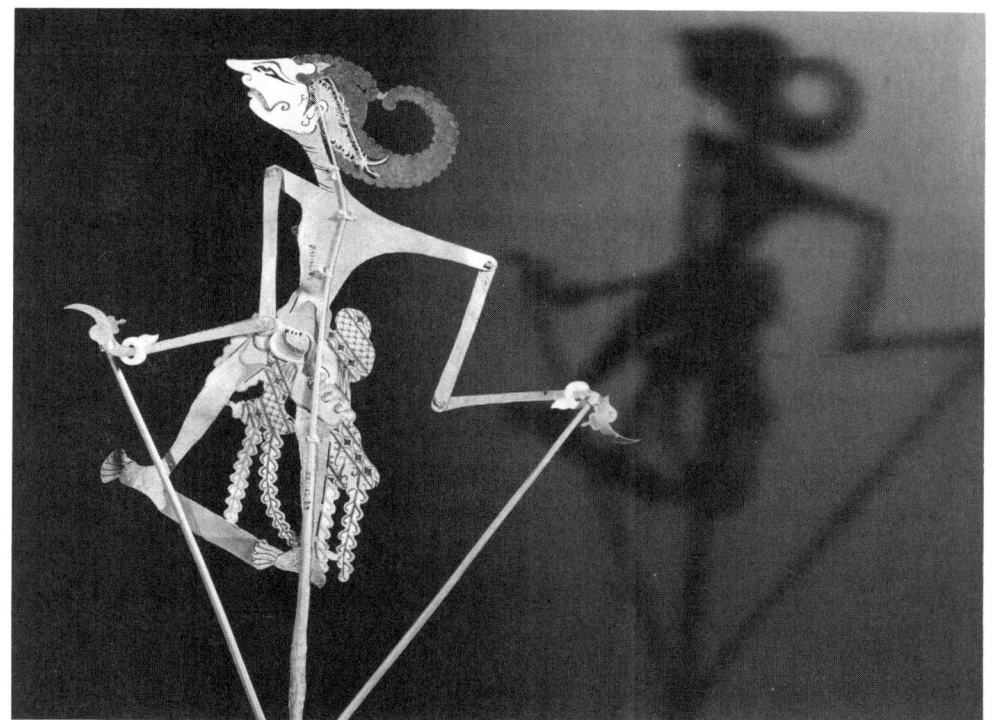

Performance of wayang kulit showing dalang (puppeteer) behind screen with his repertoire of puppet characters. Instruments of gamelan are seen in foreground. Electric light behind screen illuminates puppets. Courtesy of the American Folklife Center, Smithsonian Institution, Photo No. 91-15091-34.

Most wayang kulit present the age-old conflict between good and evil, with a set of characters representing each. The audience never doubts who is good and who is evil since the former appear on the audience's left, the latter, on the right. Characters are also identified by motives played by instruments of the gamelan. A puppet show is quite apt to last most of the night. From 8:00 p.m. to midnight, the characters are gradually introduced. A conflict between good and evil emerges, with the first session of the wayang ending with a *gara-gara* or conflict. At midnight, the patet changes and the characters begin to battle. By 3:00 a.m., the patet changes once again as the battle is finally won by the forces of good, usually by 6:00 a.m.

A similar type of drama called *wayang orang* uses human characters. *Wayang golek* uses doll-shaped puppets. Drama may also be danced rather than acted. Whether the drama is wayang or one that is danced, the stories are the same. The audience immediately identifies characters by symbol, outline, and music. Stories always show good triumphant over evil.

In Central Java, the term *karawitan*, refers to all music performed on the gamelan, as opposed to music performed on other types of instruments. Karawitan accompanies dance recitals, known as *beksan*, as well as wayang orang and wayang golek, both of which use verbal dialogue and a narrator, as well as *sendratari*, which is dance-drama without dialogue. Gamelan music is also performed as concert music, too, in which case it is called *klenengan*.

Legong dance accompanied by gamelan (southeast Bali). Reyong (similar to bonang) is seen in center, suspended gongs in background. Photo by Baron Rodolphe Meyer de Schauensee (c. 1930). Courtesy of The University Museum, University of Pennsylvania, Neg. No. S4-140740.

In Bali, the gamelan is used to accompany a variety of dances and presentations, including *legong*, danced only by young girls who have not reached puberty. The story is a complex one, involving three dancers, one of whom introduces the drama, and two of whom continually change roles. The legong, in which the two principal dancers use fans, is one of the most graceful of the classic Balinese dances. The legong was originally a court dance but has become popular at temple ceremonies as well. The main dancers wear gold costumes with crowns of frangipani blooms. Dancing is slow and graceful, involving full body movements as well as minute gestures of the hands and fingers. The *barong* dance-play represents the eternal fight between good and evil, with the barong a creature of good, the rangda, a mythological, evil monster. The barong is costumed to resemble a Chinese lion while rangda is portrayed as a witch. Trance dances, such as the *sanghyang*, have a long tradition in Indonesia, in which dancers are supposedly possessed by deities or demons. There is undoubtedly some connection between trance dances and the *ketchak* dance, an ancient story accompanied by a chorus of men who imitate monkey sounds. They represent an army of monkeys who rescue Rama in a battle against an army of demons, chanting the repetitive "chak-a-chak-a-chak", as they wave their arms to exorcise demons. *Baris*, warrior dances, developed out of pre-battle rituals, allowing performers to whirl themselves into a frenzy, accompanied by music which matches.

Barong dancers with masks (c. 1930). The Barong dance represents the forces of good, represented by the mythical lion, Baron Singha, and the forces of evil, portrayed by Rangda. Photo by Baron Rodolphe Meyer de Schauensee (c. 1930). Courtesy of The University Museum, University of Pennsylvania, Neg. No. S4-140739.

Gamelans have been identified which specialize in accompanying one or another type of drama. The *gamelan wayang* accompanies puppet plays, the *gamelan semar pelugingan*, the legong and other stories derived from Hindu mythology. In general, the *gamelan gong* is considered the older, more sedate style of gamelan playing, *gamelan gong kebyar*, a more flamboyant contemporary style, full of virtuoso drumming and brilliant timbres. *Gamelan gede* is used for celebrations in the Hindu temples while *gamelan angklung*, consisting of bamboo tubes which are shaken, is used for cremation rituals. The anglung or *jegog* in Bali, basically a West Javanese instrument, uses a four-tone scale. Bamboo tubes are cut into correct lengths, soaked for several days, and then wind-dried. The clear sound of each tube is made by cutting along the top of the tube as well as down its side. They are suspended in a frame by other natural materials. It is believed the tubes must only be cut on a special day by special people to make a successful instrument.

East Kalimentan Kenyah dancer. Courtesy of the American Folklife Center, Smithsonian Institution, Photo No. 91-15067-3.

Key Terms and Concepts

Angklung
Balungen
Baris
Barong
Batangan
Bedug
Beksan
Bonang
Bonang Barung
Bonang Panerus
Bonang Penembung
Buka
Cantus Firmus
Celempung
Ceng-ceng
Ciblon
Cipher notation
Colotomic
Dalang
Gambang
Gamelan
Gamelan Angklung
Gamelan Gede
Gamelan Gong
Gamelan Gong Kebyar
Gamelan Semar Pelugingan
Gamelan Wayang
Gangsa
Gara-gara
Gender
Gender Barung
Gender Panerus
Gender Penembung (Slentem)
Gending
Gerongan
Gong Ageng
Karawitan
Kempul
Kempyang
Kendang Gending
Kendang Ketipung
Kenong
Kepatihan
Ketawang
Ketchak
Ketuk
Klenengan
Kraton
Lara
Legong
Metallophone
Niyaga
Patet
Pelog
Pengisep
Pengumbang
Pesinden
Plesedan
Pokok
Rebab
Reyong
Rincik
Saron
Saron Barung
Saron Demung
Saron Panerus (Peking)
Seka
Sendratari
Siter
Slentem
Slendro
Stratification
Suling
Taring
Trompong
Wayang
Wayang Golek
Wayang Kulit
Wayang Orang

Self-Checking Chapter Review

Match Column II to Column I	
Column I	**Column II**
1. patet 2. angklung 3. slendro 4. colotomic 5. balungen 6. gong ageng 7. bonang 8. pelog 9. gender 10. legong 11. dalang 12. panerus 13. gambang 14. saron 15. suling	A. puppeteer B. heptatonic scale C. rhythmic cycle D. cantus firmus E. xylophone F. bamboo idiophone G. Balinese dance H. ends cycle I. flute J. set of gong-chimes K. mode L. pentatonic scale M. keyed metallophone with trough resonator N. highest voicing of a family of instruments O. keyed metallophone with individual tube resonators

Answers	
1. K	9. O
2. F	10. G
3. L	11. A
4. C	12. N
5. D	13. E
6. H	14. M
7. J	15. I
8. B	

Selected Bibliography

Becker, Judith (1980). *Traditional Music in Modern Java: Gamelan in a Changing Society*. Honolulu: University of Hawaii Press.

Hood, Mantle (1977). *The Nuclear Theme as a Determinant of Patet in Javanese Music*. New York: Da Capo.

Hood, Mantle and Susilo Harja (1967). *Music of the Venerable Dark Cloud: Introduction, Commentary, and Analyses* (of accompanying recordings). Los Angeles: Institute of Ethnomusicology, U.C.L.A.

Kunst, Jaap (1949). *Music in Java: Its History, Its Theory, and Its Technique*. (Translated from Dutch by Smile Van Loo). Second edition. The Hague: Martinus Nijhoff.

Lentz, Donald A. (1965). *The Gamelan Music of Java and Bali*. Lincoln: University of Nebraska Press.

Manuel, Peter (1988). *Popular Music of the Non-Western World*. New York: Oxford University Press.

McPhee, Colin (1966). *Music in Bali*. New Haven: Yale University Press.

Oey, Eric (producer and editor) (1985). *Indonesia*. Englewood Cliffs, NJ: Prentice-Hall, Inc.

Sorrell, Neil (1990). *A Guide to the Gamelan*. Portland, Oregon: Amadeus Press.

Zoete, Beryl de and Walter Spies (1938). *Dance and Drama in Bali*. London: Faber and Faber Ltd.

Selected Discography

Bali Court Music and Banjar Music
UNESCO Collection: Musical Sources
Philips 6586-008

Bali: Musical Atlas
Odeon Co 64-17858

Balinese Theatre and Dance Music
UNESCO Collection: Musical Sources
Philips 6586-013

Gamelan Batel Wayang Ramayana
CMP Records LC 6055

Gamelan Music of Bali
Lyrichord Discs LLST 7179

Gamelan Semar Pegulingan
Nonesuch Records H-72046

Golden Rain
Nonesuch Records H-72028

Jasmine Isle, The
Javanese Gamelan Music
Nonesuch Records H-72031

Java: Historic Gamelans
UNESCO Collection: Music Sources
Philips 6586-004

Javanese Court Gamelan
Nonesuch Records H-72044

Music for the Balinese Shadow Play
Nonesuch Records H-72037

Music from the Morning of the World
The Balinese Gamelan
Nonesuch Records H-72015

Music of Indonesia
Folkways Records FE 4537

Music of the Venerable Dark Cloud
(Javanese Gamelan Khjai Mendung)
Institute of Enthnomusicology
University of California at Los Angeles

West Meets East
Folkways Records FSS 37455

Endnotes

1. Hood, Mantle (1972). "Music of Indonesia". *Handbuch der Orientalistic Dritte Abteilung*. Koln: E.J. Brill, page 9.

2. Kunst, Jaap (1949). *Music in Java: Its History, Its Theory, and Its Technique*. (Second edition). The Hague: Martinus Nijhoff (2 volumes translated from Dutch by Emile Van Loo), page 234.

CHAPTER SEVEN

MUSIC OF OCEANIA

Our next region to investigate is not an integrated country or culture, but, rather, a region which encompasses many of the Pacific islands as well as Australia. The islands of this area are located in the central and southern Pacific, close, by global standards, to Australia. The classification of *Oceania* is thus convenient and appropriate.

The collective region of Oceania spreads over an ocean area twenty times the size of the United States. The actual land mass of the region, discounting Australia and Papua New Guinea, however, is smaller than one of our Western states.

Oceania is grouped into four regions. *Australia*, of course, refers to the continent itself, while *Polynesia* ("polys" meaning "many" and "nesos" meaning "island") consists of 18 island groups lying in a triangle. Hawaii is the northern point of the triangle, New Zealand the south, with Easter Island forming the eastern point. This is the widest expanse of the four regions of Oceania, including the Hawaiian Islands, Samoan Islands, Tahiti, and New Zealand, but Polynesia is linked more by ethnic and cultural considerations than by propinquity. The third region of Oceania is *Melanesia* ("melas" meaning "black"), which lies between Indonesia and Polynesia, south of the equator and somewhat northeast of the Australian continent. The main islands include New Guinea, the Bismarck chain, the Solomon Islands, Fiji, Vanuatu (New Hebrides), New Caledonia, New Britain, and New Ireland. This region is the most diverse of the four, including over 700 different islands. *Micronesia* ("mikros" meaning "small"), lying north of the equator and of Melanesia, west of Polynesia, is the fourth region of Oceania. It includes the Marshall, Caroline, and Mariana islands, which includes Guam, and Kiribati (Gilbert Islands). In addition to the main islands cited here, each of the island regions have numerous atolls and islands which are part of the same cultural region.

Pacific Islander, Rarotonga, Cook Island.
Courtesy of the Library of Congress Collections LCUSZ62:211487.

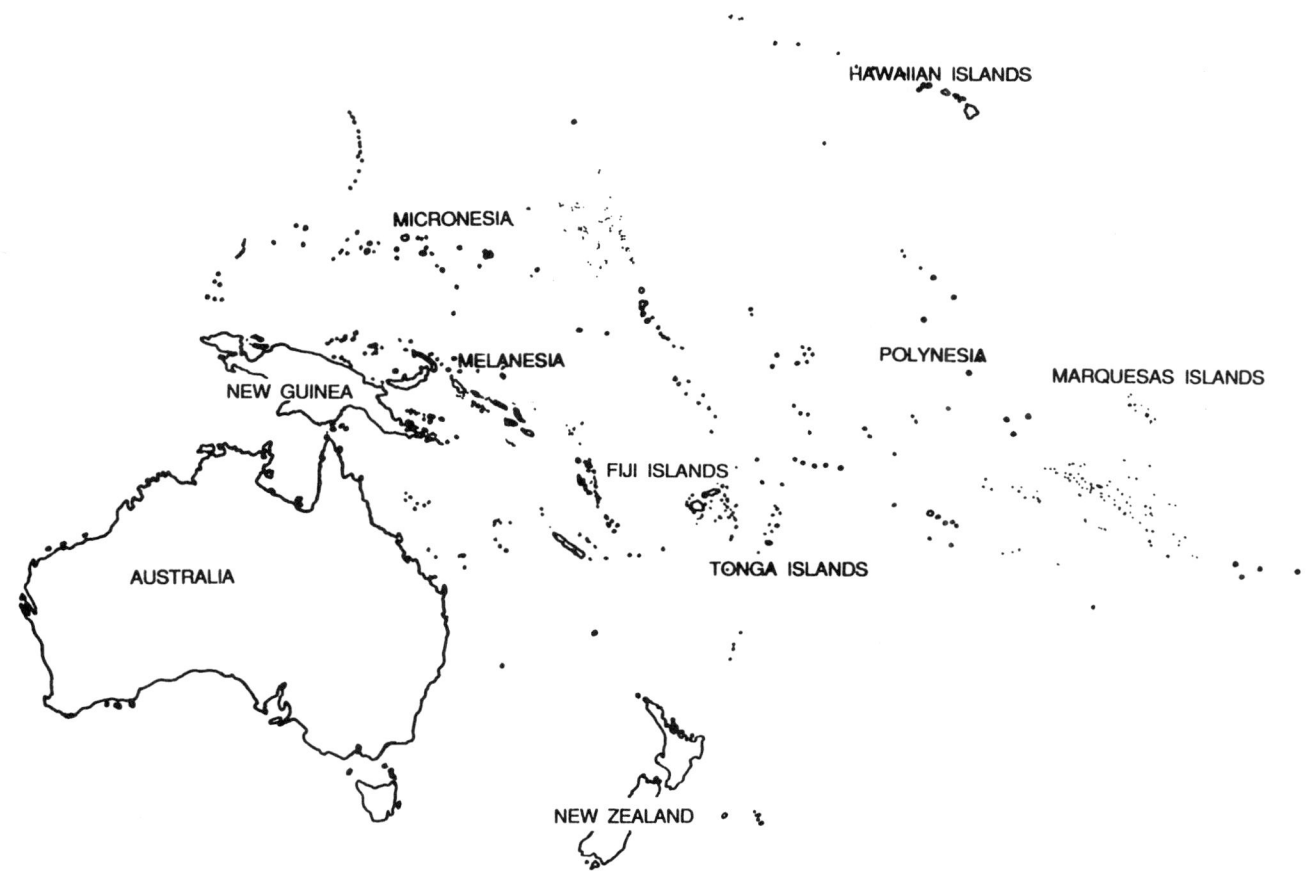

This region of the world, seemingly isolated by vast stretches of water, actually was dynamically linked throughout history. After the first wave of settlers came from southeast Asia 20,000 years ago, the ocean provided a pathway to explore, migrate, trade, and even make war. Cultural influences were similarly exchanged, with some degree of homogeneity existing throughout all of Oceania. When European explorers began to arrive in the sixteenth century, they found a stone-age culture. Captain James Cook, an eighteenth century navigator, recorded the importance of music and dance throughout these island regions. During the nineteenth century, a wave of missionaries descended on the region, influencing not only native music and dance, but values, culture, and health as well. The region came under the protectorate of Europe and the United States during the late nineteenth century, being important, particularly for the United States, as a strategic defense chain. Many of the island groups are better known as battle zones for World War II than as cultural entities. Since the mid-twentieth century, these islands have achieved independence and importance within the commerce and culture of the Pacific Rim. We will examine the music of each of these regions independently, beginning with Polynesia.

Drawing of women's night dance in Rapaso, Tonga. Copied from Cook's *Voyages of Discovery, Atlas No. 17.* Courtesy of The University Museum, University of Pennsylvania, Neg. No. NC35-296.

Music of Polynesia

Since the region of Polynesia is so far from the Asian mainland, it is easy to understand why this region was settled most recently of all Oceania. The Polynesians are believed to have originated in southeast Asia, migrated to Melanesia, and gradually sailed east from Fiji to Tonga and Samoa, arriving to the far points of the triangle, Hawaii, Easter Island (Rapa Nui), and New Zealand, most recently. There is also a theory that the region was settled from South America, not Asia at all.

Most of the music of the region is vocal, including lullabies, prayers, work songs, games, and love songs. Music is part of acculturation, songs being important to convey history as well as genealogy. *Himene* is a term which refers to the hymn-like choral songs of Polynesia, including actual church songs derived from missionary influence as well as choral singing in general. Clear, resonant, and blended singing is typical of all of Polynesia and himene are sung in two-, three-, and four-part harmony.

Since it has been one of the United States since 1959, *Hawaii* is the best known region of Polynesia. A melting pot of Oceanic, Asian, and American traditions, the true music of Hawaii consists of *mele*, chanted poetry, the *hula*, dances which interpret poetic texts, and accompanying instruments.

Within the category of mele, there are two singing styles. *Kepatepa* refers to rhythmic recitation while *oli* is less rhythmic, more of an intonation, emphasizing vowels and feeling, quasi-recitativo. The former is more a parlando style of delivery, the latter, improvisatory, with colorations of pitch and vowels by individual singers. The inflections and ornaments between pitches are more important than actual structural pitches that are sounded.

Hawaiian dancers performing with ipu hula (dance gourd).
Courtesy of the American Folklife Center, Smithsonian Institution,
Photo No. 89-17120-36.

Singing which accompanies the hula, *mele hula*, is somewhat like oli style, with vowel coloration and sustained breathing. The hula, which may be performed standing (*hula ku i luna*) or seated (*hula noho i lalo*), requires graceful movements of the performers' fingers, wrists, hands, arms, and entire torso. The words of poetry chanted are, to some degree, pantomimed through movement, using gentle and undulating movements. Instruments are used by dancers when they are seated. When they stand, a seated drummer (*ho'opa'a*) accompanies them. Hawaiian singing is not complex, usually using two or three pitches in repetitive patterns as recitation tones for poetry. The interval of a descending minor third, untempered by European standards, is a common occurrence in melodies with a limited range. Modern chants may use a slightly wider pitch spectrum, five or six pitches, and sound somewhat tonal. Melodies tend to have undulating contours, ascending and descending within their narrow range, accompanied by simple rhythmic patterns in duple time. Melodies and chants are repeated strophically with little variation or elaboration between sections, other than to accommodate different syllables in the poetic text. Hulas are often titled by the instruments which accompany them, such as hula pi'uli.

Hula requires graceful movements of the dancer's fingers, wrists, hands, arms, and torso. Courtesy of the American Folklife Center, Smithsonian Institution, Photo No. 89-17174-26.

The instruments of Hawaii, used to accompany mele and mele hula, include the well known *ipu hula* or dance gourd. It is actually consists of two gourds joined together at the neck, the bottom one long and larger, the upper, short and squat, with a resonating hole cut at very the top. The ipu hula is stamped against a mat with one hand as well as slapped with the free hand during performance, creating a percussive accompaniment with two basic sounds. The *pahu hula* is a wooden cylinder drum made from a log, with a larger upper chamber, smaller lower. Its single head is covered with either shark- or calfskin, laced down with cords, and struck with the hands. Pahu hula are often played in groups of two or three, particularly for ceremonies and festive occasions. The *puniu* is a small knee drum made from coconut shell covered with fish skin. It is struck with a small mallet made from braided fiber. Although the puniu is used either individually or with the ipu hula, it is commonly combined with the pahu hula and played by one percussionist, who uses one arm for each drum.

Additional Hawaiian accompanying instruments include the *kala'au*, wooden clapping sticks and *'uli'uli*, a gourd rattle with a decorative fringe of feathers around its handle. It was observed by and recorded in the diary of Captain James Cook when he visited the islands in 1779. *Hi'ili* are a type of lithophone, stone castanets, used as self-accompaniment for a seated dancer. *Ka eke'eke* are pairs of stamping pipes, each a different length to create a different pitch, made from bamboo tubes. The *'ulili* is a type of spinning rattle made of three gourds attached by cord. The *pu'ili*, an instrument which combines music performance and dance, is a pair of bamboo tubes about 20 inches long split lengthwise at the top. They are struck together to provide rhythmic accompaniment as well as on the ground, on the performer's shoulder, or on palms of the hand.

Seated hula dancers playing ipu hula. 'Uli'uli are seen on each dancer's right. Courtesy of the American Folklife Center, Smithsonian Institution, Photo No. 89-17117-2.

Hula accompanied by pu'ili, paired and split bamboo tubes. Courtesy of the American Folklife Center, Smithsonian Institution, Photo No. 89-17119-18.

Although most Hawaiian instruments are membranophones or idiophones, the *'ohe hano ihu* is a bamboo nose flute. It represents one of the few aerophones of the culture. In Polynesia, it is believed breath from the nose has more spiritual power than breath from the mouth. The *pu kani* is a shell trumpet used as a signalling device more than musical instrument. This is true for the *oeoe*, a bullroarer, and the *pu la'i*, a leaf trumpet, as well. Chordophones are represented by the *ukulele* (meaning, in Hawaiian, "leaping frog"), a Portuguese instrument introduced through Madeira in the late nineteenth century. It is used to accompany singing and dance, basically with Western-style triadic harmony and progressions. The Polynesian word comes from *ukeke*, a small zither of Hawaii with two strings. It was placed against the player's mouth, which then acted like a resonator for the small instrument.

Tonga, which includes about 150 islands lying in an archipelago southwest of Samoa, has a tradition blended with the music of other parts of Polynesia. Its music is basically chanted poetry accompanied by instruments and dance. Work songs, called *tau'a'alo*, depicting group activities that accomplish a mutual task, as well as game songs are common. Mourning songs are called *tengihea* and songs conveying historical aspects of the culture, including its mythology, are called *fakaniua*. Many songs begin slowly, are executed within a five-pitch range, and then intensified by increasing tempo and density as the music develops. Part singing, as in Hawaii, is common, often including as many as six vocal lines. The indigenous instruments include bamboo stamping pipes, sounding boards beaten with wooden mallets, and the slit-drum or *nafa*, which produces different pitches depending where it is struck. The *fangufangu*, a nose flute, and *mimiha*, panpipes, are examples of aerophones. The former was used to awaken a sleeping chieftain when it was forbidden to speak to him.

French Polynesia is centered in Tahiti, but also includes the Society Islands, Marquesas, Australs, and Gambiers, as well as numerous atolls. This region was settled via Samoa in the first century A.D. Although it was discovered by the Spanish in the late sixteenth and early seventeenth centuries, it was not really opened to the European world until English explorer, Samuel Wallis, arrived in 1767.

Most French Polynesian music is vocal, either as an activity in its own right or to accompany dancing. Two- and three-part textures, often duplicated at the octave as both men and women sing, are somewhat common. Music acculturates all members of these island cultures, continually reminding theme of societal norms. In the Gambier Islands (Mangareva), the *kapa* is a call-response song in which a leader, *pou-kapa*, asks a question and a group responds, phrase after phrase. This structure is used in Tahiti as well, usually with leader questioning, answering, and then the group responding, resulting in AAB form. Himene singing is common to French Polynesia, including adaptations of the religious style to native culture. The *himene tarava* is a style of singing in which the women maintain a smooth melodic line while the men interpolate percussive vocal sounds. Music is generally strophic, with words changing as the song develops. Intensification occurs through the addition of instruments and patterns of greater complexity.

In the Marquesa Islands, music is integral to all aspects of society, with more than fifty types of chants recognized. Each has special significance, it is believed, that contributes to some event or condition, whether fishing, fertility, devotion, or death. Most melodies in Polynesia are narrow in range, using seconds and thirds. They are made exciting through the addition of various vocal registers and instrumental timbres.

Dance in Otaheite (Tahiti), drawn during Cook's *Third Voyage*, Atlas No. 28.
Courtesy of The University Museum, University of Pennsylvania, Neg No. G8-299.

In Tahiti, the conch-shell trumpet (*pu*) is used in ceremonies, including dance. Long, single-headed drums, as well as the slit-drum, *to-ere*, are common. The Tahitians also use a metal drum, made from a large can, called *tini*, which provides a metallic accompaniment for dancing. The *tariparau*, a double-headed, cylindrical drum is part of many ensembles. These instruments are used to accompany dances such as the *'ote'a*, a vigorous dance in which the women swing their hips rapidly while the men use energetic knee and leg movements. In the Marquesas, a wooden xylophone is used as well as wooden sticks for clapping. In the Gambiers, the *pu-ko'e*, a nose flute, and the *pa'u*, drum, are used.

The Samoan Islands in the central region of Polynesia include nine inhabited islands. The region consists of both American Samoa as well as Western Samoa. The music, as with most of Polynesia, is basically vocal. Songs are identified by their utility. In Samoa, legends, called *fagono*, depict some historical aspect of the culture. Part of the legend is sung and these songs are known as *tagi*. There are several hundred legends and each may employ as many as sixteen songs. Music is also used as a curative in the Samoan culture. Most singing uses close intervals in the range of a perfect fourth. Singing includes both unison and part-singing, as well as solo leaders. Call-response is common.

Each Samoan village has a designated composer who creates songs for societal needs, whether birth, death, marriage, or festivity. This person also teaches the village singers these songs, which become property of the entire village. Medicinal songs, however, are presented by the village doctor. Singing occurs while the performers are seated, walking, or standing.

Instruments of the culture include the omnipresent slit-drum, used in three basic sizes. The *logo*, the largest, was apparently used by European missionaries to call natives to church service. The Samoans also use a beaten or stamped floor mat as a percussive accompaniment.

Drawing of Maori war canoe. From John Hawkesworth, *An Account of the Voyages...Undertaken...for Making Discoverines in the Southern Hemisphere...* Courtesy of The University Museum, University of Pennsylvania, Neg. No. S8-85518.

The last Polynesian group is the *Maoris*, the indigenous people of New Zealand, who presently number about 95,000. The Maoris migrated from Pacific islands to New Zealand after their legendary hero, Kupe, discovered the island, arriving in long canoes in several small fleets rather than one massive invasion. Maori singing, which is also used to accompany dance, is heightened speech, using clearly articulated words that tell a story. The *haka* is a fighting dance that uses threatening gestures, hoots, and words, including slapping the chest, forearms, and thighs and stamping the feet. It results in much syncopation. Because of over-population and perennial inter-island migration which necessitated fighting for new islands or defending inhabited ones, war-like dances and songs have always been associated with Polynesia. This bellicose posturing is reflected in music. In addition to frightening an enemy who might observe it, the haka also prepared warriors both mentally and physically for battle, requiring great aerobic conditioning to execute properly. Presently, however, a haka is also considered appropriate as a dance of welcome.

The Maori *poi*, however, is a gentler dance done by women as they swing colored beads over their heads. The *karakia* is a magical dance, sung in monotone to evoke a spell or placate a deity, of whom the Maori have many. *Patere* are songs delineating genealogy or history of the culture. This aspect of Maori tradition, based on male lineage through first-born sons, *primogeniture*, is integral. Lineage is conveyed to crib babies in lullabies since this, it is believed, joined humans with the gods. Lullabies are called *oriori* or *popo*. Laments are known as *tangi* while a death chant is called *maemae*.

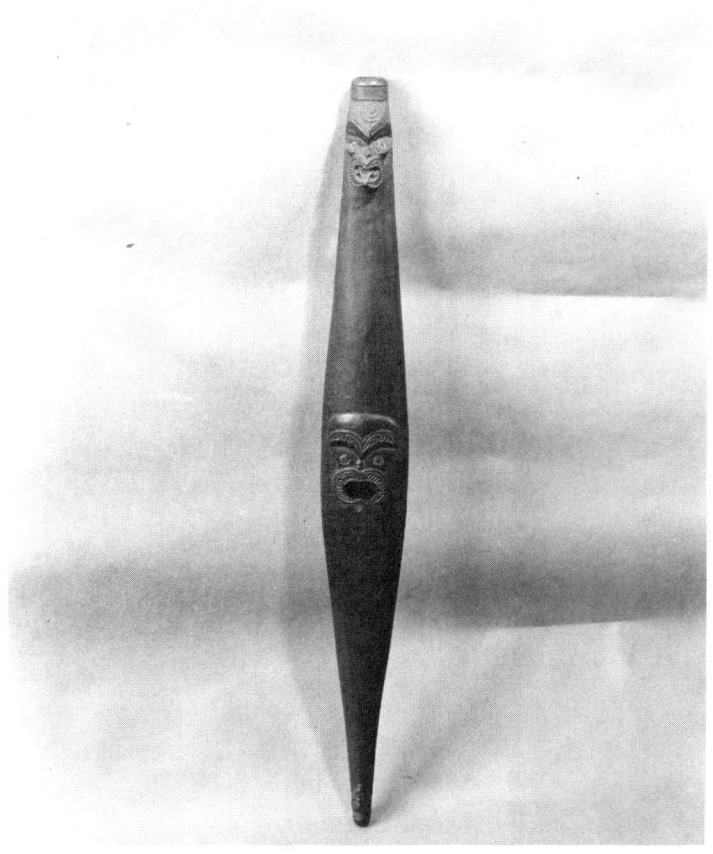

Maori wooden trumpet (putorino). Courtesy of The University Museum, University of Pennsylvania, Neg. No. S8-40531.

Ranges and intervals are both narrow in singing, and most songs focus on a reciting tone, *oro*, which serves as tonic. Part-singing is typical of this region, as it is for all of Polynesia. Instruments of the Maori include shell-trumpets, whistles made from shark or whale teeth, and the nose-flute.

It is interesting to observe how human creativity allowed the Polynesians to use resources in their environment to enhance their culture through musical instruments. Coconut shells, palm branches, conch shells, fish skin and teeth, and island tree wood were the building blocks of the musical instruments described here. Even the earth itself is a musical instrument, such as Easter Island's *keho*, a pit in the ground covered by a large stone. The performer simply pounds on the stone to provide musical accompaniment.

Nagahate: Big Numbers
Man from Pacific Islands.
Courtesy of the Library of
Congress Collections
LCUSZ62:72162.

Music of Micronesia

Micronesia is a region of over 2,000 small islands lying north of the equator in the Pacific. Two categories of islands form most of the region: low coral atolls and high volcanic formations. The latter provide more abundant natural resources because of the rich soil, thus enabling them to support larger populations than on atolls. The region was settled from the Philippines Islands as well as from the Solomons in Melanesia. Inhabitants originally came from the Asian mainland. Many of these islands were known as strategic defense positions and battle zones during World War II. As some have gained independence, however, names have been changed to reflect distinct ethnicity.

Micronesia consists, as we have seen, of the Mariana Islands, the Carolines, the Marshalls, and Kiribati (the Gilberts). The Marianas, discovered by Magellan in 1521, lie closest to the Asian mainland and include Guam, which is the largest island in Micronesia. In the Marianas, the inhabitants are a blend of American, Korean, Filipino, and neighboring Carolinian as well as indigenous people called *Chamorro*. Chamorro music is a blend of Spanish and Filipino elements, reflecting ethnic assimilation and adaptation as a result of the coming of Europeans. The *chamorita*, based on European melodies, is a song with Chamorro words, usually sung as solo or chorus in harmony. The form is strophic and lyrics concern work (fishing), lullabies, love, and leave-taking.

Two indigenous instruments that still exist, possibly similar to ancient prototypes, are the *belembaupachot*, a bamboo jew's harp, and *belembautuyan*, a musical bow. Hibiscus wood is used to fashion a bow about 6 feet in length. A single string, either fiber or wire, is attached to both ends. A gourd or coconut shell resonator is then placed half-way down the bow. When played, the resonator rests on the performer's stomach while he fingers the single string with one hand and hits the string with a grass mallet held in the other. The term, belembautuyan, translates as "vibrations of the stomach." In Guam, the music is synthetic, providing a blend of Chamorro, Latin, and Western music.

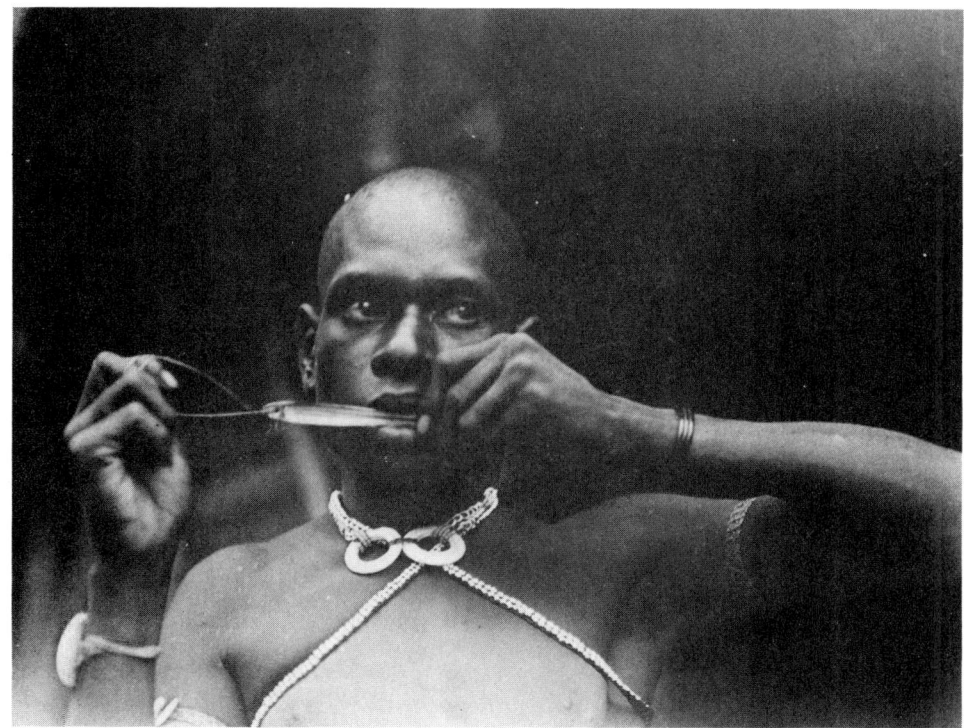

Performance on the jew's harp. Courtesy of Field Museum of Natural History, Chicago, Neg. No. A37415.

In the Marshall Islands, which consist of two parallel chains called Ratak and Ralik, both lying far to the east in Micronesia, music is vocal. The *eb* is one of the oldest types of song, depicting legends through dance and accompaniment of bamboo sticks. If the sticks are short, they are called *jimokmok*. These are used in sitting dances by women while men use longer sticks, *made*, for standing dances. In addition to eb, there are songs associated with navigation, canoe making, fishing, and tattooing, all vital activities in the region. Other instruments include a shell trumpet, *jilel*, and *aje*, a single-headed hourglass drum used to accompany dance and gesture. Since many practices were prohibited during the late nineteenth century when missionaries arrived to convert native populations, hymn singing, usually in four parts, supplanted or replaced indigenous music. Western instruments, including guitar, harmonica, and ukulele, generally replaced native instruments.

Outrigger canoe. Courtesy of the Library of Congress Collections LCUSZ62:66993.

The Caroline Islands, consisting of 963 islands lying in the middle of Micronesia, are culturally diverse. Most song is poetry enhanced through pitch and gesture. Melodic lines are narrow, using microtones with repetitive patterns in psalmodic style. Songs are performed with dance, using either line position or while seated. Dance is basically a pantomime of the text. When harmony occurs, it is in form of pedal tone or drone. In Ifaluk, a coral island, a love-song, sung by either men or women, is known as a *bwarux*. *Arueru* are songs of honor, either used as lament or praise for village leader while the *ur* is a dance used to entertain gods. In the Palau Islands, formed from volcanic action, men and women sometimes sing together, often separately. *Derebesbes* is sung by male members of the town council in turn, each person adding a strophe. It is punctuated between stanzas by hoots. Women sing *eldolem*, dirges, at funerals while both genders participate in the *alall*, a sarcastic song delivered by teenage boys and girls as a mock quarrel. In the Carolines, songs have a narrow range, a second or third at most, and a descending vocal glissando, covering an octave, often terminates each. This vocal descent is rather typical throughout Micronesia. Harmony occurs through parallel intervals, often at the fourth, sounding somewhat like Western parallel organum. Carolinian instruments include the *ngaok*, a bamboo flute with fipple mouthpiece, and *debusch*, shell trumpet. Development of Micronesia instruments, compared to other regions of Oceania, is somewhat minimal.

Funeral gifts of stone money and pearl shells, Yap (Caroline Islands) (1903). Photo by William H. Furness, 3rd. Courtesy of The University Museum, University of Pennsylvania, Neg. No. S4-139881.

Tribal group from Pacific Islands. Courtesy of the Library of Congress Collections LCUSZ62:66993.

Music of Melanesia

Melanesia is perhaps the most culturally diverse of all Oceania, including, on one extreme, the Trobriand Islanders who have had much contact throughout the region as well as indigenous people of Papua New Guinea, on the other, who have lived in relative isolation for centuries. Unlike Micronesia or Polynesia, music has been used more as an aesthetic experience in its own right, rather than merely accompanying dance or enhancing poetry. There are thus more inherent musical qualities in this region, reflected in the frequent use of archaic words, language, and nonsense syllables that have literary meaning to neither performer nor audience. Songs, too, are composed by identifiable community musicians, who then "own" the song. Songs may be commissioned by political leaders or musical groups. Singing style is largely monophonic, often employing antiphony between leader and chorus. Harmony, when it occurs, is a drone or the result of overlapping between leader and chorus, a type of polyphony.

Drummer from West Nakanai, New Britain, with kundu (c. 1954). Photo by Ward H. Goodenough. Courtesy of The University Museum, University of Pennsylvania, Neg. No. S4-57313.

Papua New Guinea, which became independent in 1975, includes the eastern portion of New Guinea (the western portion is Irian Jaya, which is part of Indonesia) as well as the Bismarcks and part of the Solomon Islands. It is the largest land mass of Melanesia. The *sing-sing* is one of the most important musical events in the culture. Held at night and including several groups of performers, they celebrate puberty and fertility rites, social feasts involving the roasting of a pig, courting, death, warfare, and other cult rituals. Young women at their first menstruation, for example, celebrate at a five-day sing-sing with other girls their own age. Sing-sings are held in the village center or outside a large meeting hall. Emphasis is on group, not solo, singing, reflecting the emphasis on communal activities in the culture.

Indigenous instruments of Papua New Guinea, made from natural materials such as wood, clay, shell, or bamboo, include the *garamut*, a wooden slit-drum, hit with wooden mallets. Garamut are made in both small and large models, with the largest being 12 feet long. The largest have also been used throughout history to communicate with neighboring villages. Smaller ones are suspended in a cord frame while the larger sit on the ground. The *kundu* is an elongated hourglass drum covered with snake- or lizard-skin, often with an attached handle. Wooden instruments are carved and painted as well, being art objects in their own right. A large transverse flute, about a yard long, is made from bamboo. The mouthpiece is in the center of the instrument. End-blown flutes, generally smaller than the transverse, are also used. The *bullroarer*, a piece of wood or parchment on the end of a string whipped in the air in a circle to sound, is also an instrument of Papua New Guinea. Use and nomenclature of all instruments and rituals varies from highlands to lowlands of the island.

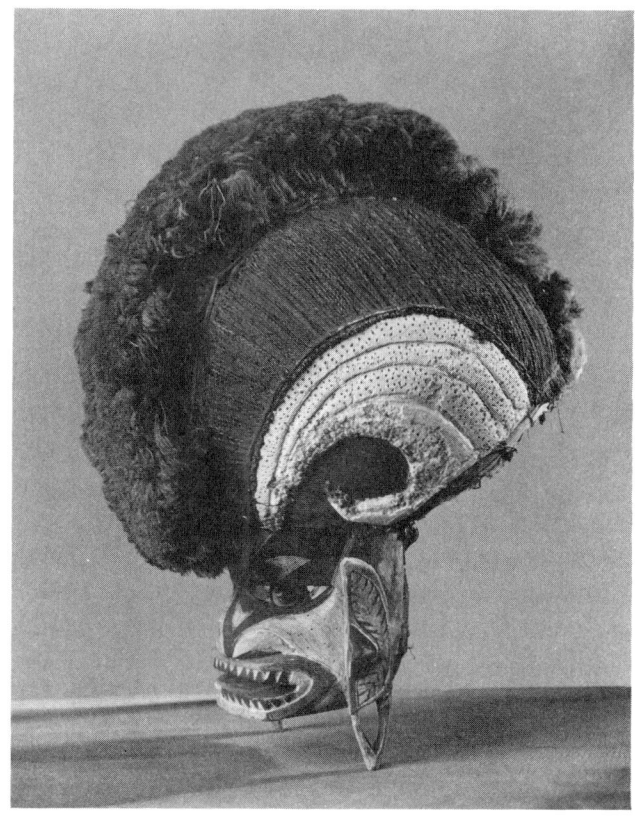

Mask (tatanua) used in funeral processions, Northern New Ireland. Courtesy of The University Museum, University of Pennsylvania, Neg. No. S8-40907, Object #P4548.

In the Solomon Islands, *panpipes*, bundles of tubes, are used, either in single or double rows. These are called *hoko ni'au* and may have as many as 13 tubes. They are used both as solo and ensemble instruments. The natives of the Solomons also use struck-bamboo instruments as well as musical bow and stamping tubes. The bamboo instruments are rafts of tuned pipes tied together, much like xylophones. The set which produces the highest pitches usually plays melody while lower instruments provide abbreviated versions, drones, or accompaniments. Nose-flutes and conch-shells are also part of musical performance, as are guitars and ukuleles.

Although Fiji is part of Melanesia, much of its musical practice is more aligned with Polynesian practice. The Fijian slit-drum is known as *lali*. It is used to accompany music as well as to signal. *Derua* are stamping tubes made of bamboo and the conch-shell trumpet is called *davui*. The nose-flute is called *dulali*. *Meke* is the most complex form of Fijian music, combining dance, song, and instruments. Meke is part of the kava-drinking ceremony that may be created by a composer upon the village's commission. Although many meke are warlike, some are contemplative. The *seasea* is inspired by stillborn children who never had a chance to sing on earth. Their melodies, it is believed, can be heard and taken from their graves.

South Pacific islander playing the nose flute.
Courtesy of Field Museum of Natural History, Chicago, Neg. No. A37457.

Although many Melanesian melodies have a narrow range, using two or three pitches, some are pentatonic, others triadic. This reflects absorption of Western practice into local culture. Music is an integral part of life in most regions, with songs reflecting cycles of the day, year, and life, whether lullaby, game, lament, war, harvest, marriage, or magic.

Music of Australia

Tribal elders of the Wailbri and Pintubu tribes (central Australia) celebrate the arrival of important visitors from Darwin with a corroboree. Photo by Michael Jensen (1973). Courtesy of Australian Overseas Information Service.

Indigenous music of the Australian continent perhaps represents the oldest continuing practice on earth, dating back 40,000 years. Although the art music of Australian is European-derived, much like American art music, its native music, as with Native Americans, is far older and quite different.

The indigenous people of Australia are called *aborigines*. They migrated from Southeast Asia, across a bridge of land, at least 40,000 years ago and possibly much earlier. As the land receded and water covered what had been an isthmus, the Australian continent became isolated from the rest of the world. Since the aborigines practiced neither farming nor animal husbandry, their survival depended on hunting and gathering. They developed an elaborate religious practice reflecting closeness to nature, including plants and animals. Inherent in this religious practice was the use of music, largely as a device to help remember what was transmitted orally, since the culture had no written language. It has bound the culture together, conveying beliefs, values, imagery, and sense of beauty.

To speak of the aborigines as one group is as incorrect as referring to Native Americans or Africans as homogeneous groups. The indigenous people of Australia are actually different clans that live throughout the Northern part of the continent, identified by region. As an anthropological term, "clan" means an extended family, linked by a common parent. Offspring marry outside the clan. "Clan" is a broader term than "family", but represents a smaller grouping than "tribe". Although definitive treatment of each grouping would be impossible in a general, introductory text, a few regions will be discussed as representative as the culture and its music in general.

Australia is a highly urbanized society with main cities lying in coastal regions. Thus, the majority of the European-derived population lives in Brisbane, Sydney, Melbourne, Adelaide, and Perth. The areas lying inland or on the Northern coast are less hospitable to Westerners and are therefore sparsely populated. These are regions where aboriginal clans roam, seeking food and shelter. Arnhem Land, the northern-most region of the Northern Territory, is home to many aborigines, as is the Broome district and Kimberley region of Western Australia, Alice Springs and Ayers Rock area in central Australia. There are also aboriginal clans in central and southern Queensland. With a population less than 140,000, the aborigines represent less than 1% of Australia's population.

Aborigines are nomadic, which, in the classification of economic systems, places them at a subsistence level of existence. They depend on nature, the immediate environment, to fulfill their basic needs. Aboriginal art, including music, therefore exists neither for its own sake nor as a result of leisure time, but, rather, to appease nature or to reinforce a social condition. Art is inexorably tied to the economics of survival and religion. Weapons are endowed with special properties through song and dance to ensure hunters will be successful when they go into the bush. A kangaroo dance, in which the aborigines role-play the ensuing event, ensures hunters return with food. A rock engraving depicts hunters who have successfully killed an emu. Although the individual artist may take pride in the finished product, art is the means to achieve economic, social, and religious ends.

As with many world cultures, art and music socializes the individual clan member in Australia. Through song and dance, the aborigine learns religious beliefs and laws of the clan, its heritage, its taboos, and its techniques for survival. Belief in *Dreamtime*, the aboriginal time of pre-existence when giants created all landmarks on earth, is learned through music. Aborigines have no written language and therefore no epic narratives in print.

Culture is transmitted orally. Acculturation occurs in the *corroboree*, an event or celebration combining music and dance. In the informal community corroboree, which may occur almost every night around a campfire, men dance and sing while women watch from a distance or hold their own dances, uninvolved with the men. Although community corroborees often include some local gossip and commentary, dances may convey traditional stories such as that of Imoraka and his wife, two turtles who emerged from the sea. During Dreamtime, they camped on the coast and their bodies later became two huge rocks. Aborigines still make a pilgrimage to these rocks to sing appropriate songs that will make female turtles lay many eggs, thus assuring the tribe an abundant food supply. Most natural formations have religious significance to aborigines, representing an animal-spirit, typical of *animism*, a belief that the wind, mountains, trees, and so on have a spirit.

Children give an impromptu dance outside the school at Mormega Homeland Centre, Northern Territory (1975). Courtesy of Australian Overseas Information Service.

By contrast, the sacred corroboree, such as initiation rites, is more formal and requires extensive preparation, including rehearsal. Elaborate body make-up, important to the ritual, is used. Young boys undergoing official admission to the clan learn their initiation songs in seclusion, often over several weeks. The traditional form of this corroboree ensures the security, stability, and welfare of the tribe. Songs of the aborigines are used for lovemaking, to accompany the birth of a baby, to begin the rain as well as end it, and for penance. Songs are even used to place a hex on a tribal non-conformist, since this individual becomes a threat to the very survival of society.

As a historical footnote, the first Europeans who arrived in Australia over 200 years ago regarded aborigines as less than human. They hunted them as wild animals, purely for sport. In Tasmania, the indigenous people were annihilated by white settlers within a few years. Although aborigines lived in peace and harmony with one another for millennia, too busy with survival to make war on neighboring clans and tribes, they took to arms in the eighteenth century as retaliation to an invading white civilization.

To demonstrate the non-warlike qualities of aborigines, it is interesting to observe what objects in their environment have become part of their decorative art. Paintings on everyday utensils, religious objects, and weapons demonstrate a love of beauty. In addition, the human body, in corroboree, as well as paintings on sheets of bark, show similar qualities. Most objects are similarly carved, whether modeled, fluted, or incised, to be decorative. The use of feathers on objects and their own bodies is part of their visual art. So is modeling animals and humans in wood or clay. Personal ornaments are part of the culture--in short, almost everything in the aboriginal environment is art. The same may be said about music. Almost every event, every ritual, every passage can be marked by song and dance. These communicate, symbolize, and acculturate.

Aboriginal music is almost totally vocal. Each song has a religious or magical significance. Songs are often owned by the clan. Trading of songs occurs in a process called *djambar*, in which learners of one clan sit in rows for three nights while watching the dancers and singers who own the songs. On the fourth night, they may join in.

Melodies are chained together to create a cycle of songs, each song identified by unique contour or progression. Some songs are conjunct, others disjunct, both using microtones. Pitches which are held over some type of beat are frequent, as is the use of melismatic passages. Some vocal production is high-pitched falsetto, which can include ululating and hissing. Some melodies have a two-pitch range, others use a range as wide as a twelfth. A typical contour descends, following the natural tendency as breath is expelled. The use of melisma obscures the actual words used in a song. The effect often becomes more important than the actual verbal denotation, vocal utterances functioning somewhat as nonsense syllables.

Although polyphony occurs in songs associated with dying, the melodic line in most songs is monophonic. Melodies are sung over a beat played by clapping sticks, but the two musical lines will not necessarily be synchronized. This results in two beat structures known as *heterorhythm*, where each part seems almost incidental to the other.

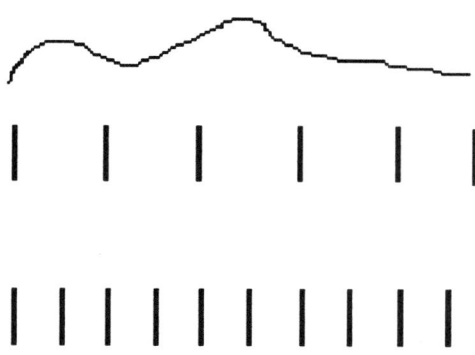

Heterorhythm

Melodic units are additive in meter, using five, seven, or even thirteen beats. Each unit is repeated, resulting in *isorhythm*, that is, reiteration of a rhythmic pattern cyclically. This pattern creates syncopation with the underlying beat through shifting accents and downbeats.

There are few aboriginal instruments. The most characteristic instrument is the *didjeridu*, an aerophone made from a tree branch, four to six feet in length. It is hollowed out by termite action and then burned and carved to create the appropriate conical bore inside. There is no reed or mouthpiece, however. Sound is produced by buzzing in one end with an embouchure using very loose lips. This produces a low pitch, used as drone to accompany singing. By breathing in continuously through his nose while expelling breath through his mouth, the performer produces a continuous pitch. Higher pitches are produced by overblowing, which produces a harmonic. The instrument is also used for hooting and shrieking to punctuate key words of the singing. The singer does not match his tune to the didjeridu, but, rather, chooses a didjeridu and player which matches his. The player holds the long tube with his two hands around the top part. The bottom end is balanced between his two crossed feet.

The only other instruments used by aborigines are sticks and boomerangs which are struck together. Hand clapping is used idiophonically as well.

Aboriginal musicians with didjeridu (left) and tapping sticks (right).
Courtesy of Australian Overseas Information Service.

The following list of instruments places the instruments from Oceania into appropriate categories.

CHORDOPHONES	IDIOPHONES
Belembautuyan	Balembaupachot
Ukulele	Derua
AEROPHONES	Garamut
Bullroarer	Hi'ili
Davui	Ipu Hula
Debusch	Jimokmok
Didjeridu	Ka Eke'eke
Dulali	Kala'au
Fangufangu	Keho
Hoko Ni'au	Lali
Jilel	Logo
Mimiha	Made
Ngaok	Pu'ili
Oeoe	Tini
'Ohe Hano Ihu	To-ere
Panpipes	Uli'uli
Pu	**MEMBRANOPHONES**
Pu Kani	Aje
Pu-Ko'e	Kundu
Pu La'i	Pahu Hula
	Pa'u
	Puniu
	Tariparau

Key Terms and Concepts

- Aborigine
- Aje
- Alall
- Animism
- Arueru
- Australia
- Belembaupachot
- Belembautuyan
- Bullroarer
- Bwarux
- Chamorita
- Chamorro
- Corroboree
- Davui
- Debusch
- Derebesbes
- Derua
- Didjeridu
- Djambar
- Dreamtime
- Dulali
- Eb
- Eldolem
- Fagono
- Fakaniua
- Fangufangu
- French Polynesia
- Garamut
- Haka
- Hawaii
- Heterorhythm
- Hi'ili
- Himene
- Himene Tarava
- Hoko Ni'au
- Ho'opa'a
- Hula
- Hula Ku I Luna
- Hula Noho I Lalo
- Isorhythm
- Ipu Hula
- Jilel
- Jimokmok
- Ka Eke'eke
- Kala'au
- Kapa
- Karakia
- Keho
- Kepatepa
- Kundu
- Lali
- Logo
- Maemae
- Made
- Maori
- Meke
- Melanesia
- Mele
- Mele Hula
- Micronesia
- Mimiha
- Nafa
- Ngaok
- Oceania
- Oeoe
- 'Ohe Hano Ihu
- Oli
- Oriori
- Oro
- 'Ote'a
- Pahu Hula
- Panpipes
- Patere
- Pa'u
- Poi
- Polynesia
- Popo
- Pou-Kapa
- Pu
- Pu'ili
- Pu Kani
- Pu-Ko'e
- Pu La'i
- Puniu
- Samoa
- Seasea
- Sing-sing
- Tagi
- Tahiti
- Tangi
- Tariparau
- Tau'a'alo
- Tengihea
- Tini
- To-ere
- Tonga
- Ukeke
- Ukulele
- 'Ulili
- Uli'uli
- Ur

Self-Checking Chapter Review

Match Column II to Column I	
Column I	**Column II**
1. kundu	A. Australian aerophone
2. Polynesian	B. large slit-drum
3. Micronesia	C. indigenous people of the Mariana Islands
4. Melanesia	D. double-gourd idiophone
5. pu'ili	E. bundled tubes
6. ipu hula	F. pit instrument of Easter Island
7. didjeridu	G. Region including Marshall, Caroline, Mariana, and Gilbert Islands
8. fagono	H. Region including Hawaii, Tahiti, Tonga, and Samoa
9. logo	I. Samoan legends
10. keho	J. whipped aerophone
11. Chamorro	K. hourglass drum of Papua New Guinea
12. sing-sing	L. communal gathering in Papua New Guinea
13. corroboree	M. bamboo idiophone
14. bullroarer	N. communal gathering in Australia
15. panpipes	O. Region including Papua New Guinea, the Solomon Islands, and Fiji

Answers	
1. K	9. B
2. H	10. F
3. G	11. C
4. O	12. L
5. M	13. N
6. D	14. J
7. A	15. E
8. I	

Selected Bibliography

Baglin, Douglass and Barbara Mullins (1972). *Aborigines of Australia.* Belrose, New South Wales: Mulavon Pty. Ltd.

Berndt, Ronald M. and E.S. Phillips (eds.) (1973). *The Australian Aboriginal Heritage.* Sydney: Australian Society through the Arts.

Blackwood, Alan (1991). *Music of the World.* Englewood Cliffs: Prentice-Hall, Inc.

Gunther, John (1974). *Inside Australia and New Zealand.* (Completed and edited by William H. Forbis.) London: Coronet Books.

"Lives and Laws of the Early Aborigines". *Australia's Heritage: The Making of a Nation.* (Volume 1: *The Great Southland.*) Sydney: Hamlyn House Pty. Ltd., pages 7-11.

McCarthy, F.D. (1974) *Australian Aboriginal Decorative Art.* Sydney: V.C.N. Blight, C.B.E., Government Printer, Trustees of the Australian Museum.

Mountford, Charles Pearcy (1966). *Aboriginal Art from Australia.* Worchester, Massachusetts: Commonwealth Press.

Selected Discography

Aboriginal Sound Instruments
Australian Institute of Aboriginal Studies
EMI (Australia) Limited AIAS/14

An Introduction to Music of New Guinea
Prestige International 25013

Arnheim Land
EMI (Australia) Ltd.
OALP 7504 and 7505

Australia and New Guinea
Columbia KL 208

Australian Aboriginal Heritage, The
Record Set accompanying *Aborigines of Australia*
(See bibliography above)

Bayanihan: Philippine Dance Company
Monitor MF 322

Fataleka and Baegu Music/Malaita, Solomon Islands
UNESCO Collection: Musical Sources
Philips 6586 018

Fijian Songs and Dances
Musical Heritage Society Inc. MHS 3425

Gauguin Years: Songs and Dances of Tahiti, The
Nonesuch Records H-72017

Hawaiian Chant: Hula and Music
Folkways Records FW 8750

Hawaiian Chants, Hula, and Love-Dance Songs
Ethnic Folkways Library FE 4271

Island Music of the South Pacific
Nonesuch Explorer Series H-72088

Maori Songs of New Zealand
Ethnic Folkways Library FE 4433

Music of Hawaii: From the Missionaries through Statehood
Ala Moana
Mele O. Hawaii

Music of Hawaii, The
National Geographical Society #706

Music of the Magindanao in the Philippines
Ethnic Folkways Library FE 4536

Music of Tonga, The
National Geographic Society #3516

Samoan Song and Rhythm
Musical Heritage Society Inc. MHS 3326

Songs from North Queensland
Australian Institute of Aboriginal Studies
EMI (Australia) Limited   AIAS/12

Songs from the Kimberleys
Australian Institute of Aboriginal Studies
EMI (Australia) Limited   AIAS/13

Songs from Yarrabah
Australian Institute of Aboriginal Studies
EMI (Australia) Limited   AIAS/7

Tahiti: Bora-Bora "A Polynesian July"
Musical Heritage Society Inc. MHS 3093

Tribal Music of Australia
Folkways Records FE 4439

World of the South Pacific
Musical Heritage Society Inc. MHS 3132

CHAPTER EIGHT

MUSIC OF NATIVE AMERICANS

Leon Albert, White Mountain Apache Crown Dancer.
Courtesy of the Arizona Historical Society Library,
Photo No. 61913.

During the same period that Oceania was settled from Southeast Asia, Mongoloid people of Northeast Asia were migrating across the Bering Strait, which was an isthmus, into North America. This migration occurred during the last ice age, between 20,000 and 35,000 years ago. These people, over their period of migration, spread out across the entire continent and extended even into all of South America through the isthmus of Panama. These waves of migration did not involve vast numbers of people, probably less than two million in the entire North American continent and about seven million in South and Central America. Presently, there are over 600,000 Native Americans in the United States. In this chapter, we will examine traits of North American indigenous people, including the Eskimos.

Yaqui harp used at Fiesta de San Ignacio (July, 1955). Courtesy of the Arizona Historical Society Library, Photo No. 22614.

The names of Indian tribes are well known to all who live in the United States, including:

>Apache
>Comanche
>Crow
>Hopi
>Iroquois
>Kiowa
>Navajo
>Pawnee
>Sioux
>Taos
>Ute
>Yaqui

Yaqui musician with shakers. Magdalena, Sonora.
Photo © David Burckhalter (1972).

Anthropologists divide Native American tribes by language and region into six categories:

1. Eastern tribes (East of the Mississippi River), including Iroquois, Wabanaki, Chippewa (Ojibwa), Cherokee, Creek, and Seminole;

2. Great Basin tribes (Nevada, Utah, interior California), including Paiute, Ute, and Shoshoni;

3. Plains-Pueblo tribes, including Arapaho, Blackfoot, Sioux, Hopi, Taos, and Zuni;

4. *Athabascan* tribes, including Navajo and Apache as well as Northern Athabascans in Western Canada, generally in the inter-mountain plateau;

5. Californian-Yuman tribes; and

6. Northwestern-Eskimo tribes, including Salish, Bella Coola, Nootka, and Kwakiutl.

There are more than 200 different tribes and 100 distinct languages in the United States alone. Although each tribe has music which is unique in form, dialect, and utility, all are related to Native American practice in general. These generalities will be the thrust of this chapter.

Native Americans are people who are at peace with their environment, that is, they live in harmony with it rather than change it drastically. Music has thus been able to maintain stability over hundreds of years and changing external conditions because of this attitude. Native Americans think holistically, which means the arts are not compartmentalized as separate disciplines done only by experts. Most people sing, dance, carve, paint, and weave as part of being human. Specialists, such as a medicine man or *shaman* may be present in a tribe. He will not be the only performer, but, rather, supervisor and organizer of artistic activities. Music is utilitarian in that it heals, soothes, punctuates, motivates, and inspires. Participating in music means participating in the life of the tribe.

Ze de Ki, Navajo medicine man (Fort Wingate, New Mexico, c. 1886). Photo by Barthelmess. Courtesy of the Arizona Historical Society Library, Photo No. 542.

Native American music is basically monophonic and linear. It is vocal with sparse instrumental accompaniment, whether drum, rattle, or sound-makers worn on dancers' bodies. Unlike Polynesian dances, in which hand movement is important, Native American dances emphasize stamping of the feet and patterns of movement on the ground. Gesture is bold and direct. The words to songs often allude to a story or tradition without telling the entire tale. In other words, a phrase may be recited to remind listeners of the story. In many cases, nonsense words, *vocables*, borrowed from other tribes or corrupted from the tribe's own language, are the basis of lyrics.

Wishram bride (Celilo Falls, Washington). Courtesy of the Library of Congress Collections LCUSZ62:105387.

Throughout history in North America, indigenous tribes used music as a key ingredient in social and religious life. Music, as with most world cultures, was never an isolated phenomenon for listening, but, rather, accompanied dances of healing, warring, hunting, birthing, marrying, and dying. Music was also important in rituals associated with peer group societies and gambling games. Music often personified supernatural spirits, such as the Hopi kachinas, who mysteriously emerged on occasions from the village kiva to dance and bring presents to the children. Music's value was rooted in its efficacy, that is, the result that came from performance, whether rain began, crops sprouted, or healing occurred. In the present world, these ancient traditions have helped tribes maintain ethnic integrity, even when utility is no longer strictly observed. Some tribes believe songs were actually handed down by their gods, with inspiration for new songs being revealed through dreams and trances.

Music is frequently dominated by male performers. Similarly, songs are passed by father to son. The tradition is learned by rote. Some tribes in the Northwest region consider precise rendition important. As a result, their music has changed little over generations. Other tribes, particularly the Plains Indians, are more casual in their approach. Their music continues to modify and change over time.

In general, there is little systematic development of musical abilities in most tribes. Music education occurs as natural acculturation to tribal ways. Similarly, there are few terms related entirely to musical practice alone, no words for scale and pitches. Instruments, of course, have names, but few are used.

Vocal style, as we have observed, is monophonic. Men and women, when they sing together, are in unison or octaves. Incipient polyphony occurs when parts overlap, more as incident than structure. Drones may be used. Vocal tone is often falsetto or produced on high pitches. Vocal tension is common, with ululations or pulsations on pitches of longer duration. The sound is often strident. Many melodies have a descending contour which follows the singers' natural breath span. Common intervals are either major 2nds or minor 3rds, often microtonal compared to Western intervals. Melodies may fall into tetratonic or pentatonic scales as well as hexatonic. Strophic form is common where a section of three to ten short phrases is repeated. This section may then be slightly varied or abbreviated in subsequent iterations, resulting in processive form.

We will now examine practices of some Native American tribes.

Music of the Pueblo Indians

The Pueblo Indians inhabit regions of the Southwestern United States and were rather distinctive in that they built city-states consisting of multi-storied mud houses. These were either perched high on mesas or in caves and fissures. The tribes that are classified as Pueblo Indians live principally in Arizona and New Mexico, consisting of Hopi, Zuni, Taos, and Tewas. Since these tribes were not nomadic, their economy was agricultural, thus allowing aggregation of population and the need for social hierarchy. Since crops formed the basis of their society, they did not need to compete for territory and game as did nomadic tribes. They were therefore generally peaceful people. Their cities were arranged around communal plazas that included a special meeting place, often underground, called a *kiva*. From the kiva, dancers would emerge on ceremonial occasions, dressed as gods to instruct the people in moral ways or provide gifts to the children.

Kiva dancers, representing *kachinas* are still part of the Hopi tradition. They can be observed by tourists during special seasons. Kachinas are not really gods, but, rather, symbolic representation of plants, animals, birds, and ancestors in human form. They return to the village on occasion to hear and then convey village prayers to important deities. They also bring clouds and rain as well as promote the general welfare and harmony of the Hopi. Over 200 different kachinas, often represented as dolls which are given to children for study and understanding, are recognized by the Hopi.

Pueblo Indians are the only group of Native Americans to develop work songs, undoubtedly to accompany activities associated with an agrarian society. Compared to many Native American people, the community-conscious Pueblo Indians developed a complex society. Their music is equally complex, using scales consisting of either five, six, or seven pitches. Their vocal style is tense, low, and growling, using beat pulsation. Melodic contours tend to descend, as described above. Many of their songs are binary based on the strophic principle, with repetition being incomplete rather than exact. Their music is often performed by a chorus of men accompanied by a single drummer, rather than a soloist, reflecting the cooperative nature of these tribes. The pitch of the drum matches the general register of singers, that is, low-pitched singers tend to use a drum that is low in pitch as well.

Butterfly Dance (1947) performed by Hopi dancers from Second Mesa, Arizona (1947). Courtesy of the Arizona Historical Society Library, Photo No. 8854.

To demonstrate some of the Pueblo practices, a few dances of the region will be described. The Hopi *Butterfly Dance* is held after crops, particularly corn, are harvested as a ceremony of thanksgiving. It is described as a social dance in which both single young men and women dance. The girls wear black manta dresses with bright capes, their hair arranged in buns or whorls on each side of their head. Each may design her own headdress which is then provided by an uncle or male first cousin, who then becomes part of the dance. The young men wear black velvet outfits with colored sashes attached to shoulders and waist. Preparation for learning songs and dances requires several weeks and, unlike typical Native American practice, participants both sing and dance rather than being confined to one or the other. Women generally dance with very small steps while the men use high, springy steps, accompanying themselves with rattles. The singing has clearly differentiated phrases which often and abruptly change tempo. The entire ceremonial is a continual shifting of patterns, colors, and rhythms as the dancers interact. Participants frequently take breaks and then re-enter the ceremony which lasts an entire day. The Butterfly Dance is a dance of young people, celebrating harvest as well as courtship. Since the men who dance the Butterfly are relatives of the maidens, young men from neighboring pueblos often come to observe the repertoire of available maidens in the village. In former times, too, maidens were required to reveal their "true loves" at the conclusion of the ceremony.

Music of the Plains Indians

The Plains Indians, which include Pawnee, Crow, Kiowa, Comanche, Sioux, Arapaho, Blackfoot, and Flathead, include tribes in the region between the Rocky Mountains and the Mississippi River. Unlike the Pueblo dwellers, these tribes were nomadic, dependent upon hunting, particularly of buffalo, and gathering. Their social structure was consequently less rigid, based more on competition than cooperation. It was often directed to preservation of territory and war, as they pursued the mercurial buffalo herds.

Music of these tribes is more individualistic with different styles for men and women. Melodic contour usually descends, incorporating either minor thirds or major seconds. Scales are tetratonic as well as pentatonic and hexatonic. Pulsation is typical of melodies, men achieving this by dynamic pulsation, women by slightly varying the pitch. Vocal quality is harsh and strident, using high tessituras. Lyrics are frequently vocables, rather than recognizable text. The incomplete binary form, occurring somewhat as AABCD BCD, is common, but material from the opening strophe may be repeated at the conclusion in a lower octave. The accompanying instruments are drum and rattle, with the instrumental beat occurring slightly before or after the vocal beat.

Unlike Pueblo tribes, Plains Indians do not take as much time to rehearse songs and dances, most of which can be assimilated in a short period of time. This may represent the more transient nature of their society, based on a nomadic mind-set. Neither melody nor choreography is elaborate, permitting individual movement and interpretation. Songs are frequently begun by a solo voice and followed by group participation. Men are the primary music makers, accompanying themselves on a single drum. When women join in, they duplicate the melody at the octave.

The Sioux *Sun Dance*, for example, was held during the full moon of mid-summer, danced by men to affirm their vows to Wakantanka, the Great Mysterious. Devotion to this deity ranged from mere body deprivation, such as fasting, to attaching skewers from a sacred pole into their bodies, thereafter dancing individualistically until the movement ripped the attachment from their flesh. This dance was finally prohibited by the U.S. government in 1881. Such rituals demonstrated the individual physical strength and fortitude of young warriors.

Everyday objects may be incorporated into musical ensembles in some cultures, whether North or South American tribes. Chocó Indians from the upperpart of the Sambu River on the Panama-Colombia border. (1949) Photo by Per Host. Courtesy of the Library of Congress Collections LCUSZ62:6046A.

The Flathead *Canvas Dance* was sung to prepare a war or hunting party to depart camp. A small group began at one end of the village, going from tepee to tepee, adding people as they progressed. By the end of the dance, most of the village was involved, providing moral support to the departing braves. Today, this dance is done with a large piece of canvas, eight feet square, which is held tightly by all performers and struck with their hands to produce a rhythmic accompaniment. It demonstrates the historical need to hunt and make war in order to survive.

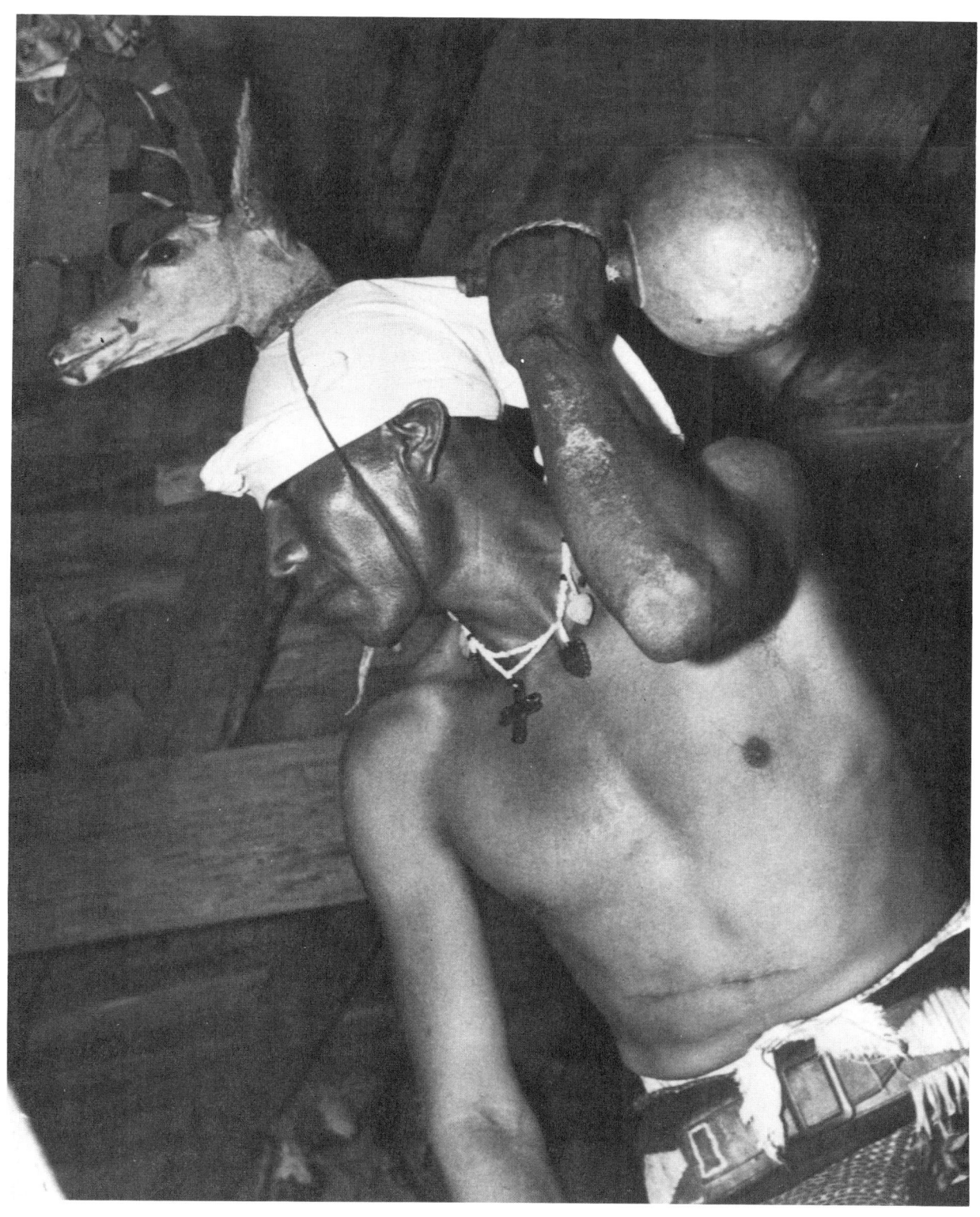

Deer dancer at the feast of San Ignacio at Pascua (July, 1955).
Courtesy of the Arizona Historical Society Library, Photo No. 22611.

Music of the Athabascan Tribes

The Athabascan group includes Navajo and Apache, the former which is the largest Indian tribe of the North American continent. There are approximately 150,000 Navajo living on 15 million acres of reservation land in the Southwest United States. Although similar to the Plains Indians in socio-economic structure, the language of the Navajo and Apache links them more to tribes of Western Canada, from where they migrated during the sixteenth century.

Navajo and Apache singing is distinctive from both Pueblo and Plains tribes. It is relatively free from pulsation and has a light, nasal sound. Although the Navajo sing in a register higher than the Apache, both commonly use the interval of a third. Apache musical structure is simpler, using a two-phrase structure, identical except for the pitch level, thus representing a sequence or transposed version. Navajo music is slightly more involved, reflecting contact with Pueblo culture, and using ranges of an octave. Navajo songs also alternate between a high, falsetto melody and a low, drone-like pitch.

The Navajo *Squaw Dance* originally functioned as a purification for warriors who had been defiled in battle by contact with another tribe, demonstrating the importance of curative chants and music throughout this culture. It presently functions as an occasion in which young women are introduced into the society and pronounced marriageable. It is still a curative rite for those who have had contact with non-Navajos. Elaborate preparations are required, beginning with a sacred stick which is decorated and exchanged between contracting parties. The shaman is engaged and singers procured. The site is chosen and food prepared. The dance, which may last three days, then commences. The entire ceremony begins with round dances, usually two circles differentiated by gender, which change direction each time the song ends. This is followed by courting songs, in which young women invite eligible men to dance with them. A man may only end this partnership by paying his partner or offering a small trinket. The escort dances, which follow, are couple dances, in which a circle movement is observed by all couples in the dancing area. The entire ceremony is terminated with quitting songs, which last until the singers are exhausted and everyone goes home.

The *Night Dance* is also a healing ceremony which lasts from two to nine days. It is sung by a male chorus, accompanied by gourd rattles. Also called the *Yei-be-chai* chant, after *Yei*, who are gods of the tribe, it is also a means whereby children are initiated into tribal ceremonies. Two dancers wear grotesque masks of buckskin to impersonate deities, alternating with other pairs throughout the long ceremony. Most of the singing is falsetto, a high-pitched sound, which is said to have restorative power. As with Squaw Dances, the Night Dance is a series of short songs and dances, some often newly created, which comprise the entire ceremony.

Navajo Yei-be-chai dance (c. 1941).
Courtesy of the Arizona Historical Society Library, Photo No. 8846.

Music of Eskimos

Eskimos are more loosely organized than many Native American tribes, functioning as local communities which exercise dominion over a given hunting and fishing area. They number fewer than 50,000. Although elders have a degree of influence within the community, there is no tradition of strong tribal leaders.

Eskimo music, which is part of Native American music in general, is closely related to functions of the community, such as launching boats, hunting seals and whales, exchanging gifts, as well as reducing social pressure and resolving conflicts. Eskimos have song duels which provide musical means to ridicule and satirize without coming to blows. Included in the repertoire of Eskimo music are game songs, story songs, lullabies, love songs, weather songs, and dirges. Most use no instrumental accompaniment and frequently use vocables in the refrain.

In Eskimo culture, the *Messenger Feast* was an important celebration in former years. Sometimes referred to as the "Inviting-In" Dance, it was sponsored by a single individual who saved cash for years in order to pay for the festivities. By so doing, fame was achieved and other Eskimos were obligated to the host. In the Messenger Feast, the host indicates his intention to have a feast, sending a messenger throughout the community to invite the guests. Preparation then requires dances and songs be learned by all groups who will attend. This requires several weeks. Melodies, usually purchased from a wise man of the village, must be reproduced exactly. When the feast days finally arrive, each chorus, consisting of six men, leads singing in turn for the entire community, competing with other groups to be the best. The feast is held within the communal lodge, called a *kazgi*, which has separate entrances for performers and audience. Once inside, however, both mingle freely. Since it is believed spirits are also present, food and drink are placed on tables for them. Face masks are worn by performers, symbolizing these animal spirits. Over the three days of the festival, dances move from the comic, entertaining to more serious ones, culminating in dances which actually portray animals. As a finale, the shaman of the group dances, eventually falling into a trance. When he awakens, he announces the animal spirits have been placated and the festivities end.

Whale feast at Point Hope, Alaska, Yenisei-Ostyak peoples. Original photo by Froelich Rainey. Courtesy of The University Museum, University of Pennsylvania, Neg. No. S4-140579 and the Department of Library Services, American Museum of Natural History, New York. Neg. No. 2A 3815.

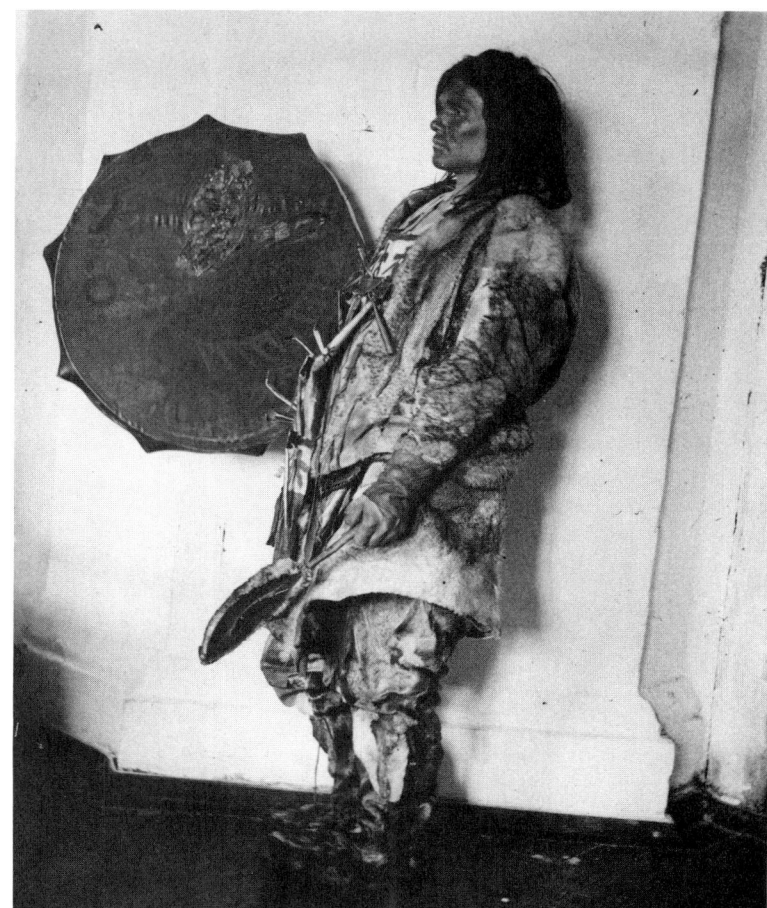

Shaman and drum (Siberia, near Turukhansk), Yenisei-Ostyak peoples (c. 1914). Photo by F. Schoch/F. Sarin Courtesy of The University Museum, University of Pennsylvania, Neg. No. S4-140730.

Instruments of Native Americans

The music of Native Americans is largely vocal, incorporating instruments derived from tools and objects in each tribe's immediate environment. Most instruments are therefore either idiophones or membranophones. The *container rattle* is one of the most universal idiophones, consisting of gourd, wood, horn, shell, or leather container filled with rocks or seeds. Yuman and Apache tribes often make rattles from baskets and Mexican tribes have even used turtle shells. *Strung rattles*, worn as wristbands or anklets, are made of strung bones, wood, teeth, and hooves. Metal rattles and bells have been adapted into many cultures since Europeans introduced these types of sleigh bells. The *rasp*, a notched stick which is scraped, is used among the Athabascans and Plains tribes. An additional idiophone used on the West cost is the split-stick clapper.

Cocoon rattles attached to dancers' legs at Yaqui celebration. Courtesy of the American Folklife Center, Smithsonian Institution, Photo No. 89-17178-23.

Membranophones of Indian tribes are most commonly single-headed frame drums, held in one hand and struck by mallet with the other. Except for Californian tribes, this is indigenous to all regions. The double-headed drum occurs in the Great Lakes, Great Basin, and Eastern regions. These are usually played by several percussionists. With both types of drums, the mallets are usually padded on the playing end with rawhide. As we have seen, a piece of canvas or leather, stretched taut by performers, can function as a drum without frame.

The bow is the only indigenous chordophone of Native American people, confined to the Great Basin region. The Apaches adapted a resonator for it, suggesting utility beyond mere hunting. The *Apache fiddle* (Navajo violin), which is hybrid between the primitive Indian bow and European string instruments, is made from a wooden tube with a single string passing over a bridge. It is bowed with a tiny horsehair bow.

Yaqui drummer with flute. Courtesy of the American Folklife Center, Smithsonian Institution, Photo No. 89-17178-30.

Chesley Goseyun Wilson, White Mountain Apache, playing one-string Apache fiddle. These instruments are made from agave stalks and strung with horsehair. (1989). Photo by Jim Griffith. Courtesy of the Southwest Folklore Center, Tucson, Arizona.

Aerophones have been made by Indian tribes from cane, wood, bark, pottery, and even bone. Most are end-blown flutes, using three to six finger holes. Nose flutes were used in the Great Basin as were panpipes in California. The bullroarer, a whipped aerophone, was used by Western tribes. Instruments, however, were exclusively adjunct to singing and dancing, adding interesting effects and accompaniments rather than providing the entire musical structure.

"Southern Scratch", a Tohono O'odham band, playing waila music at Tucson Meet Yourself. (1990). Photo by David Burckhalter. Courtesy of Jim Griffith and the Southwest Folklore Center, Tucson, Arizona.

Key Terms and Concepts

Apache Fiddle
Athabascan
Butterfly Dance
Canvas Dance
Container Rattle
Eskimo
Kachina
Kazgi
Kiva
Messenger Feast
Night Dance
Plains Indians
Pueblo Indians
Rasp
Shaman
Squaw Dance
Strung Rattle
Sun Dance
Vocable
Yei
Yei-be-chai

Self-Checking Chapter Review

Match Column II to Column I	
Column I	**Column II**
1. Night Dance	A. Great Basin Indians
2. Canvas Dance	B. Hopi dance of Thanksgiving
3. vocables	C. Northwest Indians
4. Zuni and Hopi	D. Athabascan Indians
5. kiva	E. medicine man
6. Salish and Kwakiutl	F. Eastern Indians
7. Apache and Navajo	G. bowed chordophone
8. Shoshoni and Ute	H. healing ceremony
9. Sun Dance	I. nonsense syllables
10. Cherokee and Iroquois	J. Pueblo Indians
11. Squaw Dance	K. scraped idiophone
12 Butterfly Dance	L. underground lodge
13. Apache fiddle	M. deprivation rite
14. shaman	N. yei-be-chai
15. rasp	O. war party ceremony

Answers			
1.	N	9.	M
2.	O	10.	F
3.	I	11.	H
4.	J	12.	B
5.	L	13.	G
6.	C	14.	E
7.	D	15.	K
8.	A		

Selected Bibliography

Herndon, Marcia (1980). *Native American Music*. Hatboro, PA: Norwood.

Johnston, Thomas (1976). *Eskimo Music by Region: A Comparative Circumpolar Study*. Ottawa: National Museum of Man.

McAllester, David P (1949). *Peyote Music*. New York: Viking Fund Publications in Anthropology (#13).

Merriam, Alan P. (1967). *Ethnomusicology of the Flathead Indians*. Chicago: Aldine.

Nettl, Bruno (1965). *Folk and Traditional Music of the Western Continents*. Englewood Cliffs: Prentice-Hall, Inc.

_____ (1952). *North American Indian Musical Styles*. Philadelphia: American Folklore Society.

Roberts, Helen H. (1936). *Musical Areas in Aboriginal North America*. New Haven: Yale University Press.

Vennum, Jr., Thomas (1982). *The Ojibwa Dance Drum*. Washington, DC: Smithsonian Institution Press.

Selected Discography

American Indian Dances
Folkway Records FD 6510

American Indian Music for the Classroom
(4 records)
Canyon Records C-3001-04

American Indian Sings, The
(Louis W. Ballard)
The New Southwest Music Publications

Apache
Canyon Records C-6053

Authentic Music of the American Indian
Everest Records SDBR 3450

Eskimos of Hudson Bay and Alaska, The
Folkway Records FE 4444

Folk Music of the United States from the Archive of American Folk Song

Seneca Songs from Coldspring Longhouse	AAFS L17
Music of the Cora, Seri, Yaqui, Tarahumara, Huichol, Tzotzil, and Tzeltal	AAFS L19
Songs of the Chippewa	AAFS L22
Songs of the Sioux	AAFS L23
Songs of the Yuma, Cocopa and Yaqui	AAFS L24
Songs of the Pawnee and Northern Ute	AAFS L25
Songs of the Papago (Tohono O'odham)	AAFS L31
Songs of the Nootka and Quileute	AAFS L32
Songs of the Menominee, Mandan and Hidatsa	AAFS L33
Kiowa	AAFS L35
Indian Songs of Today	AAFS L36
Delaware, Cherokee, Choctaw, Creek	AAFS L37
Plains: Comanche, Cheyenne, Kiowa, Caddo, Wichita, Pawnee	AAFS L39
Sioux	AAFS L40
Navajo	AAFS L41
Pueblo: Taos, San Ildefonso, Zuni, Hopi	AAFS L43

Great Plains Singers and Songs
Canyon Records C-6052

Hopi Butterfly
Canyon Records ARP 6072

Indian Music of Mexico
Folkways Library FE 4413

Indian Music of the Southwest
Folkway Records FW 8850

Memories of Navajoland
Canyon Records C-6057

Natay: Navajo Singer
Canyon Records C-6160

Navajo
Canyon Records C-6055

Navajo Squaw Dance Songs
Canyon Records ARP 6067

Music of the American Indian: Apache
Archive of American Folksong AAFS L-42

Music of the American Indians of the Southwest
Ethnic Folkways Library FE 4420

Music of the Sioux and the Navajo
Ethnic Folkways Library FE 4401

Navajo Sway Songs
Indian House IH 1501

Night and Daylight Yeibichei
Indian House IH 1502

Ojibwa Choir, The
Montaigne Limited LPG 106 (CT 31087)

Papago Dance Songs
(2 records)
Canyon Records C-6084 and C-6098

Peyote
Canyon Records C-6054

Philip Cassadore Sings
Canyon Records C-6056

Popular Dance Music of the Indians of Southern Arizona
Canyon Records C-6085

Promised Land, The: American Indian Songs of Lament and Protest
Folkways Records FHS 37254

Pueblo Indian Songs from San Juan
Canyon Records ARP 6065

Pueblo Songs of the Southwest
Indian House IH 9502

Round Dance Songs of Taos Pueblo
(2 records)
Indian House IH 1001-02

Sioux Favorites
Canyon Records C-6059

Song of the Indian, The
(2 records)
Canyon Records C-6050

Songs and Dances of the Flathead Indians
Ethnic Folkways Library P 445

Songs from Laguna
Canyon Records C-6058

Songs from the Pima
Canyon Records ARP 6066

Songs of the Sioux
Canyon Records C-6062

Sounds of Indian America
Indian House IH 9501

Traditional Navajo Songs
Canyon Records C-6064

Yaqui: Music of the Pascola and Deer Dance
Canyon Records C-6099

Yaqui: Ritual and Festival Music
Canyon Records C-6140

Yei-Be-Chai Songs
Canyon Records ARP 6069

Zuni
Canyon Records ARP-60601

CHAPTER NINE

MUSIC OF AFRICA
(SOUTH OF THE SAHARA)

As with many cultures discussed in this text, Africa is neither a distinct culture nor country. It is actually the second largest continent of the world. It has 20% of the world's land mass, representing some 50 countries, 3,000 tribal cultures, and 15% of the world's people, over 800 million. The music of each distinct group cannot be covered in one chapter, not only because of its sheer diversity, but, equally, because not every tribe has had its music observed, documented, and codified by ethnomusicologists. Nonetheless, some generalizations of musical practices can be made concerning the continent. In this chapter, only music of Africa south of the Sahara Desert will be discussed.

The countries of Africa have become familiar to Westerners as many nations have sought, won, and attempted to deal with independence. These include Zaire, Nigeria, Ghana, Kenya, Angola, Ivory Coast, Cameroon, Sudan, Zambia, Zimbabwe, Uganda, and so on. The tribes are not as well known as Native American tribes, but include Ashanti, Bemba, Chopi, Baule, Ibo, Hausa, Zulu, Shona, Masai, Lele, Senufo, Nupe, Teso, and Swazi. Tribes are not necessarily concentrated in one country either. Colonialists, realizing what strength a concentrated tribe might have within one country, often carved up regions and drew boundaries so large tribes were split into two or more countries. Consequently, discussing the music of one country often means including several tribes, or when discussing one tribe, several countries.

Acrobatic dancer with face makeup, age 9. Dan peoples, Ivory Coast. Photo by Eliot Elisofon, 1971. Courtesy of the National Museum of African Art, Eliot Elisofon Archives, Smithsonian Institution, Neg. No. VIII-48,10.

In general, Africa, as discussed in this chapter, is divided into five principal regions. These are:

Khoi-San area

This is the Western part of the tip of South Africa, including South Africa, Lesotho, and Namibia, as well as Bushmen and Hottentots, primarily nomadic groups;

Eastern Africa

> This region extends from Ethiopia southward, including the eastern cattle region, such as Kenya, Tanzania, and Mozambique. Tribes include the Masai and Watusi;

Guinea Coast, the southern coast of the Western extension of Africa

> This region includes Ghana, Nigeria, Ivory Coast, and Liberia;

Congo area

> This region extends across the equatorial zone of the continent, including Zaire, Central African Republic, Uganda, and Cameroon, as well as pygmy and negrito tribes;

> and

Sub-Saharan Africa

> This is the strip above the Congo area and to the east of the Guinea Coast, including Mali, Niger, Chad, and Sudan.

Drummers at a masked dance. Yoruba peoples, Meko, Nigeria. Photo by Eliot Elisofon, 1970. Courtesy of the National Museum of African Art, Eliot Elisofon Archives, Smithsonian Institution, Neg. No. II-19a, 35.

In such a wide and diverse area, what generalizations can be made about music? One is its communal aspect. It is integral to society and part of each person's daily experience. Over eighty percent of Africans live in villages. Their life, although harsh and unpredictable, is based on traditions and rituals, social frameworks, and aesthetic expressions which transcend written documentation. Little was known about Africa, other than coastal regions that could be easily reached by sea, earlier than a century ago. Tribes did not have written expressions of their culture, but, rather, depended on oral tradition. Nonetheless, tribal music today undoubtedly reflects each culture uniquely. Music is vital to birth, death, puberty, marriage, hunting, planting, and harvesting, as well as rites associated with secret societies and initiation. Music is part of acculturation, used to teach children tribal mores and taboos. Epic songs convey the history of the tribe. Music inspires and ennobles. It is used purely for entertainment, to amuse and divert. It may relieve social and political tension by allowing one person to litigate against another in song without libel. It is used to praise as well as criticize tribal leaders. In short, most daily transactions are somehow integrated by music into the communal aspect of the tribe and village.

Since music in Africa is so integral to the local unit, almost everyone participates. Nonetheless, there are trained professionals who oversee and direct musical occasions. In West Africa, this is the *griot*, a highly gifted musician who may be employed by a political leader to sing his praises. Independent griots are hired by those who can afford them, again to extol their virtues in public. The griot may be associated with witchcraft and magic, therefore being both respected and feared by most acquaintances. He is not only musician, but news-bearer, dancer, story-teller, and repository of tradition.

Griot playing the kora: Batourou Sekou Kouyate and his wife, Dinotan Tounkara. Bamana peoples, near Bamako, Mali. Photo by Eliot Elisofon, 1970. Courtesy of the National Museum of African Art, Eliot Elisofon Archives, Smithsonian Institution, Neg. No. VII-9, 30.

Music is basically communal, frequently done in groups for a special reason. On some occasions, it permeates an entire event, such as a celebration. On other occasions, it provides prelude to an event, such as preceding a hunt. Spontaneous musical activities often may spring up as well. Music is also used by individuals for personal entertainment, usually in seclusion or without awareness of any audience. In all cases, music is part of life and human awareness, rarely isolated from its social context. With the exception of praise-singers, griots, who pass their traditions within their family, members of villages learn their music by observing and participating. There is little organized music education for most people. It simply occurs as part of tribal socialization.

Musical performance in Africa is usually structured one of four ways. One important way is the use of leader and chorus, using a *call-response*, that is, *antiphonal* structure.

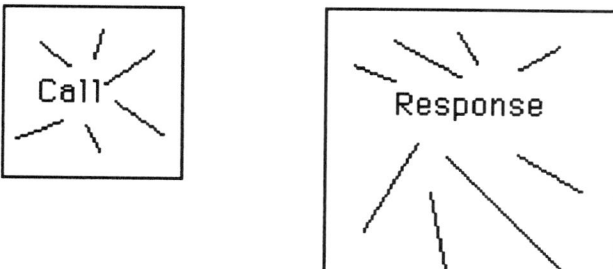

Those who lead are usually specialists, griots, while the chorus consists of community members who simply imitate the same phrases. Antiphonal singing may occur between male and female choruses as well. A second structure, using two people, is similar. They have equal roles, sometimes echoing one another, other times, singing together. This requires rehearsal and preparation, rather than imitation. A third way is the use of soloist, whether accompanied by instruments or not, who does all of the singing. The fourth, undoubtedly the most complicated, is the interlocking of soloist and chorus in *hocket*, that is, interdependent lines, each part contributing various melodic pitches or segments.

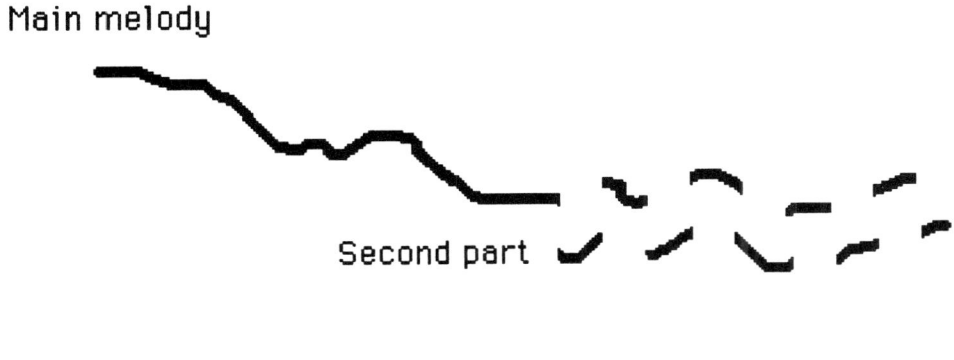

Hocket

Unlike antiphony, the complexity of this structure results from rehearsal and preparation, rather than mere imitation. Although most members of a community might participate in musical activities, the leaders and preparers of the music would be the most highly regarded. Next in recognition would be talented instrumentalists or solo singers. General chorus members would not be highly regarded as musicians.

What generalizations can be made about the structure of African music? One often thinks of rhythmic vitality as a keyword in African music. This is undoubtedly true. Rhythmic complexity may be added to this. African music is generally based on a steady beat, undeviating in its consistency. This steady beat, felt by all participants, is the underlying structure for musical events. Rhythmic cycles are *additive*, which means a cycle might consist of 5 + 7 beats or 2 + 5 + 3, that is, unequal divisions. This occurs against other cycles which have different combinations, such as:

```
5 + 7        S w w w w S w w w w w w S w w w w
2 + 5 + 3    S w S w w w w S w w S w S w w w w
3 + 2 + 3    S w w S w S w w S w w S w S w w S
```

This, of course, results in syncopation and shifting accents that rarely converge because major downbeats do not occur with any degree regularity. This phenomenon is known as *polyrhythms* or *polymeters*. Nonetheless, these layers of accent groupings are all ruled by a single metronomic beat.

In addition and as a result of polyrhythm, African music frequently superimposes duples against triples, a phenomenon called *hemiola*.

```
duple     S w S w S w S w S w S w
triple    S w w S w w S w w S w w
```

Hemiola occurs in European music, but is more an anomaly than a regularity, to create a special feeling or signal a cadence. In African music, it is the norm, much like six-eighth and three-quarters time occurring simultaneously.

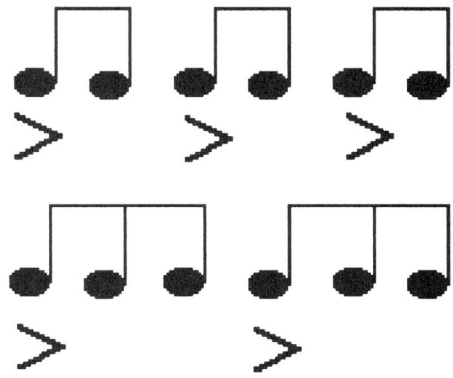

Circle dance. Men wear loincloth of beaten bark and caps with parrot feathers. Mangbetu peoples, Medje, Zaire. Photo by Eliot Elisofon, 1970. Courtesy of the National Museum of African Art, Eliot Elisofon Archives, Smithsonian Institution, Neg. No. I-2, 19A.

Some African music, however, is based on two beats which do not necessarily coincide. Using the quarter as well as the dotted quarter as basic beats, each moving at a slightly different tempo, might be the best way to characterize this phenomenon. Most African tempos are robust, the beat moving at 120 to 225 per minute. This is what creates much of the energy of African rhythms, which seemingly have relentless drive. Musicians are able to maintain the same tempo for minutes and even hours.

By contrast, African scales are not particularly complex. Most are either pentatonic or heptatonic, at least as measured by fixed-pitched xylophones and other keyed instruments. This gives the music a diatonic flavor, not unlike Western music. Although common intervals are similar to major and minor seconds, thirds, sixths, and sevenths of European music, neutral thirds and sevenths, which lie between major and minor, also occur. These sound much like flatted intervals we associate with American jazz, particularly the so-called "blue tones". Note bending is also common.

Since many African languages, particularly the Bantu, are inflected or tonal, what happens in a melody is influenced by the pitch of certain words. Melodies tend to occur in one of three ways. The descending line, beginning with a high pitch and occurring over a phrase or breath-span, is one. Undulating from low to high to low in a bell-shaped curve is a second. The third melodic structure is rather like a pendulum that swings from low to high back to low. Within these basic contours, a melody may center around a core pitch or a series of them. It may also jump in thirds, outlining triads, at least in a Western sense. It may descend by fourths. All melodic structure is typically short, using repetition or slight variation of the basic melodic unit. This unit, heard against a complex rhythmic accompaniment, is continually modified because of its convergence in the entire polyrhythmic structure with shifting accented beats. It is important to realize, however, that simultaneous events in African music are perceived as horizontal events, not by vertical regularity. This simply means Africans think of these musical events as layers of sound, some melodic, some rhythmic, that occur at the same time. Each line is usually differentiated by distinct timbre, accent grouping, and structure.

Although timbre will be discussed later in this chapter, texture and form will be examined here. Texture is often polyphonic, occurring through several techniques. In call-response, the overlapping of leader and chorus results in polyphony. Often, a solo melody will be supported by an *ostinato*, a short, repeated melodic unit sung by chorus or played by instruments. It may occur either below or above the melody.

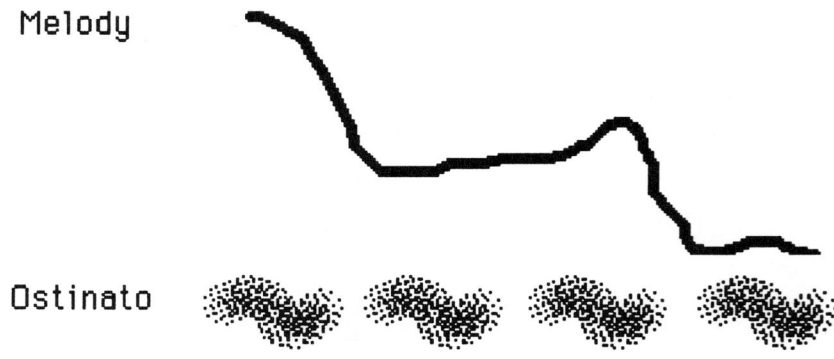

Numerous ostinati may be used simultaneously, building tension through complexity. Periods of repose occur when some of these ostinati are terminated or converged. Rounds and canons also occur. Melodic lines may be duplicated at a set interval, commonly thirds, fourths, or fifths, resulting in a texture like parallel organum, which is neither truly polyphony nor monophony. Finally, the interlocking lines of hocket described earlier are also polyphonic. Although all of these examples are not based on harmonic vocabulary that is culturally defined, they occur as a result of the cooperative social nature of the music as well as the interplay of numerous and simultaneous melodic and rhythmic events. The predominant intervals appear to be those which are favored in European music as well, making this music seem familiar and friendly to those schooled in Western traditions.

Bekete drummer, Zaire.

Finally, form of African music is basic repetition or slight variation of a musical idea. Although most units are short, some are longer, integrating contrasting phrases. There is little development of musical ideas, but, rather, processive variation, through accretion of layers and shifting of accents in techniques reminiscent of American minimalism. In musical events which accompany lengthy ceremonies, each part is based on a short musical idea, much like new material in each movement of a sonata or suite.

To move these abstractions into more concrete understanding, we will explore some of the countries and cultures of Africa, using the five regions outlined above:

> Khoi-San area
>
> Eastern Africa
>
> Guinea Coast
>
> Congo area
>
> Sub-Saharan Africa

Music of the Khoi-San Area

This area includes Namibia, Lesotho, South Africa, as well as Bushmen and Hottentots. The language that unifies this region is characterized by clicking sounds in speech. Only a few examples can be discussed here, but these are representative of the area. Bushmen are semi-nomadic people roaming in bands of 20-50 people in Botswana, Namibia, and Angola. Their singing is characterized by high tessituras with yodeling. The texture is often polyphonic, the metric structure, polyrhythmic. Handclapping typically accompanies the singing, which is not based on meaningful texts, but, rather, vocables. Two instruments are also used, the musical bow, using the mouth as a resonator, and a small thumb piano, generically referred to as *lamellophone*, specifically as *mbira*. Lamellophones, which occur in many regions of Africa, have small metal or wooden keys that are plucked, thus giving rise to the nomenclature "thumb piano". They may be attached or placed in a resonator to augment the sound.

Among Bushmen, women and children do most of the singing, which is used to accompany men who imitate animals in their dancing. Vocal lines of the polyphonic structure are differentiated by timbre, that is, each line has a distinct range and color.

Mbira, a lamellophone. Zaire.

Lesotho is named for the Sotho people who inhabit this landlocked South African country. Since this is a cattle region, many of the instruments of the Sotho are used to herd and control cattle. The Sotho identify two types of instruments. Those controlled by the hand, *liletsa tsa matsoho*, include a single-headed drum, the *moropa*, which accompanies female puberty rites and dancing. The double-headed drum, *sekupu*, is often used in healing ceremonies. Liletsa tsa matsoho also includes bullroarers, shaken and scraped rattles, metal bells as well as struck chordophones such as the *thomo*. Those instruments controlled by mouth, *liletsa tsa molomo*, include the *lesiba*, a stick zither which uses the mouth as resonator. It is used to herd cattle since it makes birds' sounds. Mouth resonance is considered as part of the instrument, not merely a performing technique. Other instruments controlled by the mouth include the *lekolilo*, flute, *lekhitlane*, megaphone, and *sekebeku*, a jew's harp.

The Sotho use music in various utilitarian ways, reflecting their cattle-herding culture, such as tanning hides, as well as rites of passage, such as puberty, where the initiates learn *mangae*. These instructional songs, sung to the entire village by individuals upon their return from isolation, are joined responsorially by the other initiates. The villagers then admit the young men into society by providing appropriate gifts.

Songs and dances are not usually performed by mixed groups, except for the *motjeko*, in which both boys and girls dance in a circle while one girl reveals her affection for a certain boy. Songs are usually divided into two groups, those performed while dancing, *ka maoto*, and those sung in place, *ho engoe*. The former may be individualistic, reiterative, and energetic, the latter, more in the nature of religious singing, such as for weddings and funerals. Lullabies are in the ho engoe category.

Music of the Sotho is frequently responsorial, a soloist or small group leading, while a larger group, the entire village, responds. Solo singing and dancing, often of virtuosic proportions, is responsorially commented upon by the group. Lyrics reflect work situations as well to build group spirit. In the past, musical activities were equally distributed throughout village groups, but contact with Western influences has given rise to professionalism and specialization in the culture.

Two Masai girls (Kenya, East Africa), draped with jewelry. Photo by Carol Beckwith. Courtesy of The University Museum, University of Pennsylvania, Neg. No. S8-133053 and Carol Beckwith.

Music of Eastern Africa

Both Ethiopia and Kenya are part of East Africa, a region which is based on a grazing and herding economy. This region also has the most pronounced highlands of any African region, formed by the Rift Valley, which, in the case of Ethiopia, provided relative isolation for many of the cultures. Since cattle are the mark of wealth and power in this region, society is based on the cattle economy and tends to be complex and differentiated. The power of authority is often concentrated, musically, in drums, particularly kettledrums. The language group used in this region of the continent is Afro-Asiatic. In Kenya, dominant tribes are Pokomo, Gikuyu, Embu, Meru, Nandi, Pokot, and Masai. In Ethiopia, tribes include the Nuer, Dorze, Gimira, and Amhara.

Call-response is a typical feature of Kenyan singing, which is the basis of all musical practice. Although the leader's part is sometimes elaborate and long, other times, short and concise, response by the chorus in either case is typically short and repetitious. When overlapping occurs between leader and chorus, polyphony occurs. Scales are either heptatonic or pentatonic, frequently using C, D, or even G as a tonal center. Rhythmic meters are free if dancing is not involved, stricter when movement accompanies the music. Strict meters are basically simple duple or triple. Complexity comes as a result of superimposing different meters as well as adding syncopation.

Although some performers are recognized by their superior musical ability, there is not really a system of professional musicians who only ply this craft. Most tribes involve everyone in music making. Songs and dances are performed to celebrate birth, engagement, matrimony, and death, as well as to praise, heal, protest, and satirize. There are also songs for working and playing. Music is a catalyst which binds the culture through common references and practices, both socializing and codifying.

Kenyan instruments include various types of *lyres*, chordophones which have strings attached to a resonator at one end, a yoke which is supported by two protruding arms at the other. There is no fingerboard, but, rather, numerous strings, four to eight, tuned to a given pitch array or scale. These are plucked or strummed by the hand. Among the Gusii, this lyre is called the *obokano*, among the Luo, *thom*, and the Pokot, *pagan*. It is played while the performer is seated.

There are also various types of end-blown flutes, made of bamboo or reed, as well as trumpets made from gourds or animal horns. The Luo tribe call their trumpet the *abu*. Some aerophones show Arabic influence, which is not surprising, given the propinquity of Eastern African to the Middle East. The double reed *zumari*, an oboe-like instrument, is an example. Drums, predominantly double-headed, are common as are shakers and rattles made from gourds.

When pitched instruments are used with singing, they duplicate the melody in unison or provide a pitch ostinato as accompaniment. Some performances include bridging sections between strophes which are entirely instrumental.

Ethiopian melody, which shows traits of African as well as Islamic culture, is undulating rather than merely descending in each phrase. Ranges are wide. Polyphony occurs in many contexts, often through duplication of the melodic line at octave or fifth, which is known as *magadizing*.

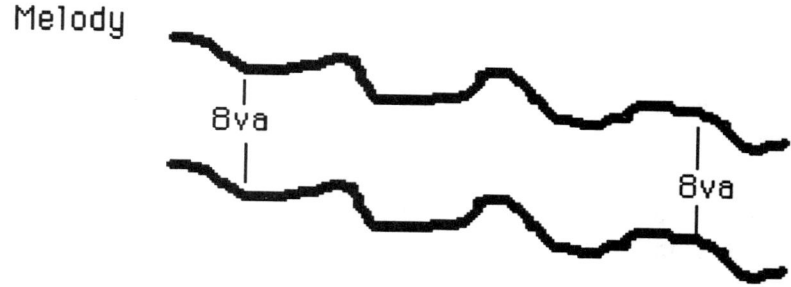

Lyrics are derived from poetic forms. Compared to much African singing, the style in Ethiopia is constrained and tense, using frequent melismas, which may reflect the absorption of Arabic traits.

Instruments of Ethiopian tribes include the *masenqo*, a small spike-fiddle with one string which is bowed. It is characterized by its diamond-shaped resonator. Masenqos are played predominantly by *azmari*, wandering minstrels who carry the news from village to village. The performance style is elaborate, incorporating numerous melismas and embellishments typical of Ethiopian singing. The masenqo is joined in ensembles by the *embilta*, a notched flute, as well as panpipes and drums.

Lyres of the region include the *beganna*, a large lyre with a rectangular resonator, often with as many as ten strings, and the *kerar*, a smaller lyre with a bowl-shaped resonator and fewer strings. Since the former is large, it rests on the ground when played. The smaller kerar (also *krar*) is held in the performer's lap or arms. These instruments may duplicate the melody that is sung or provide ostinati as accompaniment. The beganna is played predominantly by male aristocrats while the kerar is used by women of all classes to accompany romantic ballads.

Music of the Guinea Coast

The Guinea Coast is the region of West Africa that bulges into the South Atlantic Ocean, including Sierra Leone, Ivory Coast, Ghana, Togo, Benin, and Nigeria. Historically, it is important since many slaves brought to the New World were imported from this region. They are the true ancestors of today's African Americans. The music of this region, too, was one of the antecedents of American jazz, combined with Protestant hymn-tunes to form a unique hybrid musical style in the United States during the post-Civil War era. Since this area was relative accessible to navigators, it is an area that has had long contact with European civilization.

Ghana, which achieved independence from the United Kingdom in 1957, has retained much of its indigenous music, even in the face of Westernization. Music is largely a social event, used for ceremony, festivities, or merely as entertainment. It is used to accomplish communal tasks, such as building, weeding, or pounding. There are songs which convey tribal culture and history, games, and group sentiments. Men's songs include hunting and warring music while women sing dirges

Musicians with gourd shakers accompanying Goli society dancers. Baule peoples, Kondeyaokro, Ivory Coast. Photo by Eliot Elisofon, 1972. Courtesy of the National Museum of African Art, Eliot Elisofon Archives, Smithsonian Institution, Neg. No. XIII-17, 36A.

or songs representing domestic chores. Music, as with most tribal cultures, celebrates life passages: birth; circumcision; marriage; and death. Music is also a safety valve, allowing one to criticize a relative, pretentious chieftain, or tax collector. In a society in which newspapers and the editorial page are not daily occurrences, music functions somewhat as an aural pillory. Victims of social protest sometimes pay singers to stop as the only way to avoid communal derision. Social protest is a component of West African music that carried to the spirituals and field hollers of early slave music in America.

The Akan people of Ghana use complex drumming in their music, showing rigid differentiation by function. Each drum is known for its specific function--speaking, signaling, or dancing. Even within these three categories, some drums may be used for only *one* type of dancing. Drums of signaling are used to communicate short, repetitive patterns to which meanings have been assigned. Drumming occurs all on one pitch. In speech drumming, however, the pitches of the

Shrine house musicians, shaker and horn. Ashanti peoples, Besease, Ghana. Photo by Eliot Elisofon, 1970. Courtesy of the National Museum of African Art, Eliot Elisofon Archives, Smithsonian Institution, Neg. No. V-19, 8A.

drumheads are different to convey inflected speech patterns, which is characteristic of the Bantu languages spoken here. The listener interprets the meaning by the phrasing of the drums as well as the series of highs and lows heard. The Bantu languages, of which there are 150, have as many as nine different pitch levels. The listener therefore is decoding what is heard, not merely hearing a known signal. Slit drums are used to convey inflections in speech drumming. In dance drumming, the third category, there is much repetition of typical rhythms used in movement. A metronomic beat might be provided by bell or rattle. Each drum, whether used for signaling, speaking, or dancing, requires a different technique. No drummer would consider using a signal drum for dancing. Contrast this to the West, where Joplin, Beethoven, and Cage might all be performed on the same piano within the same concert!

Travelling minstrels, including bolon (center) player. Dan peoples, Man region, Ivory Coast. Photo by Eliot Elisofon, 1971. Courtesy of the National Museum of African Art, Eliot Elisofon Archives, Smithsonian Institution, Neg. No. VIII-50, 33.

Music performed in Ghana by a special group may be named for it or for the instrument used. Among the Akan, *ab fo* means music performed by hunters as well as the hunters themselves. Puberty rites are called *bragors* and music for puberty rites is called *bradwom*. *Adenkum* means a gourd trumpet as well as the music it performs.

The Ashanti are the largest tribal group in Ghana, consisting of over 1,500,000 or 10 per cent of the entire population. As a unit, they are politically organized under chieftains who owe allegiance to the Assantehene, chief executive of the entire tribe. The status of each chieftain in this national hierarchy is reflected in the number of musical ensembles and the types of instruments that are used, since court music is largely instrumental. One of the most important instruments of the court is the *atumpan*, a single-headed talking drum, grouped by size in ensembles. Each is played with a forked stick mallet. The *twenesin* is a signal drum while the *donno* is a double-headed, hourglass drum. Although there are few chordophones, aerophones include trumpets made of animal horn or tusk. These are played in ensembles of five to seven performers, each contributing one or two pitches of the melodic line. The *atenteben* is a bamboo flute which is played at court as well. Single and double bells without clappers, known respectively as *dawuro* and *nnawuta*, are also used.

By contrast, community music is mostly vocal, using few instruments. The basic scales are diatonic, each phrase descending as part of the natural breathing process. Melodies are duplicated at the third and call-response is typical.

Nigeria, also a Guinea Coast country, is one of most heavily populated in all of Africa, estimated at 90 million. This country is home to numerous tribes associated with musical prowess, including Yoruba, Fulani, Hausa, Igbo, Ibibio, and Nupe. In such diversity, united by independence in 1960, it is hard to generalize about Nigerian music.

Drummers accompanying Egungun mask. Yoruba peoples, Ede, Nigeria. Photo by Eliot Elisofon, 1970. Courtesy of the National Museum of African Art, Eliot Elisofon Archives, Smithsonian Institution, Neg. No. II-25, 30.

Among the Hausa, who inhabit the Western central region, there are recognized professional musicians who compose and perform. They specialize in either vocal or instrumental music, making their living entirely through their craft and owning the songs they create. By contrast, Yoruba musicians make their living by agriculture, plying their musical craft when an event requires it. Igbo performers, who are not professional musicians, interpret music of the entire village rather than creating new songs.

Instruments in Nigeria, as in all of Africa, may be grouped into families to symbolize the roles inherent in society itself. In the uta orchestra of the Ibibios, there are seven instruments. Seven is an important number among the Ibibios and this ensemble consists of two drums, one woodblock, and four horns made from deer antlers with gourd resonators. The smallest and most talkative is the mother uta. The other three horns are considered male, playing lower and fewer pitches. The purpose of this ensemble fittingly is for funerals of prominent women of the tribe or for aging women who want to rejuvenate themselves. This family relationship, one woman and three men, applies to other sets of drums throughout the culture, the female drum typically being the most active. Among the Yoruba, concentrated in the Western coastal region as well as neighboring Benin, each drum and rhythm is associated with a god. A particular god cannot be petitioned on the incorrect drum.

The Yoruba's principal music is called *dundun*, which is also the name of the hourglass drum used in its performance. The strings which tension its two heads are squeezed to raise the pitch, simulating inflections of the language as well. The Yoruba also use the *agogo*, a clapperless iron bell, the *agidigbo*, a lamellophone which has a resonator, and the *goje*, a one-stringed fiddle which is bowed. Vocal music is divided into regular song and praise chant, the latter known as *oriki*. Although there is a distinction between instrumental and vocal music, the former is nonetheless based on speech inflections and patterns, performed by drums which can vary their pitch.

A rather unique chordophone of Senegal, Sierra Leone, Gambia, Guinea, as well as Mali in the sub-Saharan region, is the *kora*, a 21-string harp-lute, which is played only by professional musicians. It is used to accompany songs and poetry.

Music of the Congo Region

Musicians accompanying circle dance (nebembo). Mangbetu peoples, Medje, Zaire.
Photo by Eliot Elisofon, 1970. Courtesy of the National Museum of African Art,
Eliot Elisofon Archives, Smithsonian Institution, Neg. No. I-3, 10.

The Congo area is the region of equatorial Africa between the Guinea Coast and East Africa, including the countries of Cameroon, Zaire, Central African Republic, and Uganda.

Cameroon has numerous tribal groups, including the northern Fulani as well as the southern Bassa, Duala, Bulu, Fang', and Mvele. The southern area is more homogenous than the rather isolated northern lands, which are dominated by the Islamic-based culture of the Fulani.

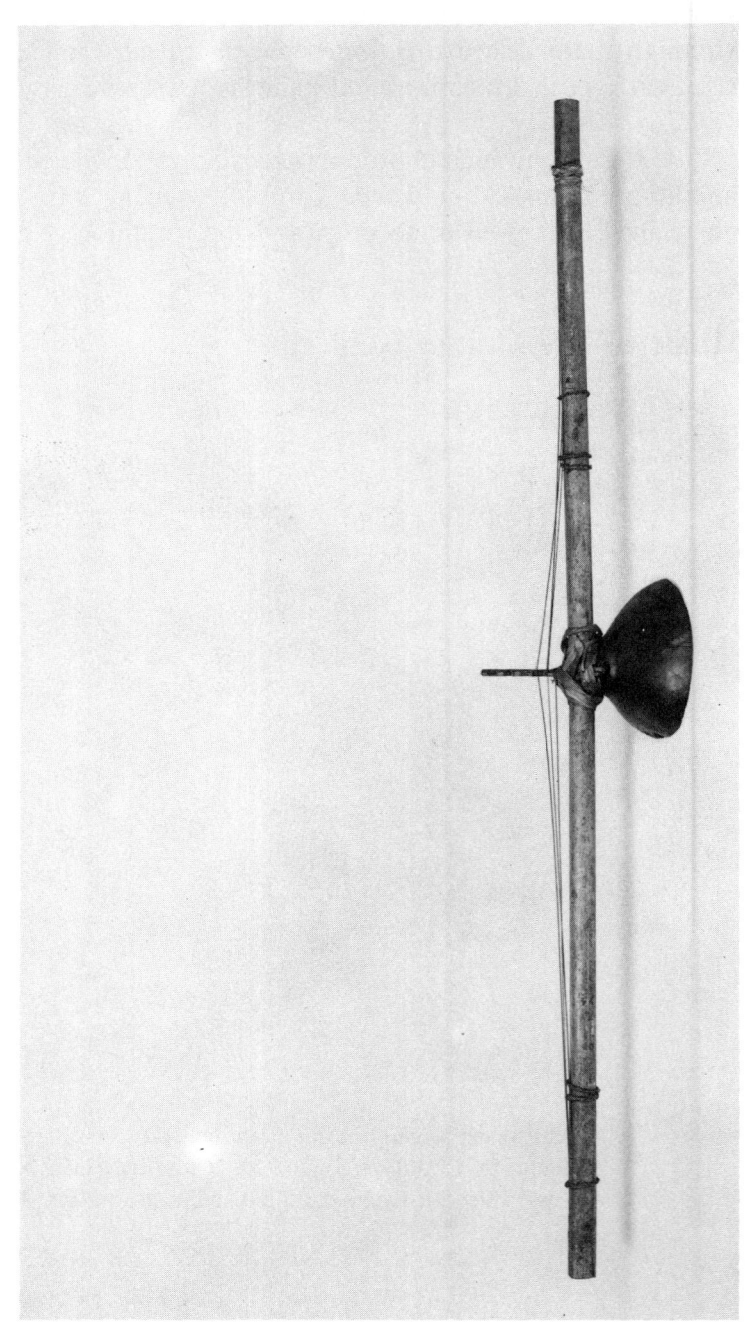

Mvet, central African chordophone, also called rafia harp or Fang harp (Fang peoples). Courtesy of The University Museum, University of Pennsylvania, Neg. No. S8-80256, Object #AF 268.

The Fulani use music for court ceremonies. It is often festive and militaristic, using the *algaita*, a double-reed aerophone, and *kakaki*, metal trumpet, both of which are reminiscent of Near Eastern instruments. They also use various types of drums. Southern Cameroon musical instruments include the *mvet*, a stick zither, usually with five strings, used to accompany the recitation of epic poetry. *Balophons*, portable xylophones of different dimensions with gourd resonators, are common. They are usually heptatonic, using equal division of the octave, and are played in ensembles of three or four, accompanied by drum and rattle. It is common for each resonator to have a hole cut through, over which is placed paper. When the key is struck, the paper vibrates or buzzes sympathetically, providing pitch and accompaniment simultaneously. Lamellophones, known as *timbrh* or *mbo tong* are common in Cameroon as well, using as many as eighteen keys. Some are attached to box resonators and others are single boards placed inside a drum for added resonance. Keys are wood (raffia branch) or pounded metal. The Fang' use a harp with eight strings known as the *ngombi*.

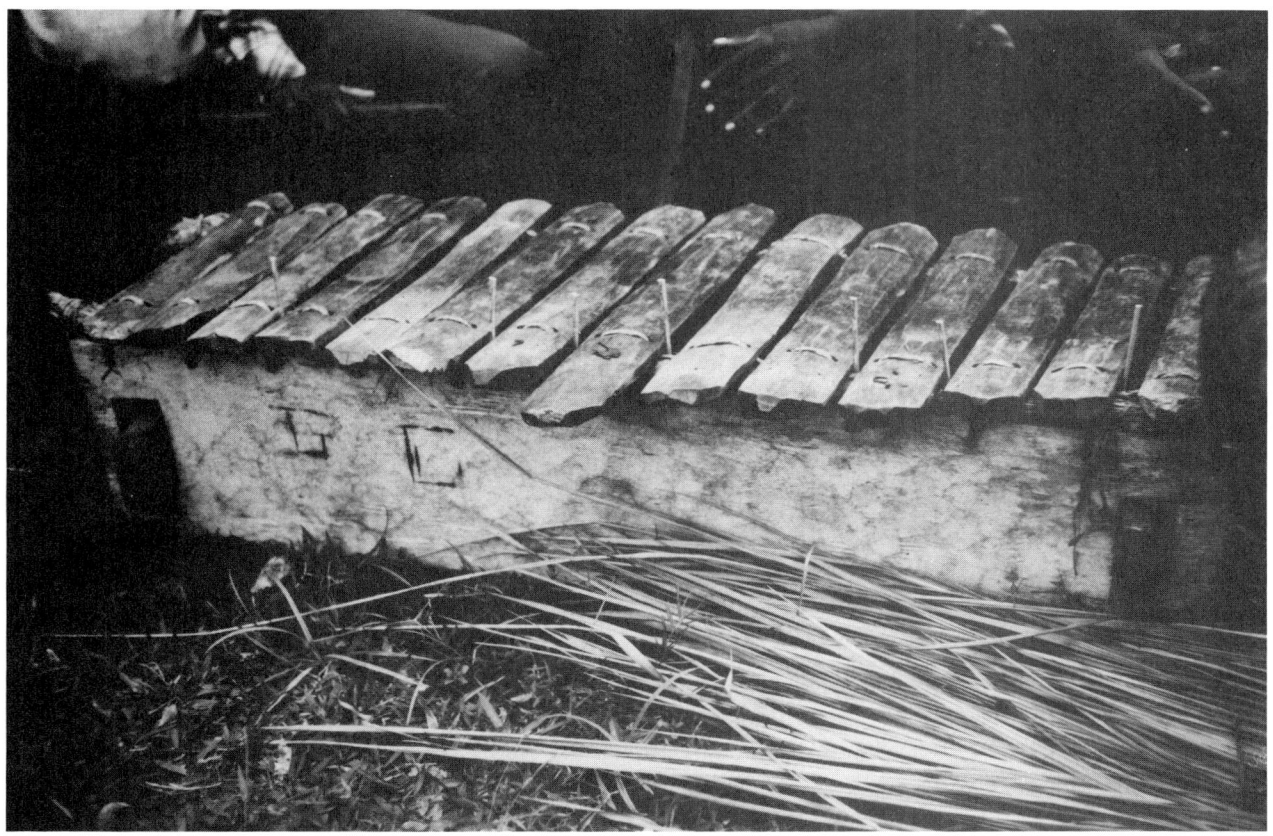

Balaphon from Zaire. The entire instrument can be disassembled for transport.

Zaire, which was formerly the Belgian Congo, is also a densely populated region of equatorial Africa, including over 25 million people. Third largest country on the continent, occupying a land mass as large as the United States east of the Mississippi River, it is home to numerous tribal groups, including the Lulua, Bakete, Ipanga, Kuku, Banji, Pende, and Lokele. Over 250 different tribal cultures were once part of this vast country.

Tundandi dance of boys after circumcision. Lulua peoples, Bashila Kasonge, Zaire.
Photo by Eliot Elisofon, 1947. Courtesy of the National Museum of African Art,
Eliot Elisofon Archives, Smithsonian Institution, Neg. No. 22923, C-4, 16.

Bantu languages are used by many groups of Zaire, providing cultural unity in music as well. Bantu music is characterized by a metronomic pulse which motivates all melodic and rhythmic ideas. Syncopation and superimposition of accent groups are added over the regular beat. Singing is open-throated and resonant, often incorporating nasal resonance as a secondary sound source. Melodic ideas are based on scales which are heptatonic, using the interval of the third predominantly. Songs are built up by improvisation using the same text repetitively, gradually varying the melodic idea, much as in theme and variation. Singing is accompanied by instruments, which include slit-drums, lamellophones, harps, zithers, and bows. Balophons, with either individual gourd or trough resonators, are used as well.

Pygmy music is also part of the Congo region. Pygmy refers to people who are less than 4.5 feet tall and, in Africa, they live in Gabon, Cameroon, Zaire, Central African Republic, Uganda, Rwanda, and Burundi. Less than 170,000 in number, half live in Zaire. Their tribes are the Binga, Twa, Mbuti, Ngombe, Aka, and Benzele and almost all are part of a hunting-gathering economy. As with Bushmen, they survive in small, nomadic bands.

Ituri (Congo region) forest pygmy beside Alfred M. Collins, a European (c. 1926), Mbuti peoples. Courtesy of Alfred M. Collins and The University Museum, University of Pennsylvania, Neg. No. NC35-1031.

One of the most unique attributes of pygmy music is the presence of yodeling, using vocables. Melodic phrases are short with a descending contour. Group participants sing their version of this contour simultaneously, adding ostinati and parallelism at will. Unlike most African music, call-response is not typical. There is a preference for pentatonic melodies and harmony at the fourth or fifth. As might be expected from nomadic people, there is no tradition of instrumental music, other than the use of small flutes and drums.

Mbuti dancers, edge of Ituri forest, near Beni. Photo by Eliot Elisofon, 1970. Courtesy of the National Museum of African Art, Eliot Elisofon Archives, Smithsonian Institution, Neg. No. I-12a, 34.

Music of the Sub-Saharan Region

The region of Africa that lies above the Congo region is known as sub-Saharan Africa. It includes the countries of Mauritania, Mali, Niger, Chad, and Sudan. Most of these countries are huge land masses incorporating numerous tribes. Nonetheless, because of the harshness of the region, most areas are sparsely populated as compared to the Congo or Guinea Coast regions. Since the region was transversed from early times by trade routes from the East, as might be expected, it has been influenced by Arabic and Islamic traditions.

N'tomo mask covered with cowrie shells. Bamana peoples, Bamako region, Mali. Photo by Eliot Elisofon. Courtesy of the National Museum of African Art, Eliot Elisofon Archives, Smithsonian Institution, Neg. No. VII-8, 36.

Sudan, the second largest country of Africa in land mass, is unified by the Arabic language as well as the Islamic religion. The principal tribal groups are Nubians, Nilotes, Funge, Nuba, and Maha. Although religious music is part of most cultures, the secular use of music is more pronounced, including its use in weddings, birthings, and funerals. The *sayra* is a processional song used to accompany a groom and his family to the bride's house. It is sung by women and the leader is an elderly family member. The refrain is provided by the entire group. A *dobeit* is a nomadic song, sung by men to praise one's camel. It is based on poetry, a typical Arab practice, and most dobeits use the same melody with different words. *Gardagi*, sung by both men or women, are songs of either praise or criticism. They begin with known lyrics, the performer gradually improvising new ones as the occasion demands. The singing style is unmeasured and may be accompanied by a single-stringed chordophone.

Among Sudanese instruments are *nihass*, copper-bottomed kettledrums, used only by and for leaders. These are similar to nakars, a precursor of European timpani. The goblet drum, similar to the darabukka, is called *daluka*. Sudanese lamellophones are called *kundi*, using ten keys. Each key is attached to a small ring under the bridge, which is furthest from the performer's hands. When each key is plucked, its attached ring vibrates sympathetically, producing two sounds at once, a preference noted earlier with other types of instruments as well as vocal production. The *rongo* is the Sudanese balophon with ten ebony keys. These are pentatonic, covering a two octave range played in parallel octaves. Individual resonators for each key produce a secondary vibration through the placement of paper or spider web over a hole cut into each. Drums include the *gugu*, a slit-drum shaped as an animal. Aerophones include the *zumbara*, a flute, and *penah*, a gourd trumpet. Bundled pipes consisting of as many as thirteen tubes are called *baal*. The *bangia* is a lyre, also known as *tambour*. The *umkiki* is a Sudanese rabab with one string used as accompaniment in the singing of gardagi.

Instruments of Africa

Kora player, Senegal.
Courtesy of the American Folklife Center,
Smithsonian Institution,
Photo No. 87-0666-25.

It is a common misconception that drums are the only indigenous instruments of the continent. In reality, as we have observed throughout the five regions of Africa, there are a variety of idiophones, aerophones, and chordophones as well. As with many cultures that live close to nature, as the predominantly rural Africans do, natural resources are used to construct musical instruments and accompany daily activities, religious ceremonies, and festivities. Therefore, the variety of responses by 3,000 tribal groupings is truly amazing and overwhelming in world cultures. Prototypes emerge throughout the continent, based on what material is available. These have tribal names which vary from region to region yet are generically referred to as xylophones or lamellophones, flutes or trumpets.

Drummer on dundun and young girls performing for the Timi of Ede. Yoruba peoples, Ede, Nigeria. Photo by Eliot Elisofon, 1971. Courtesy of the National Museum of African Art, Eliot Elisofon Archives, Smithsonian Institution, Neg. No. VII-34, 21A.

In general, since rhythmic vitality is omnipresent in all music of Africa, the percussive quality of sound producers is perhaps most pronounced, giving rise to this misconception. Although drums of various sizes and shapes are ubiquitous, so, too, are xylophones, lamellophones, slit-drums (which are really idiophones), shakers, rattles, and body adornments. In reality, the majority of African instruments *are* idiophones. Aerophones, whether flutes, oboes, or trumpets, and chordophones, whether lyre, harp, zither, lute, or bow, are all used for their percussive quality, infrequently for merely playing the melody. Even singing is percussive, using repetitive pitch units. Music making is largely a group activity in which the entire tribe participates. There is no music for sitting and listening.

Balaphon players accompanying Tiebleke dance. Bamana peoples, Bin village, Mali. Photo by Eliot Elisofon, 1959. Courtesy of the National Museum of African Art, Eliot Elisofon Archives, Smithsonian Institution, Neg. No. XII-R2, 6.

Key Terms and Concepts

Abu
Additive
Agogo
Algaita
Antiphonal
Atumpan
Azmari
Balophon
Beganna
Call-response
Congo Region
Dobeit
Donno
Dundun
Embilta
East African Region
Gardagi
Goje
Griot
Guinea Coast Region
Hemiola
Hocket
Ho Engoe
Kakaki
Ka Maoto
Kerar (Krar)
Khoi-San Region
Kora
Lamellophone
Lesiba
Liletsa Tsa Matsoho
Liletsa Tsa Molomo
Lyre
Magadizing
Mangae
Masenqo
Mbira
Moropa
Motjeko
Mvet
Nihass
Obokano
Ostinato
Polymeter
Polyrhythm
Sayra
Sekupu
Sub-Saharan Region
Thomo
Twenesin
Zumara

Self-Checking Chapter Review

Match Column II to Column I	
Column I	**Column II**
1. atumpan	A. chordophone with yoke
2. abu	B. mbira
3. antiphonal	C. spike fiddle
4. nihass	D. repeated pattern
5. Congo region	E. xylophone
6. ostinato	F. superimposition of different meters
7. agogo	G. oboe
8. lamellophone	H. alternation of pitches by different instruments
9. magadizing	I. equatorial Africa
10. balophon	J. kettledrum
11. masenqo	K. trumpet
12. lyre	L. call-response
13. algaita	M. singing parallel melody in octaves or fifths
14. polyrhythm	N. clapperless bell
15. hocket	O. talking drum

Answers	
1. O	9. M
2. K	10. E
3. L	11. C
4. J	12. A
5. I	13. G
6. D	14. F
7. N	15. H
8. B	

Selected Bibliography

Akpabot, Samuel Ekpe (1976). "Fugitive Notes on Notation and Terminology in African Music," *The Black Perspective in Music* 4:1 (Spring), pages 39-45.

_____ (1975). *Ibibio Music in Nigerian Culture.* Michigan State University Press.

_____ (1971). "Standard Drum Patterns in Nigeria," *African Music* 5:1, pages 37-79.

Arom, Simha (1991). *African Polyphony and Polyrhythm: Musical Structure and Methodology.* (Translated by Martim Thom, Barbara Tuckett, and Raymond Boyd.) New York: Cambridge University Press.

Bebey, Francis (1975). *African Music: A People's Art.* (Translated by Josephine Bennett). New York: Lawrence Hill & Company.

Brandel, Rose (1961). *The Music of Central Africa.* Martinus Nijhoft.

Chernoff, John Miller (1979). *African Rhythms and African Sensibility.* Chicago: University of Chicago Press.

Dietz, Betty Warner and Michael Babatunde Olatunji (1965). *Musical Instruments of Africa.* New York: John Day.

Ekwueme, Lazurus E.N. (1974). "African-Music Retentions in the New World," *The Black Perspective in Music*, 2:2, (Fall), pages 128-44.

Nketia, J.H. Kwabena (1963). *Drumming in Akan Communities of Ghana.* London: Thomas Nelson and Sons, Ltd.

_____ (1963). *Folk Songs of Ghana.* Accra, Ghana: Ghana University Press.

_____ (1974). *The Music of Africa.* New York: W. W. Norton & Company.

Tracey, Hugh T., Gerhard Kubik and Andrew Tracey (1969). *Codification of African Music and Textbook Project: A Primer of Practical Suggestions for Field Research.* Johannesburg: International Library of African Music.

Tracey, Hugh (1948). *Chopi Musicians.* New York: Oxford University Press.

Van Dam, Theodore (1954). "The Influence of the West African Songs of Derision in the New World," *African Music*, 1:1, pages 53-56.

Warren, Fred and Lee Warren (1970). *The Music of Africa: An Introduction.* Englewood Cliffs: Prentice-Hall, Inc.

Wachsmann, Klaus P. (Ed.) (1971). *Essays on Music and History In Africa.* Evanston: Northwestern University Press.

Selected Discography

Africa: Drum, Chant, and Instrumental Music
Nonesuch Explorer Series H-72073

Africa: Music of the Princes of Dahomey
Counterpoint/Esoteric Records #537

African Concert (Sung by the Troubadours of King Baudouin)
Philips PCC 214

African Musical Instruments
ASCH Records Ah 8460

African Music
Folkways Records FW 8852

African Tribal Music and Dances
Counterpoint/Esoteric Records CPT-513

Aka Pygmy Music
UNESCO Collection: Musical Sources
Philips 6586 016

Anthology of Music of Black Africa
Everest Records 3254 (Three record set)

An Anthology of African Music
UNESCO Collection: Barenreiter-Musicaphon
BM 30 L 2301-2310
- Volume 1: **The Music of the Dan (West Africa)**
- Volume 2: **Music from Rwanda**
- Volume 3: **Music of Ba-Benzele Pygmies (Cameroon)**
- Volume 4: **Ethiopia I Copts (Ethiopian Christianity)**
- Volume 5: **Ethiopia II Cushites (Highlands of Southwest Ethiopia**
- Volume 6: **Hausa Music I (West Africa)**
- Volume 7: **Hausa Music II (West Africa)**
- Volume 8: **Music of the Senufo (West Africa)**
- Volume 9: **Chad (Kanem: West Central Africa)**
- Volume 10: **Central African Republic**

Banda Polyphony: Central African Republic
UNESCO Collection: Musical Sources
Philips 6586 022

British East Africa
World Library of Folk and Primitive Music
Columbia Masterworks 91A 02017

Ceremonial Music from Northern Dahomey
UNESCO Collection: Musical Sources
Philips 6586 032

Dahomey: Bariba and Somba Music
EMI (Odeon) C 064-18217

Folk Music of Ghana
Folkways Records FW 8859

French Africa
World Library of Folk and Primitive Music
Columbia Masterworks 91A 02015

Ivory Coast
EMI (Odeon) C 064-17842

Music and Dances of Occidental Africa
Olympic Records OL 6110

Peuls (Niger) and Northern Dahomey, The
UNESCO Collection: Musical Atlas
EMI (Odeon) C 064-18121

Savannah Rhythm: Music of Upper Volta
Nonesuch Explorer Series H-72087

Songs of the Congo
Epic Records LF 18005

CHAPTER TEN

MUSIC OF THE LATIN WORLD

Martin Kondori playing panpipes, Tiwana Ku, Bolivia. Courtesy of the American Folklife Center, Smithsonian Institution, Photo No. 91-15028-12.

The final category of music to explore is that of the Latin world, which includes Central and South America as well as the Caribbean. This region includes Mexico on the north as well as Cape Horn on the South. The countries of the region are well known, including Argentina, Brazil, Columbia, Venezuela, Panama, Cuba, Paraguay, Chile, and Mexico. Our survey will allow only for general observations and exploration of a few cultures.

The region here has a population in excess of 350 million. Its history antedates the coming of Columbus. Latin music is therefore a blend of pre-Columbian Indian culture, African influence, as well as European, primarily Spanish and Portuguese. As we have done throughout this text, the emphasis will be primarily upon indigenous music that characterizes the culture, not European-derived art music. The African component of Latin music is undoubtedly most concentrated in Central America and the Caribbean where slaves were imported during colonial times. Indian music is predominant in rural areas of South America and Mexico. European influence has been felt throughout the entire region, primarily in the use of instruments which were imported and adapted in local cultures. The most important of these has been string instruments, particularly the guitar. In addition, European harmony has been integrated into much of the indigenous music.

Norteno musicians, playing violin and baja sexto at Tucson Meet Yourself (1988).
Photo © David Burckhalter. Courtesy of Jim Griffith and the Southwest Folklore Center, Tucson, Arizona.

The Spanish, who came to Central and South America during the late fifteenth and early sixteenth century, found well-established and elaborate Indian cultures, notably the Incas, Aztecs, and Mayas. The Mayas in Mexico worshipped their gods with music and dance. The Aztecs of Central America similarly used music to propitiate gods and control natural events, whether rain, hunt, or harvest. In Peru, the Incas developed elaborate ceremonies to worship the sun. They used the same word, *taqui*, to represent both music and dance. Although there is no recorded evidence how their music sounded, there are extant instruments which show the level of sophistication these cultures attained in music. The Aztecs used drums made of hollowed-out tree trunks called *huehuetis* for signalling and calling warriors together. The *tiapitzalli* was a pottery flute, much like an ocarina while the *ayacachtli* was a bone maraca filled with small pebbles. They also used conch shell trumpets and various types of rasps made of bone or wood. The music of these Indian cultures included ceremonial, love, epic, and liturgical songs. In short, the Spaniards found a well established culture, including musical activities, when they began to colonize the New World. These cultures were also quick to adopt musical instruments of Europe. Philip II of Spain issued a warning against local Indian musicians who spent their time solely in playing instruments, but it came too late. Indian craftsmen began to imitate European instruments and add them to ensembles. By the middle of the sixteenth century, Indian music took on the flavor of what we call Latin music.

The period of colonization was generally three hundred years, sixteenth through eighteenth centuries, and was a period of assimilation of the three basic cultures of Latin America. The Indians' natural love of music and its place in their cultures made them ready converts to Catholicism. The Spanish used the *auto*, a religious play acted out largely through pantomime, to instruct and involve the Indians in liturgy. Importation of African slaves provided an additional dimension of music. Church music and European instruments, along with genres and forms of Spain and Portugal, became the catalyst of Latin music.

Music of Mexico and Central America

The history of Mexico is long, its culture rich and diverse, including the music of Indians before the coming of the Spaniards as well as the entire colonial period, 1521-1821. During this period, European music was part of worship in Mexican churches and cathedrals. In this section, we will examine a few recent popular traditions that are often heard in the United States, particularly in the Southwest.

European music became part of the culture during the Spanish conquest of Mexico, allowing diatonic scales and triadic harmony to be heard and incorporated into Mexican traditions. A typical Mexican song uses a profusion of parallel thirds to accompany a melodic line. For this reason, music of Mexico has a European flavor, colored by local interpretation, which makes it easy to understand. Many of the instruments, too, are traditional orchestral instruments or adaptations.

Rural or peasant music in Mexico was known during Colonial times as *son*, a generic term to set it apart from *musica*, which means court or city music. Although the distinction is not as clearly drawn in present day, son is considered grassroots music which can be either sung or danced, or, often, both. One of its most striking characteristics has been complex rhythmic patterns, often shifting between duple and triple divisions in six beats, either successively or simultaneously:

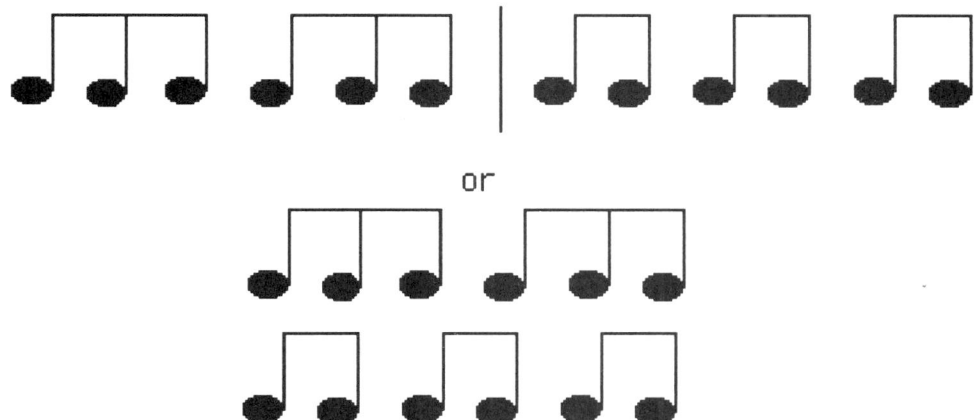

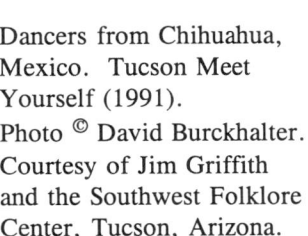

Dancers from Chihuahua, Mexico. Tucson Meet Yourself (1991). Photo © David Burckhalter. Courtesy of Jim Griffith and the Southwest Folklore Center, Tucson, Arizona.

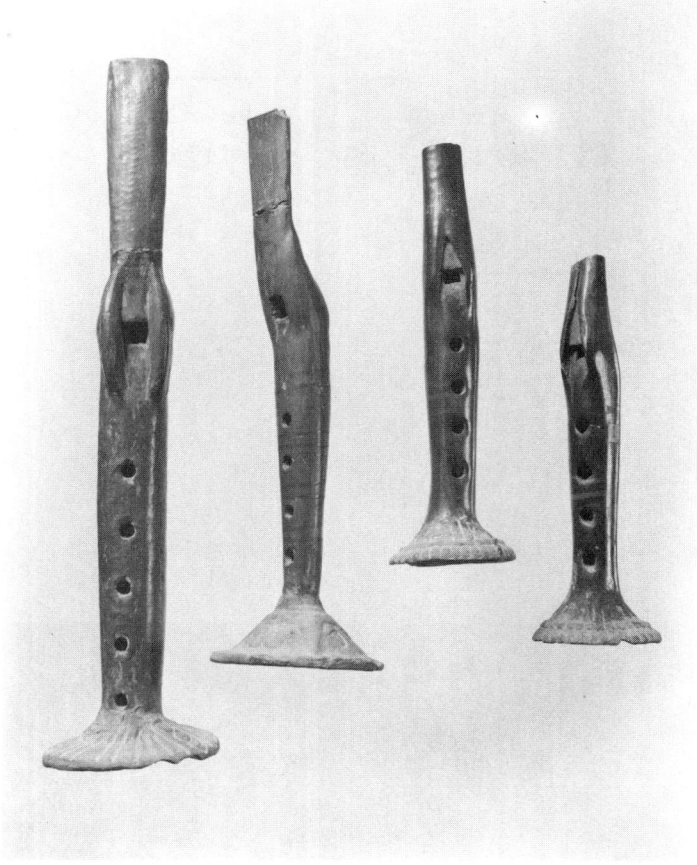

Mexican pottery flutes. Courtesy of The University Museum, University of Pennsylvania, Neg. No. S8-62779.

There are many categories of son, depending on the region from which it is derived, including *chilena*, which comes from the Pacific coast region in Mexico, *huapango*, which derives from the Huastec region, that is, the Gulf Coast below Tampico. The huapango is a fast and complicated dance, done by one couple or several. It typically has three accompanying figures, one in two-four, one in three-four, and one in six-eight, creating interesting cross-rhythms. The *jarocho* comes from Veracruz while the *jarana* is from the Yucatan peninsula. Dances and instruments used for accompaniment vary, depending on the region from which the son comes, but typically has verses and refrains, including alternation between voices and instruments. When guitars are used for accompaniment, the typical strumming pattern used is called *rasqueado*.

When son is sung, the text is stereotypical, dealing with women and love or reciting the attributes of a city or region. When dancing is included, it only occurs in instrumental sections. Son are danced by couples, not in group formations, and the feet are used in a percussive manner on floor or platform, a style called *zapateado*. Many son end with a *despedida*, a "leave-taking", in which the composer and performers are identified.

Mexican guitarist, Huatabampo, Sonora. Courtesy © David Burckhalter (1990).

One type of son, the *corrido* is a folk idiom that has evolved into a popular form of music, much like a folk ballad. It tells an epic story, when sung, about current events or people, whether revolutionary figures or bandits. The corrido evolved during the nineteenth century, a period of political uncertainty in Mexico. It therefore can be satirical, serving as an artistic vehicle to comment on social and economic problems. The form is strophic, even when totally danced. Dancing occurs in a line, not as couples. The corrido is derived from the Spanish *romance*, a genre which extolled the virtues of legendary Spaniards as early as the fourteenth century. Both romance and corrido are based on poetry set in quatrains, rhymed stanzas in four lines, each with eight syllables. Interest occurs in the music for listeners because of the interplay between the metrical nature of the lyrics and the irregular meter of the music. Although the instrumental accompaniment is the same for each strophe or stanza, the performers often slightly vary the musical interludes that occur between strophes. The corrido, as expected, ends with a despedida, such as "Now with this I say farewell."

Conjunto, with baja sexto and button accordion. Guaymas, Sonora.
Courtesy © David Burckhalter (1990).

The *canción*, by contrast, is less epic than the corrido, using sentimental and emotional lyrics. It is not designed for dancing, but, rather, to express great pathos or at least a broken heart. Whereas the corrido will have a steady tempo, there are many deviations in a canción, particularly the use of rubato. A special category which developed during the Mexican Revolution of 1910 is the *canción ranchera*, which deals with soldiers and war. Both the canción and corrido are active genres, with contemporary musicians expressing sentiments about the farm labor movement or pollution through these genres.

Norteno musicians at Tucson Meet Yourself (1991). Photo © David Burckhalter. Courtesy of Jim Griffith and the Southwest Folklore Center, Tucson, Arizona.

The instrumental groups of Mexican son are varied, depending on the region from which the music derives. There are two rather standardized ensembles which appear as universal groups. The *conjunto* (ensemble), associated with Mexican music of Texas and northeastern Mexico, uses a button accordion, undoubtedly derived from German influence in Mexico during the nineteenth century, and the *baja sexto*, a twelve-string guitar. The accompaniment is typically simple 1-2-3-4 or 1-2-3, undoubtedly derived, respectively, from the European polka (*polca*) and waltz (*vals*), two forms popular in Mexico in the nineteenth century. The better known *mariachi* group uses two violins, a *vihuela*, five-course guitar, *jarana*, larger five-course guitar, and *guitarron*, a bass guitar with four strings. The guitarron is a recent addition to mariachis, the harp formerly having been used. During the 1930s, partly due to the need for greater definition in the musical group for radio broadcast, trumpets were added. Compared to the conjunto, mariachis accompaniments are more complex and rhythmically involved.

"Los Changitos Feos", a mariachi group at Tucson Meet Yourself (1991). Photo © David Burckhalter. Courtesy of Jim Griffith and the Southwest Folklore Center, Tucson, Arizona.

Panama, a Central American country bound by Costa Rica on the north, Colombia on the south, is a blend of Indian, African, and European cultures as well. This region, as compared to Mexico, had large populations of Africans who were imported as slaves. They consequently influenced local musical practice. Panama is at a geographical confluence of all Latin cultures, creating some of the most colorful music of the entire region.

Many of its string instruments are derived from European models, including the *mejoranera*, a small five-string guitar, and the *bocona*, a larger model. These are tuned to sound a triad in second inversion, the six-four position, which provides a unique flavor to harmonic progressions. The *rabel* is a three-string fiddle, derived perhaps from the Arabic rabab. The modern violin is frequently used in Panamanian music as is the accordion. By contrast, percussion instruments are derived from Indian and African prototypes. The *tambora* is a large cylindrical double-head drum played with two mallets while the *pujador* (medium-sized) and *repicador* (small) are smaller, single-headed drums with frames that conically taper downward. They are struck by the performer's hands and sound much like Cuban bongo drums. Timbre can be varied by striking location as well as slightly raising the drum from the floor with one's knees. The *guachara* is a rasp or guiro made from a large gourd with notches scored on its surface.

Mariachi violinist.
Photo © David Burckhalter.
Courtesy of Jim Griffith
and the Southwest Folklore
Center, Tucson, Arizona.

The *tamborito* is the national dance of Panama, a dance that once was considered licentious. It dates from the seventeenth century and is usually presented by a female singer with chorus echoing on a refrain, reflecting an African antiphonal structure. The sung portion of the tamborito is called *tonada* and is in duple time. It is frequently major in tonality. The singing is typically accompanied by the three Panamanian drums, tambora, pujador, and repicador, as well as hand clapping which uses these three rhythmic patterns:

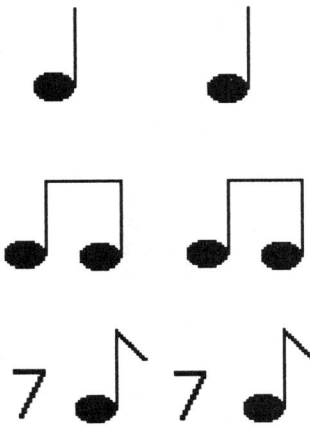

Drums maintain the steady beat, which accelerates as the dance progresses, as well as added triplet rhythms and anticipatory syncopations. A single couple face each other within a circle of hand clappers and singers in the tamborito. Drummers are also placed within the enclosed circle.

The Panamanian *cumbia*, which refers both to singing and dancing, is derived from Africa. It is also in duple time. Melody is played on the violin, rabel, or even accordion while accompaniment is provided by bocona or mejoranera and tambora. Harmonic structure alternates between tonic and dominant chords. This dance has been termed the "representation of the erotic struggle between the male and the female." Several mixed couples participate when the cumbia is danced, revolving around the instrumentalists. Women dancers each carry lighted candles in one hand. Since this dance was integrated into polite society, it integrated movements similar to the polka and was known as the *cumbia de salon*. The rustic, more sensuous dance became known as the *cumbia plebeya*.

The *mejorana* is a dance or song. When vocal, men are the performers, and it is called *socavon*. It is performed antiphonally, the leader calling in a falsetto voice. When danced, two rows, one of men, the other of women, face each other, much like a Yankee square dance. Movement includes advancing to the opposite row, retreating, and even passing through. There are two types of steps used in mejorana, the *paseo*, which is a strolling step, and the *zapateado*, a stamping movement.   The mejorana is accompanied by two guitars. The metric structure is both simple and compound duple, sometimes superimposed, creating hemiola through rhythmic intricacy.

Another dance of Panama the *punto* is a spirited one in compound duple time, that is, a triplet flow over the beat. The melody, however, is simple duple time, arranged into a period, with antecedent and consequent.

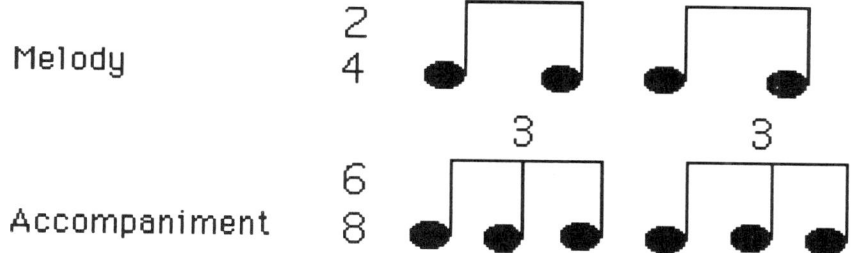

The punto is danced by engaged couples as viewers toss money at their feet. Both paseo and zapateado steps are used. Although most puntos are major, a minor version is called *coco*.

Guatemalan musicians, guitar and marimba, in studio picture. Courtesy of The University Museum, University of Pennsylvania, Neg. No. S4-140732.

Music of the Caribbean

Musician and his marimba on the move, Guatemala. Courtesy of The University Museum, University of Pennsylvania, Neg. No. S4-140733.

The Caribbean refers to Cuba, Jamaica, Haiti, Dominican Republic, and Puerto Rico, as well as the Lesser Antilles grouping, which includes Antigua, Guadeloupe, Martinique, Trinidad, Grenada, Tobago, and Curacao. This area is commonly referred to as the West Indies. Since these cultures had considerable contact with Africa, they have produced unique musical styles which continue to permeate many styles of contemporary popular music as well, particularly reggae. Although this area was first contacted by Spanish explorers, it was generally neglected because of the abundant resources that were more available in South and Central America.

Steel drummers from Trinidad. Courtesy of the American Folklife Center, Smithsonian Institution, Photo No. 88-15009-30.

Puerto Rico, which has territorial status with the United States, was visited by Columbus during his second trip to the New World. Colonization began in the early sixteenth century. The predominate traits of its music are African and Spanish with little incorporated of the Arawak, the native tribe. The Puerto Rico *plena* is much like the Mexican corrido, a topical ballad, but is considerably shorter. It may be satirical, describing a person or event. Compared to the corrido or the Spanish romance, the derivation for both of these New World genres, its melody and accompaniment are more rhythmic vital, suggesting derivation from African models. The plena consists of verse and refrain, the former often improvised by the soloist, with chorus joining in on the repetitive refrain. Most plena are simple duple time, incorporating this rhythmic pattern:

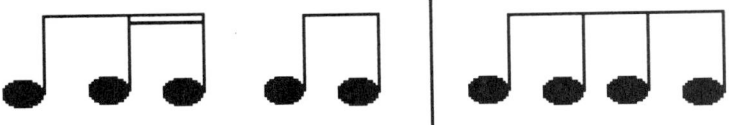

Puerto Rican bomba dancers. Courtesy of the American Folklife Center, Smithsonian Institution, Photo No. 89-17185-10.

Other genres of Puerto Rico include the *bomba*, which is danced by individuals or couples enclosed by a circle of singers. Antiphony between leader and chorus is typical, and accompaniment is provided by drums. It has been associated with the *bamboula*, a dance of the Antilles islands, as well as the *belen* and *cunya*, other dances of the Caribbean region. The *baquine* is a lament sung for a dead child the night before burial while the *seis* is a genre derived from Spain. It is based on stanzas of poetry arranged in ten-lines (*decima*) and sung by a soloist with guitar accompaniment or two singers who compete with one another in the lyrics they create. When danced, it is done as couples. The seis alternates six-eight and two-four time in spirited tempos. The *aquinaldo* is a Christmas song which is sung by carolers from house to house. It is characterized by its syncopated accompaniment.

Samba school. Courtesy of the Library of Congress Collections LCUSZ62:211487.

Puerto Rican instruments include the *cuatro*, a guitar-like instrument derived from the Spanish vihuela. It has either four double courses, which provide its name, tuned in fourths, but often an added fifth string, whether single or double, added to extend the lower range. The *tiple* and *tres* are smaller versions of the cuatro, the latter, as its name suggests, with three strings. Maracas and guiros are indigenous idiophones but the *marimbula*, a lamellophone which provides bass accompaniment in many ensembles, is derived from the African mbira.

Cuatro player, Jalq'a, Bolivia. Courtesy of the American Folklife Center, Smithsonian Institution, Photo No. 91-15028-34.

Cuba is the largest island in the West Indies. The names of its music and dance are well known in the United States because of their popularization from the 1930s on. The genres are numerous yet distinct and include the *areyta*, *guaracha*, *danzon*, *zapateo*, *punto*, *son*, as well as *rumba*, *mambo*, *chachacha*, and *bolero*. A few will be examined here.

The *guaracha* is a solo dance used in theatre performances or a sung piece based on quatrains in which solo and chorus alternate in binary form. The texts are topical, often mischievous and satirical. As a genre, it is frequently associated with popular opera. The Cuban *habanera* (Havana air) is characterized by one of these patterns:

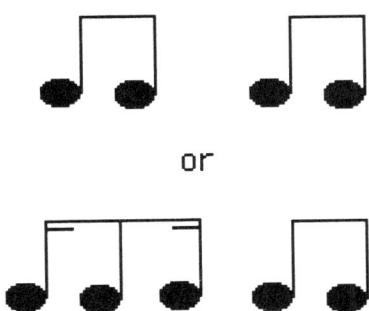

the former, a rhythm used by Bizet in his famous habanera from *Carmen*. *Zapateo* is a rustic dance characterized by stamping of the feet, using short steps and heel blows. The meter is six-eight, with each eighth note of the six receiving vigorous strumming on the accompanying Cuban guitars. Most dances, which are also sung, tend to incorporate satirical and topical lyrics to provide interest for listeners, making improvisation of words an important component. Tempos are exuberant and rhythms a combination of simple and compound time. These are linked successively to create hemiola or simultaneously to create polyrhythm. Rhythmic vitality is an integral component of most Latin music, particularly Cuban.

More contemporary dances are the *rumba*, which is danced as couples, the *chachacha*, which is named for the three stamps the feet make during performance, the *mambo*, and *bolero*, which is a two-part song form. Most of these, when vocalized, use meaningless vocables in a regular phrase structure. The Cuban *conga*, the official dance of *comparsas*, that is, carnival parades preceding Lent, is characterized by this rhythmic motive:

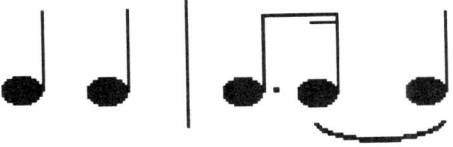

It is danced during Carnival by paraders in bright, colorful costumes and is characterized by a repeated eight-bar phrase accompanied by syncopated ostinati.

Carnival dancers.
Courtesy of the Library of Congress Collections LCUSZ62:211487.

Cuban instruments are similar to those used in much of the Caribbean and Central America. They include the *guiro*, a scraper or rasp, also known as the *rascador*. *Claves* are two matched cylindrical hardwood sticks. One is cradled in the performer's hand, which acts as a resonator, and struck by the other. *Maracas* are a pair of gourds, filled with seeds, that are shaken. *Bongo drums* are two single-head drums, one small, one large, that are played as a unit. The *tumbadora* is a single-head drum made in three sizes, each of which is conical with a slight bulge in the middle. The largest, also called a *conga*, is nearly a yard high. The smaller conga is called *enkomo*. The *cenceroo* is a piece of metal which is struck as rhythmic accompaniment, much like an African bell. The *quijada del burro* is a tambourine made from the jawbone of an ass to which small jingles have been attached. Cubans also use common household items in their musical ensembles, including bottles and frying pans. Accompaniment is provided by guitars and cuatros. Many European wind instruments, especially the saxophone, have been integrated in contemporary Cuban popular music, but the African influence is nonetheless the compelling factor.

Conga drummer. Courtesy of the American Folklife Center, Smithsonian Institution, Photo No. 90-0099-13.

Cuban drummers. Courtesy of the American Folklife Center, Smithsonian Institution, Photo No. 89-17223-27.

Music of Spanish-Speaking South America

South American panpipes.
Courtesy of the Library of Congress Collections LCUSZ62:6042.

There are numerous nations considered as part of Spanish-speaking South America since Spain was the principal colonizer of this continent. We will discuss only two here.

Peru was headquarters for Spain during the conquest of South America, being as important as Mexico during the conquistador era. The indigenous people of Peru apparently had an active musical life long before the arrival of the Spaniards, however. The Chavin culture (1200-400 B.C.) used notched flutes and conch-shell trumpets while the Paracas people (400 B.C.-400 A.D.) had bone flutes, panpipes, and trumpets. Later cultures, including Chimu, Nazca, and Tiahuanaco, had kettledrums, rattles, and more sophisticated aerophones. When the Spaniards finally arrived in Peru, the active culture was the Incan. Most native traditions are derived from the Incas, tempered by European influence. The Indian influence is the prevailing component of Peruvian music, particularly in the more isolated highlands. Lowland areas were more directly influenced by European models. There are more than thirty native groups, including Witoto, Ocaina, Yagua, Iquito, Omagua, and Quechua. The latter are direct descendants of the Incas.

Peruvian dancers and dancers.
Courtesy of the Library of Congress Collections LCUSZ62:211487.

Among Peruvian instruments are the *quena*, the name for the notched vertical flute. It is made from either reed or the leg bone of a llama. It has five fingerholes which produce a pentatonic scale, a recurring pitch arrangement in Peruvian music. *Antara* is the name for panpipes, bundles of pipes of different length which are tied together. *Ayariche* is a clay ocarina while conical trumpets, which produce a series of overtones, are called *aylli-quepa*. These are made from either wood or pottery. Other instruments of Peru include maracas, known as *chil-chil* (undoubtedly for the sound they produce when shaken), *tinya*, a double-head cylindrical drum, and *huancar*, a single-head drum.

The music of the Incas as well as their descendants, the Quechua, fits into one of three categories. Ceremonial music, known as *huanca*, is for public presentation, sun worship, and preparation for war. *Harawi* is music of personal enjoyment and intimacy while *huaino* is dance music. Most of the these traditions are still followed by the Quechua. Hymns to the sun, an example of huanca, are still sung. Harawi are performed on flute or are solo songs performed without accompaniment. Huaino include the *cachua*, a round dance performed by betrothed couples.

It is in duple time with even rhythmic patterns and is accompanied by a small drum and flute. The *huaino*, also a dance, is duple time but with syncopation in the accompaniment.

Incan musician, Cuzco, Peru. Courtesy © David Burckhalter (1981).

Music of the lowlands people, known as *mestizo* since it blends Indian and European traditions, includes the *marinera*, a dance in either three-four or six-eight time. Although a partner dance, the couples dance apart, waving handkerchiefs. The tempo is lively. Originally called *chilena*, the name was changed after a war between Chile and Peru in 1879-1883, largely to avoid nomenclature derived from an enemy as well as to honor Peru's navy. Marinera are called *tonadero* in northern Peru. Although marinera are usually major, tonadero are minor.

Panpipe player, Taquile, Peru. Courtesy of the American Folklife Center, Smithsonian Institution, Photo No. 91-15034-3.

Creole music, which is a blend of African and Indian culture, is also present in Peru. Unlike purely Indian music, it incorporates harps, guitars, and *guitarillas*, small, four-string guitars. These play rasqueado, which, it may be recalled, refers to a strumming pattern. In this case, it is a consistent flow of triple time. Creole music includes the *triste*, similar to harawi. Additional dances include the *tanguino*, a slow dance in four-four time and *pasacalle*, a street dance performed during Carnival to accompaniment of a brass band.

Argentina, the second largest country of South America, was named for the silver that the Spanish found in abundance there. Argentina is the Latin word for Spanish *la plata*, which means silver. Its music is a blend of indigenous Andean, Creole, and European music. The style of the gauchos, Argentine cowboys, has been an important influence in music of the country.

Dancers and musicians, Tanquile, Peru. Courtesy of the American Folklife Center, Smithsonian Institution, Photo No. 91-15093-23.

Colombian dancers at Tucson Meet Yourself (1989). Photo © David Burckhalter. Courtesy of Jim Griffith and the Southwest Folklore Center, Tucson, Arizona.

Songs derived from the gaucho tradition include the *vidalta*, consisting of couplets and refrains. It is sung in parallel thirds, accompanied by drum and guitar. The meter is three-four alternating with six-eight. The term literally means "little life of mine." The *estilo* is a typical song of the gauchos, much like an American cowboy ballad, telling of life on the Argentine pampas. It has two sections, one slow and one fast, often changing meter between sections. The typical stanza is decima, that is, ten lines consisting of eight syllables each, suggesting connection to traditional Spanish poetry. Tonality swings between major and minor. The *gato*, meaning "the cat", is a dance for two couples. It is much like a fast waltz, characterized by *escobilleo*, swinging each foot to and fro in turn, while slightly scraping it against the ground. Men's movement includes toe-tapping in place while women move around them. The *escondido* is a dance similar to the gato where the female hides from her partner. *Rancheras* are ranch dances, based on the Polish mazurka, but in six-eight time. The *chamame* is a dance in three-four time, derived from Indian tradition, in which the accompaniment has three triplets followed by two groups of duplets. The *triste* is a slow, melancholy song of love and romance, derived from and similar to the Peruvian genre of the same name.

The dance par excellence of Argentina is undoubtedly the *tango*, which began in the last part of the nineteenth century and became internationally popular in the first part of the twentieth. The tango is a blend of the Andalusian tango, the Cuban habanera, and the indigenous *milonga*, a popular dance of the lower classes of Buenos Aires. Only in the twentieth century did it absorb its characteristic accompanying pattern, which is identical to the habanera, and become elevated to the status of national dance. Usually binary in form, each section consisting of sixteen measures, it is danced by couples.

Music of Brazil

Unlike much of South America, Brazil was colonized by Portugal. The national language is therefore Portuguese. This is the largest country of South America, occupying half the continent. It borders every country of the continent except Ecuador and Chile. It also contains the largest river of the world, the Amazon. As with all Latin cultures, it blends Indian, Negro (Creole), and European influences in a variety of ways. Music of African descent is referred to as *Negra* while the blending of European and Indian traditions is called *Nortista*.

Among Negra music is the *batuque*, which is danced in a circle, using drum and hand clapping accompaniments, often colored by beating on a piece of wood, glass, or iron. The characteristic rhythmic motive is:

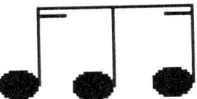

Carnival at Tobago, Trinidad. Courtesy of the American Folklife Center, Smithsonian Institution, Photo No. 88-15126-4.

Considered the forerunner of the samba, it is rhythmic vivacious, using syncopation in the accompanying patterns. The *congada* is a song consisting of short phrases which are shouted rather than sung. The term itself is derived from liturgical plays of Brazilians of color to celebrate the festival of Our Lady of the Rosary, their patron saint. It simulates African incantations and voodoo influences. The *maxixe*, in duple time and moderate tempo, is danced in couples, derived partially from the Argentine tango. The *samba*, national dance of Brazil, is as well known as the Cuban mambo, rumba, and chachacha. Sambas tend to be fast, in duple time and major tonality. There are actually two types of sambas, the rural samba, similar to the rustic batuque, and the urban samba, similar to the maxixe. Sambas are danced by couples as well as groups in circle formation. They are used as music for the infamous Carnival of Rio de Janeiro on Mardi Gras, the Tuesday before Ash Wednesday, which begins the Lenten season of the Catholic Church.

Among Nortista music is the *modinha*, a diminutive of the Portuguese moda. Although more popular in technique and mood, the modinha is much like an aria from Italian opera. It is for solo voice with chamber accompaniment, reflecting traits of Portuguese folksong as much as Neapolitan opera seria. Modinhas are frequently in minor tonality. *Toada*, which is identical to the Spanish tonada, is a folksong, musical setting of quatrains, quintrains, or decimas. When the quatrain is used, a refrain typically follows, signalling a change from slow triple time to lively compound duple. A *chula* is a rustic dance in duple time, usually in a major mode. The *cantilena* or *xacara* is a ballad which tells the story of feudal love, court intrigue, and other subjects derived from European prototypes, nonetheless colored by Brazilian interpretation.

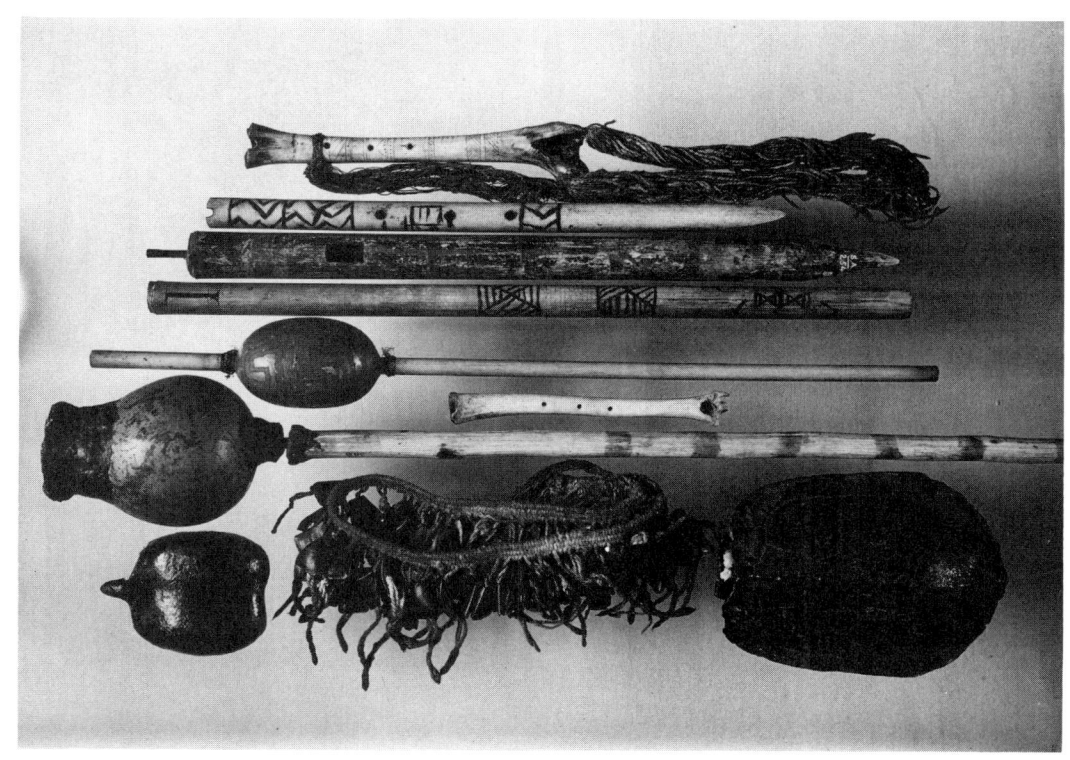

Indian instruments of Brazil (top to bottom)

Jaguar bone flute
3 bamboo flutes (quill changes tone)
Gourd rattle
Bone rattle
Bamboo flute with gourd resonator
Nut rattle (left)
String with animal hooves (middle)
Tortoise shell (right)
(It hums when the hand is rubbed over it and is a secret instrument.
Only the initiated may see it!)

Courtesy of The University Museum, University of Pennsylvania, Neg. No. G8-20794.

Panpipes and native dress, Jalq'a, Bolivia.
Courtesy of the American Folklife Center, Smithsonian Institution,
Photo No. 91-15078-27.

Key Terms and Concepts

Antara
Aquinaldo
Auto
Ayariche
Aylli-Quepa
Bajo Sexto
Baquine
Batuque
Bocona
Bolero
Bomba
Bongo
Cachua
Canción
Cantilena
Cenceroo
Chachacha
Chamame
Chil-Chil
Chilena
Chula
Claves
Coco
Comparsa
Conga
Congada
Conjunto
Corrido
Cuatro
Cumbia
Decima
Despedida
Enkomo
Escobilleo
Escondido
Estilo
Gato
Guachara
Guiro
Guitarilla
Guitarron
Habanera
Harani
Harawi

Huaino
Huanca
Huancar
Huehueti
Jarana
Mambo
Maracas
Mariachi
Marimbula
Marinera
Maxixe
Mejorana
Mejoranera
Mestizo
Milonga
Modinha
Musica
Negra
Nortista
Pasacalle
Paseo
Plena
Pujador
Punto
Quena
Quijada del Burro
Rabel
Ranchera
Rascador
Rasqueado
Repicador
Romance
Rumba
Samba
Seis
Socavon
Son
Tambora
Tamborito
Tango
Tanguino
Taqui
Tinya
Tiple

Toada
Tonada
Tonadero
Tres
Triste
Tumbadora
Vidalta
Vihuela
Xacara
Zapateado
Zapateo

Self-Checking Chapter Review

Match Column II to Column I	
Column I	**Column II**
1. corrido	A. stamping movement
2. estilo	B. Brazilian national dance
3. guiro	C. Cuban dance
4. tumbadora	D. "Mixed" music or tradition
5. mestizo	E. panpipes
6. rumba	F. strolling step
7. zapateado	G. 4-string guitar of Puerto Rico
8. habanera	H. Puerto Rican ballad
9. rasqueado	I. 5-string guitar of Panama
10. cuatro	J. Mexican ballad
11. mejoranera	K. rasp
12 samba	L. Cuban drum
13. antara	M. Havana air
14. plena	N. gaucho ballad
15. paseo	O. strumming technique

Answers			
1.	J	9.	O
2.	N	10.	G
3.	K	11.	I
4.	L	12.	B
5.	D	13.	E
6.	C	14.	H
7.	A	15.	F
8.	M		

Selected Bibliography

Brewster, Mela Sedillo (1938). *Mexican and New Mexican Folk Dances.* Albuquerque: University of New Mexico Press.

Coopersmith, J.M. (1949). *Music and Musicians of the Dominican Republic.* Washington, D.C.: Pan American Union.

Correa de Azevedo, Luiz Heitor (1948). *Brief History of Music in Brazil.* Washington, D.C.: Pan American Union.

Ferguson, Erna (1934). *Fiesta in Mexico.* New York: Knopf.

Luper, Albert T. (1950). *The Music of Argentina.* Washington, D.C.: Pan American Union.

_____ (1950). *The Music of Brazil.* Washington, D.C.: Pan American Union.

Music in Latin America: A Brief Survey (Volume III) (1942). Washington, D.C.: Pan American Union.

Music of Latin America (1963). (Reprint of the Third Edition, 1953). Washington, D.C.: Pan American Union

Pena, Manuel (1985). *The Texas-Mexican Conjunto: History of a Working-Class Music.* Austin: University of Texas Press.

Slonimsky, Nicolas (1945). *Music of Latin America.* New York: Thomas Y. Crowell Company.

Stevenson, Robert (1968). *In Aztec and Inca Territory.* Berkeley: University of California Press.

_____ (1952). *Music in Mexico: A Historical Survey.* New York: Thomas Y. Crowell Company.

Selected Discography

Amerindian Ceremonial Music from Chile
Philips 6586026

Argentina
Folkways Records FW 8841

Argentine Folk Songs
Folkways Records FW 6810

Black Caribs of Honduras, The
Ethnic Folkways Library P 435

Black Music of South America
Nonesuch Records H-72036

Calypso Travels
Folkways Records FW 8733

Cantares de Columbia
Sonolux LP 12-205/IES-49

Cantos de las Posadas
Folkways Records FC 7745

Columbian Instruments
Ethnic Folkways Library FE 4177

Corridos y Canciónes de Aztlan
Xalman SBSR 102980

Danzas del Tawantinsuyo
Odeon del Peru LD-1304

El Alma de Mexico
Gran Disco (Pickwick) K 806

El Hombre Mexicano
Audio Fidelity Stereodisc AFSD 6116

Fiestas of Peru: Music of the High Andes
Nonesuch Records H-72045

Folk Songs of Mexico
Folkways Records FW 8727

Indian Flutes, Harps, and Guitars
Musical Heritage Society Inc. MHS 3164

Indian Marimba: Flutes, Harps, and Guitars, The
Musical Heritage Society Inc. MHS 3238

Indian Music of Mexico:
Seri, Cora, Yaqui, Huichol, Tzotzil
Folkways Records FW 4413

Kingdom of the Sun: Peru's Inca Heritage
Nonesuch Records H-72029

Los Chiriguanos of Paraguay
Nonesuch Records H-72021

Magic of South American Guitar
Musical Heritage Society Inc. MHS 3259

Mariachi Aquilas de Chapala
Folkways Records FW 8870

Mariachi! The Sound of Mexico
Columbia Records ES 1810

Marimba Music of Tehuantepec
University of Washington Ethnic Music Series UWP 1002

Musica Indigena Venezolana
Ministerio de Justicia
Comision Indigenista Nacional

Music of Peru
Folkways Records FE 4415

Music of the Incas
Capitol Records SP-10545

Music of Trinidad
NGS 3297

Music of Guatemala (2 volumes)
Ethnic Folkways Records FE 4212-13

Music of the Maya: Quiches of Guatemala
The Rabinal Achi and Baile de la Canastas
Ethnic Folkways Library FE 4226

Real Mexico, The
Nonesuch Records H-72009

Ritmos de Venezuela
La Compania de Venezuela

Saludos Amigos
Sutton SSU 108

Saudades do Brasil
Musical Heritage Society Inc. MHS 3260

Selecciones de Zarzuela
Columbiana de Discos T 100106

Serenata
Sutton SSU 113

Sones de Jalisco
RCA Victor MKS-1653

Sones of Mexico
Folkways Records FW 6815

Sones y Huapangos de Jalisco
Gran Disco (Pickwick) K 802

Songs and Dances of Bolivia
Folkways Records FW 6871

Songs of Chile
Folkways Records FW 8817

Songs of Mexico
Folkways Records FW 6853

Traditional Music of Mexico
Olympic Records Corporation 6119

Traditional Songs of Mexico
Folkways Records FW 8769

Trio San Antonio
Arhoolie Records 3004

Trinidad Steel Band
Audio Fidelity AFLP 1809

SOURCES OF MATERIAL FOR WORLD MUSIC

Archives of Traditional Music
Morrison Hall
Indiana University
Bloomington, IN 47405

Arhoolie Records
Box 9195
Berkeley, CA 94709

Asch Recordings
701 Seventh Avenue
New York, NY 10036

Audio Fidelity
770 Eleventh Avenue
New York 19, NY

Australian Institute of Aboriginal Studies
P.O. Box 553
Canberra City, A.C.T. 2601

Barnes and Noble Bookstores
126 Fifth Avenue
New York, NY 10011

Canyon Records
834 N. 7th Avenue
Phoenix, AZ

Celestrial Harmonies
P.O. Box 30122
Tucson, AZ 85751
      Phone (602) 326-4400

Center for Music Television
Eugene Enrico, Director
School of Music
University of Oklahoma
Norman, OK 73019
    Phone (405) 325-2081

Chinese Music Society of North America
P.O. Box 5275, One Heritage Plaza
Woodridge, IL 60517
    Phone (708) 910-1551
    Fax   (708) 910-1561

China Record Company
Distributed by Guozi Shudian
China Publications Centre
P.O. Box 399
Beijing, The People's Republic
    of China

CMP Records
P.O. Box 1129
5166 Kreuzau

Coyote Oldman Music
Perfect Pitch
1450 6th Street
Berkeley, CA 94710

Counterpoint/Esoteric Records
1313 North Vine Stree
Hollywood 28, CA

D.K. Agencies
313/74-D, Inderiok
Old Rohtak Road
Delhi-110035, India
    Phone   568445
    Fax   Dikay ND-3616

Everest Records
10920 Wilshire Blvd., Suite 410
Los Angeles, CA 90024

Fortuna Records
P.O. Box 32016
Tucson, AZ 85751

IASPM-Japan
c/o Toru Seyama
2-10-9 Aoba-dai
Takarazuka, Hyogo 665
Japan

Indian House
P.O. Box 472
Taos, NM 87571

Kuckuck Schallplatten
Habsburgerplatz 2
8000 Munchen 40
Germany
      Phone (089) 332078

Lyrichord Discs Inc.
141 Perry Street
New York, NY

Mele O. Hawaii
P.O. Box 3920
Honolulu, Hawaii 96812

Monitor Records
Music of the World
156 Fifth Avenue
New York, NY 10010

Musical Heritage Society Inc.
1710 Highway No. 35
Oakhurst, NJ 07755

Music of the World
P.O. Box 258
Brooklyn, NY 11209-0005

National Geographical Society
Washington, D.C. 20036

Nonesuch Records
1855 Broadway
New York, NY 19923

Olympic Records Corporation
200 West 57th Street
New York, NY 10019

Original Music
418 Lasher Road
Rivoli, NY 12583
    Phone (914) 756-2767
    Fax   (914) 756-2027

Rounder Records Corporation
One Camp Street
Cambridge, MA 02140

Rykodisc
Pickering Wharf Building C-3G
Salem, MA 01970

The Scholar's Choice
622 Sibley Tower
Rochester, NY 14604
    Phone (716) 262-2048
        800- 782-0077
    Fax   (716) 262-2228

Shawanchie Records
P.O. Box 284
Newton, NJ 07860

Smithsonian/Folkways Recordings
Office of Folklife Programs
955 L'Enfant Plaza, Suite 2600
Smithsonian Institution
Washington, DC 20560
    Phone (202) 287-3262

Society for Ethnomusicology
SEM Business Office
Morrison Hall 005
Indiana University
Bloomington, IN 47405

The Southwest Music Publications
P.O. Box 4552
Santa Fe, NM 87502

Talking Taco Records
P.O. Box 40576
San Antonio, TX 78229-1576

University of Illinois Press
54 E. Gregory Drive
Champaign, IL 61829

The University of Massachusetts Press
Box 429 Amherst, MA 01004
    Phone (413) 545-2217
    Fax   (413) 545-1226

World Music Institute
40 West 27th St.
New York, NY 10001
    Phone (212) 545-7536
    Fax   (212) 889-2771

World Pacific Records
Liberty Records Inc.
Los Angeles, CA 90028

W. W. Norton & Company, Inc.
500 Fifth Avenue
New York, NY 10110

INDEX

A

Abbasid, 93, 102, 104
Ab Fo, 307
Aborigine, 254, 255, 256, 257
Absolute music, 33
Abu, 303
Accented Beat, 32, 102
Accidental, 22
Accordion, 9, 332, 333, 334, 336
Additive, 66, 257, 296
Additive Form, 36, 37
Adenkum, 307
Adhan (azan), 95, 118
Aerophone, 38, 39, 215, 217, 218, 242, 257, 282, 303, 307, 316, 317, 318, 346
Africa, 290-324, 327, 328, 334, 335, 336, 339, 341, 344, 349, 351, 352
    Congo, 293, 309-313
    East Africa, 293, 302-304
    Guinea Coast, 293, 304-309
    Khoi-San, 292, 300-302
    Sub-Sahara, 293, 314-316
Agidigbo, 309
Agogo, 309
Ai, 182
Aje, 247, 259
Ajinas (jins), 97, 98
Ajza, 102
Alall, 248
Alap, 70-72, 74, 79, 80, 101, 104
Alapana, 70
Algaitha, 311
Alto (c1) Clef, 15
Alto (contralto), 42
Amsa, 63

Anashid, 119
Angklung, 223, 228
Animism, 255
Antara, 347
Antecedent, 34, 35, 336
Antibaddha, 70
Antiphonal, 295, 296, 335, 336, 340
Anuvadi, 63
Apache, 266, 276, 277, 280, 281
Apache Fiddle, 280, 281
Aquinaldo, 341
Arab, 91-126, 206, 213, 217, 224, 303, 304, 314, 315, 334
Areyta, 342
Argentina, 349-351
Arohana, 62, 63
Arueru, 248
Assonance, 116
Astaire, Fred, 7
Asymmetric Meter, 33, 68
Ataba, 116, 117
Atenteben, 307
Athabascan, 268, 276-277, 279
Atikomal, 61
Atitvra, 61
Atumpan, 307
Augmented, 28
Australia, 234, 253-259
Auto, 328
Avarohana, 62, 63
Avarta, 66, 67
Ayacachtli, 328
Ayariche, 347
Aylli-quepa, 347
Azmari, 304

B

Baal, 316
Bachi, 190, 191
Bagpipe, 25
Bajo Sexto, 327, 332, 333
Balophon, 311, 312, 316, 318
Balungen, 216, 217, 219, 224
Bamboula, 340
Bamm, 106
Ban, 150, 151
Bangia, 316
Baquine, 340
Bardasht, 101
Barenboim, Daniel, 10
Baris, 227
Barong, 227
Bass, 42
Bass (f) Clef, 15
Batangan, 219, 223
Batuque, 351, 352
Baya, 78
Bayin System, 140
Beat, 31, 32, 66, 69, 102, 207, 212, 216, 256, 272, 273, 296, 298, 306, 336
Bedug, 218, 223
Beganna, 304
Beksan, 226
Belembaupachot, 247, 259
Belembautuyan, 247, 259
Belen, 340
Bendir, 112
Berlin, Irving, 13
Bianjing, 141, 148, 149, 151
Bian Tone, 138, 172, 213
Bianzhong, 148, 151
Bin, 72, 79
Binary, 70
Biwa, 191-192, 197
Bocona, 334, 336
Bol, 69-70, 71, 78, 79
Bolero, 342, 343
Bolivia, 325
Bolon, 307
Bomba, 340
Bonang, 221-222, 223, 224, 226

Bonang Barung, 221, 222
Bonang Panerus, 221
Bonang Penembung, 221-222
Bongo, 334, 344
Bradwom, 307
Bragors, 307
Brass Family, 39, 40
Brazil, 351-353
Buddhism, 130, 131, 135, 169, 170, 177, 194, 196
Bu'd Tanee Ny, 96
Bugaku, 166, 174, 175, 191, 192
Buka, 217
Bullroarer, 251, 259, 282, 301
Bunraku, 182-183, 190
Burmese, 40
Butterfly Dance, 272-273
Bwarux, 248

C

Cachua, 347
Call-response, 295, 298, 303, 307, 313
Calung, 222
Cancion, 332
Cancion Ranchera, 332
Cantilena, 352
Cantus Firmis, 209, 210, 216, 217
Canvas Dance, 274
Carnatic, 54, 61, 65, 98, 100
Carribbean, 326, 327, 338-345
Caste System, 48
Celempung, 217, 223
Cenceroo, 344
Ceng-ceng, 223
Cent, 17, 55, 56, 60, 96, 135, 137, 138, 139, 212, 213
Chachacha, 342, 343, 352
Chamame, 351
Chamorita, 246-247
Chamorro, 246-247
Chappa, 196, 197
Chicago Symphony Orchestra, 2, 10
Chikari, 74
Chil-chil, 347
Chilena, 330, 348

China, 127-165, 169, 171, 185, 190, 192, 193, 206, 211, 213, 224, 227
Chord, 25-31, 192
Chordophone, 38, 39, 40, 185, 189, 191, 192, 194, 215, 217, 242, 280, 303, 307, 310, 315, 317, 318
Choshi, 172
Chromatic, 24
Chula, 352
Chwago, 171
Ciblon, 218, 223
Cipher Notation, 143, 145, 215, 216
Claves, 344
Clef, 14-15
Coco, 337
Cole, Nat King, 7
Colotomic, 210, 211, 216, 222-223, 224
Comparsa, 343
Complete Cadence, 34, 35
Confucius, 128, 129, 130, 131, 135, 141
Conga, 343, 344, 345
Congada, 352
Congo Region, 293, 309-313
Conjunct, 103
Conjunto, 332, 333
Consequent, 34, 35, 336
Container Rattle, 279
Contralto (alto), 42
Corrido, 117, 331, 332, 339
Corroboree, 253, 255-256
Creole, 349, 351
Cuatro, 341, 342, 352
Cuba, 342-345, 352
Cumbia, 336
Cumbia de Salon, 336
Cumbia Plebeya, 336
Cunya, 340

D

Dadaiko, 195, 197
Dagu, 150
Dalang, 224, 225
Daluka, 316
Dan, 154, 155, 157, 180, 185
Danmono, 185, 188

Danzon, 342
Darabukka, 102, 111, 114, 316
Dastgah-ha (dastgah), 101
Davis, Miles, 1
Davui, 252, 259
Dawr, 105
Dawuro, 307
Daya, 78
Debayashi, 181
Debusch, 248, 259
Decima, 340, 351, 352
Deer Dancer, 275
Derebesbes, 248
Derua, 252, 259
Despedida, 330, 332
Dhrupad, 80
Di, 151, 151, 154, 156
Diao, 138
Diatonic, 17, 18, 23, 328
Didjeridu, 257, 258, 259
Dilruba, 72
Diminished, 28
Disjunct, 103, 104
Dissonance, 29, 63, 71, 72, 210
Djambar, 256
Dobeit, 315
Dodecaphonic, 24
Dominant, 29, 63, 78, 98, 214
Dominant chord, 29, 336
Dominant Seventh Chord, 29
Domingo, Placido, 5
Donno, 307
Dorian, 23
Dotaku, 170
Dreamtime, 254, 255
Drone, 25, 73, 74, 75, 250, 252, 257, 271, 276
Druta, 67
Duff (daff), 112, 114
Dulali, 252, 259
Dum, 103
Dundun, 309, 317
Duple Time, 32, 156, 239, 303, 328, 335, 336, 340, 348, 352
Durub, 104
Dynasties (Chinese), 132-135

E

East African Region, 293, 302-304
Eb, 247
Eighth-tone, 17
Eldolem, 248
Electrophone, 38, 39
Embilta, 304
Embu, 175
Enkomo, 344
Equal Temperament, 139
Erhu, 146-147, 151, 156
Escobilleo, 351
Escondido, 351
Eskimo, 277-279
Estilo, 351
Ethiopia, 293, 302, 303, 304

F

Fagono, 243
Fakaniua, 242
Fangufangu, 242, 259
Fasil, 105
Fifth, 28, 55, 60, 63, 98, 108, 139, 146, 313
Flat (♭), 16
Flathead, 274
Form, 33-37, 70-72, 104-105
Fret, 74, 100, 107, 144, 145, 151, 190, 191, 211
Fue, 194, 197
Fushi, 182

G

Gagaku, 166, 169, 170, 174-176, 177, 191, 192, 194, 195, 196
Gakuso, 188
Gamaka, 65, 66, 70, 188
Gambang, 222, 223
Gamelan, 205-210, 216-228
Gamelan Angklung, 228
Gamelan Gede, 227
Gamelan Gong, 227
Gamelan Gong Kebyar, 227
Gamelan Semar Peluginang, 227
Gamelan Wayang, 227
Gangsa, 219, 222
Gara-gara, 226
Garamut, 251, 259
Gardagi, 315, 316
Gat, 70-72, 79, 101
Gato, 351
Gehu, 151
Gender, 207, 220, 221, 223, 224
Gender Barung, 220
Gender Panerus, 220
Gender Penembung (Slentem), 220, 222, 223
Gending, 216, 217
Gerongan, 224
Geza, 181
Ghammaz, 98
Ghana, 293, 304-307
Ghazal, 81, 95, 117
Gidayu, 181
Gidayu-bushi, 181
Gita, 50
Gling-bu, 65
Godan, 185
Goje, 309
Gong, 131, 138, 205, 206, 207, 210, 213, 217, 221, 222, 226
Gong Ageng, 213, 216, 217, 222, 223
Gospel Motivator, 3
Grand Canyon Cowboy Band, 10
Gregorian Chant, 25, 37
Griot, 294, 295
Guachara, 334
Guaracha, 342, 343
Gugu, 316
Guinea Coast Region, 293, 304-309
Guiro, 344
Guitarilla, 349
Guitarron, 333
Guru, 51, 52, 75
Gusheh-ha (gusheh), 101

H

Habanera, 343, 351
Haka, 244
Half-step, 15, 39, 41, 213
Harawi, 347, 349
Harmonic Minor, 22
Harmony, 25-31, 248, 250, 327
Harp, 94, 266, 333, 349
Hauta, 197
Hawaii, 238-242
Hayashi, 177, 194, 196
Hemiola, 296, 336, 343
Heptatonic, 17, 18, 138, 212, 215, 303, 311, 312
Heterophony, 108, 140, 156, 179, 185, 190, 194, 210, 216, 224
Heterorhythm, 256
Hexatonic, 24, 271, 273
Hichiriki, 194, 197
Hi'ili, 240, 259
Himene, 238, 242
Himene Tarava, 242
Hinduism, 49, 50, 52, 54, 205, 208, 227
Hindustani, 54, 61, 98
Hirajoshi, 187, 190
Hocket, 210, 295, 299
Ho Engoe, 301, 302
Hoko Ni'au, 252, 259
Homophony, 30, 192
Honchosi, 190
Hopi, 270, 271, 272
Ho'opa'a, 239
Huaino, 347, 348
Huanca, 347
Huancar, 347
Huangzhong, 136, 137, 139
Huapango, 330
Huda, 92
Hueheuti, 328
Hula, 238, 239, 240, 241
Hula Ku I Luna, 239
Hula Noho I Lalo, 239
Huqin, 146-147, 151
Hyoshigi, 196

I

Idiophone, 38, 39, 194, 196, 217, 219-224, 242, 279, 317, 318
Ikuda, 187
Incomplete Cadence, 34, 35
India, 47-90, 205, 206, 211, 214, 224
Indonesia, 204-234, 235
Insen, 173
Interval, 25, 26, 39
Ipu Hula, 239, 240, 241
Iqa'at (iqa), 102-104
Iro, 182
Islam, 49, 92, 93, 95, 118, 205, 303, 310, 314, 315
Ivory Coast, 293, 305, 307
Iwato, 187

J

Japan, 166-203, 206, 211, 224
Jarana, 330, 333
Jarocho, 330
Jati, 48
Jazz, 6, 41, 42, 72, 304
Jegog, 228
Jegogan, 222
Jew's Harp, 247
Jhala, 70, 71
Ji, 182
Jiangu, 150
Jiazhong, 136
Jidaimono, 180
Jilel, 247, 259
Jimokmok, 247, 259
Jing, 154, 155
Jins, 97, 98
Jiuta, 185
Johakyu, 170, 180, 185
Jor, 70

K

Kabuki, 169, 176, 179-181, 190, 194, 196, 197
Kachina, 270, 271, 272
Ka Eke'eke, 240, 259
Kakaki, 331
Kaki, 188
Kakko, 195, 197
Kala'au, 240, 259
Kamanja, 108, 109
Ka Maoto, 301
Kampita, 65
Kangen, 174, 175, 191, 192, 194
Kapa, 242
Karakia, 244
Karawitan, 226
Karna, 64, 95, 115
Katarai, 195
Kazgi, 278
Keho, 245, 259
Kelenang, 211
Kempul, 216, 222
Kempur, 211
Kempyang, 216, 222, 223
Kendang, 204, 207, 208, 218, 224
Kendang Gending, 219, 223
Kendang Ketipung, 219, 223
Kengyo, Yatsuhashi, 184
Kenong, 216, 222, 223
Kenya, 293, 302, 303
Kepatepa, 239
Kepatihan, 216
Kerar, 304
Ketawang, 217
Ketchak, 227
Ketuk, 216, 222, 223
Key Signature, 16, 19, 20, 22
Khafif, 92, 104
Khali, 69
Khayal, 80
Khoi-San Region, 292, 300-302
Ki, 178
Kimiuta, 185, 197
Kiranam (kriti), 81
Kiri, 180

Kiva, 270, 271
Klenengan, 226
Kokyu, 192
Komabue, 194, 197
Komagaku, 171, 175
Komal, 61
Komuso, 193
Kora, 294, 309, 316
Korea, 171
Koto, 168, 184, 185-188, 190, 194, 197
Kotoba, 182
Ko-tsuzumi, 181, 195, 196, 197
Kouta, 197
Krar, 304
Kraton, 216
Kumi, 185, 188
Kumoi, 187
Kundi, 316
Kundu, 250, 251, 259
Kunqu, 154
Kyo, 178
Kyogen, 178

L

Lali, 252, 259
Lamellophone, 300, 301, 309, 311, 312, 316, 317, 318, 341
Lara, 213, 214, 215
Latin America, 325-360
Laya, 66
Layali, 105, 118
Legong, 226-227
Lekhitlane, 301
Lekolilo, 301
Lesiba, 301
Liletsa Tsa Matsoho, 301
Liletsa Tsa Molomo, 301
Linzhong, 135, 136
Lithophone, 141, 149
Logo, 244, 259
Lu, 135-140
Luo, 149
Lute, 40, 72, 94, 99, 105, 134, 144, 145, 190, 318
Lydian, 23

Lyre, 37, 303, 304, 316, 318

M

Mabda, 98
Macro-form, 34-35
Made, 247, 259
Madhyama, 67
Maemae, 245
Magadizing, 303
Mah, 103
Major, 17, 18, 19, 20, 21, 25, 28, 61, 335, 337, 348, 351, 352
Major Third, 27
Makam, 101
Mali, 293, 294, 309, 314, 315, 318
Mambo, 342, 343, 352
Mangae, 301
Maori, 244-245
Maqamat (maqam), 96-102, 104
Maracas, 344, 347
Mariachi, 333, 334, 335
Marimba, 337, 338
Marimbula, 341
Marinera, 348
Masenqo, 304
Matra, 66, 67, 68, 69, 79
Mawal, 105, 117
Maxixe, 352
Mbira, 300, 301, 341
Mbo Tong, 311
Mebachi, 195
Mehta, Zubin, 5
Mejorana, 336
Mejoranera, 334, 336
Meke, 252
Mela, 54-66, 74, 98
Melanesia, 235, 250-253
Mele, 238, 239, 240
Mele Hula, 239, 240
Melodic Minor, 22, 23
Melody, 13-24, 52-66, 96-102, 135-140, 171-173, 211-217, 239, 271, 272, 277, 298
Membranophone, 38, 39, 194, 217, 219, 242, 279, 280

Messenger Feast, 277-278
Mestizo, 348
Metallophone, 205, 206, 211, 217, 219-222
Meter, 66
Meter Signature, 32
Metric, 32
Mexico, 327, 328-333, 334, 346
Micro-form, 34, 35
Micronesia, 235, 246-249, 250
Microtone, 16-17, 40, 60, 80, 248, 256
Milonga, 351
Mimiha, 242, 259
Mind, 65
Minor, 17, 20, 21, 23, 28, 61, 337, 348, 351, 352
Minor Third, 27
Minuet and Trio, 36
Mixed Meter, 33
Mixolydian, 23
Mizmar, 111, 112
Modality, 23
Mode, 23, 24, 138, 172, 214, 216
Modinha, 352
Modulation, 24, 30
Moghul, 54
Monophony, 30, 250, 256, 270, 271, 299
Moropa, 301
Moslem, 50, 54
Motive, 34
Motjeko, 301
Mozart, Wolfgang Amadeus, 6, 41, 62
Mridangam, 67, 78
Muezzin, 95, 118
Mugam, 101
Muganeb Kabeer, 96
Muganeb Sagheer, 96
Multiplicative, 66
Munshid, 119
Muqin, 150, 151
Murchana, 65, 66
Musica, 328
Muwashshahat, 105, 119
Mvet, 310, 311

N

Nafa, 242
Nagarat, 102
Nagaski, 188
Nagauta, 197
Nagham, 102
Nagrah, 104
Nakars, 117, 118, 316
Nan, 178
Nanhu, 146
Nara, 51
Native American, 265-289
Natural Minor, 20, 22
Navajo, 266, 269, 276, 277, 280
Nawba, 104-105, 107, 116
Nay, 94, 109, 110, 114
Negra, 351
Netori, 175
Neutral Third, 96, 101
Ngaok, 248, 259
Ngombi, 311
Niagari, 190
Nibaddha, 70
Nigeria, 293, 304, 308-309, 317
Night Dance, 276
Nigin, 185
Nihass, 316
Niju Oshi, 188
Niyaga, 224
Nnawuta, 307
Noh Drama, 169, 170, 177-179, 192, 194, 195, 196
Nokan, 194, 195, 197
Nokku, 65
Nortista, 351
Note-bending, 41
Nrrta, 50
Numerical Designation, 26
Nyo, 178

O

Obachi, 195
Obokano, 303
Oceania, 235-264, 266
Octave, 14, 17, 26, 27, 54, 96, 98, 108, 110, 216, 217, 220, 223, 242, 248, 271, 276, 316
Odava, 63
Oeoe, 242, 259
'Ohe Hano Ihu, 242, 259
Okina, 178
Oli, 239
Onnagata, 179, 181
Opera, 5, 6, 134, 139, 154-157, 342, 352
Oriki, 309
Oriori, 245
Ornaments, 65, 74, 80, 186, 188
Oro, 245
Ostinato, 216, 298, 299, 303, 304, 313, 343
Osu, 188
'Ote'a, 243
O-tsuzumi, 181, 195, 196, 197

P

Padam, 81
Pagan, 303
Pahu Hula, 240, 259
Pakarena, 218
Pakhavaj, 72
Panama, 334-337
Panpipes, 252, 259, 282, 346, 347, 349, 354
Pasacalle, 349
Paseo, 336, 337
Patere, 244
Patet, 214, 215, 217
Pa'u, 243, 259
Peking Opera, 139, 146, 154-157, 196
Pelog, 212-215, 217, 222
Penah, 316
Pengisep, 224
Pengumbang, 224
Pentachord, 97
Pentatonic, 24, 137-138, 143, 172, 173, 187, 194, 212, 213, 215, 253, 271, 273, 303, 313, 316, 347
Percussion Family, 39
Perfect, 27, 28
Perfect Fifth, 27, 55, 60, 135, 137, 214

Period, 34, 35
Peru, 346-349, 350
Pesinden, 224
Phrase, 34, 35
Phrygian, 23
Piba, 145-146, 151, 154, 156, 191
Pi-wang, 60
Plains Indians, 273-275, 279
Plena, 339
Plesedan, 224
Poi, 244
Pokok, 216, 224
Polca, 333
Polynesia, 235, 237, 238-245, 250, 252, 270
Polyphony, 31, 250, 256, 271, 298, 299, 300, 303
Polyrhythm, 296, 298, 300, 343
Popo, 245
Portamento, 41, 65
Pou-Kapa, 242
Primogeniture, 244
Processive Form, 36, 37, 271, 300
Program Music, 33, 34
Psaltery, 107, 108, 114, 147
Pu, 243, 259
Pueblo Indians, 271-273
Puerto Rico, 339-341
Pu'ili, 240, 241, 259
Pujador, 334,,335
Pu Kani, 242, 259
Pu-Ko'e, 243, 259
Pu La'i, 242, 259
Pungi, 72, 79
Puniu, 240, 259
Punto, 336, 337, 342
Purvanga, 57, 70
Putorino, 245
Putra, 52, 53
Pythagorean Comma, 137, 139

Q

Qadisa, 105, 117, 119
Qanun, 94, 107-108, 114
Qarar, 98

Qin, 131, 141-142, 147, 151, 185, 186
Quadruple Time, 32
Qualitative Designation, 27
Quarter-tone, 16, 17, 96, 213
Quatrain, 116, 331, 343, 352
Quena, 347
Quijada del Burro, 344

R

Rabab, 108-109, 113, 116, 217, 316, 334
Rabel, 334, 336
Raga, 52-66, 70, 71, 72, 74, 75, 80, 81, 96, 97, 211, 214
Ragamala, 52
Ragini, 52, 53
Ranchera, 351
Range, 42, 248
Rasa, 50, 51, 52, 63, 70, 80, 101
Rascador, 344
Rasp, 279, 328, 334, 344
Rasqueado, 330, 349
Rebab, 109, 113, 207, 217, 218, 223, 224
Rei, 196, 197
Relative Keys, 20, 21, 22
Reng, 101
Repicador, 334, 335
Return Form, 35, 36, 37
Reyong, 222, 226
Rhythm, 31-33, 66-70, 102-104, 216-217, 296
Rincik, 211, 223
Ritsu, 171-173
Rock, 6, 41
Roei, 174, 175
Rokudan, 185
Romance, 331, 340
Rondo, 36
Rongo, 316
Root, 28
Ryo, 171-173
Rubato, 217
Rumba, 342, 343, 352
Ryuteki, 194, 197

S

Saibara, 174, 175, 176
Sam, 69, 71
Samba, 352
Samoa, 243-244
Sampurna, 63
Samurai, 169, 192, 193
Samvadi, 63, 64, 80
Sangeet, 50
Sansagari, 190
Sankan, 192
Sanko, 194
Sankyoku, 184-185, 194
San-no-tsuzumi, 195, 196
Sanxian, 144-145, 151, 156, 189
Sarangi, 79, 80
Saron, 218, 219, 220, 223, 224
Saron Barung, 219
Saron Penerus (Peking), 219
Saron Demung, 219
Sasara, 196
Sayra, 315
Scale, 13-24, 52, 171-173, 211-216, 272, 273, 298, 307
Se, 128, 151
Seasea, 252
Sehtar, 74, 115
Sei, 195
Seis, 340, 341
Seka, 208
Sekebeku, 301
Sekupu, 301
Sendratari, 226
Senza Battuta, 32
Seventh, 29
Sewamono, 180
Shadava, 63
Shahnai, 72, 79
Shakuhachi, 184-185, 193, 197
Shaman, 269, 276, 278, 279
Shamisen, 181, 182, 184, 185, 189-190, 191, 192, 194, 196, 197
Sharp (♯), 16
Sheng, 128, 151, 152, 153, 155
Shin, 178
Shinto, 170, 174, 176
Shishya, 51, 52, 75
Shite, 178, 179
Sho, 192, 193, 197
Shoko, 196, 197
Shomyo, 169
Shruti, 55-66
Shu, 188
Shuangmu, 150
Shudad, 98
Siamese, 34
Singing, 41-42, 80-81, 116-119, 154-158, 197, 242-245, 247, 248, 251, 256, 270, 271, 295
Sing-sing, 251
Sioux, 266, 273
Sitar, 72, 73, 74, 75, 76, 78, 79, 80
Siter, 217, 223
Slendro, 212, 215, 217, 222
Slentem, 220, 223
So, 188
Sokyoku, 188
Sonata-allegro Form, 36
Song Form, 36
Soprano, 42
Socavon, 336
Son, 328, 330, 342
Squaw Dance, 276
Species, 20, 22
Staff, 14
Steel Drum, 339
Stratification, 216
String Family, 39
Strophic Form, 36, 37, 116, 185, 242, 247, 248, 271, 272, 273, 331, 332
Strung Rattle, 279
Subdominant, 29, 214
Subdominant chord (IV), 29
Sub-Saharan Region, 293, 314-316
Suddha, 61
Suling, 218, 223, 224
Sun Dance, 273
Suona, 150, 151, 156
Swara, 54-66
Sympathetic Strings, 74, 75, 76, 79
Symphony, 5, 206, 211, 217

T

Taba, 102
Tabla, 73, 78, 95, 112, 116
Tablature, 188
Tagi, 243
Tahiti, 242-243
Tahmila, 105
Taiko, 180, 192, 195, 196, 197
Tak, 103
Tala, 66-70, 71, 72, 80, 81
Tali, 69
Tambora, 334, 335, 336
Tamborito, 335, 336
Tambour, 316
Tamboura, 72, 73, 75, 76, 77, 78, 80
Tangi, 245
Tango, 351, 352
Tanguino, 349
Taogu, 150, 151
Taoism, 130, 131
Taqm, 104
Taqsim, 105
Taqui, 328
Tar, 112, 115
Taring, 208
Tariparau, 243, 259
Tatanua, 251
Tau'a'alo, 242
Tayu, 182
Tbel, 115
Tegotomono, 185
Tejwid, 119
Tempo, 31, 66, 70, 216, 217, 218, 224, 242, 273, 298, 332, 343, 348, 352
Tengihea, 242
Tenor, 42
Tenor (c1) Clef, 15
Tertian, 28
Tetrachord, 56, 57, 70, 97
Texture, 30-31, 216-217, 298
Thaat, 54-66, 74, 98
Thaqil, 92, 104
Theme, 13, 35
Theme and Variations, 36, 185, 312
Third, 27, 28

Thom, 303
Thomo, 301
Thumri, 80
Tiapitzalli, 328
Tibet, 60
Timbre, 37-40, 73-80, 140-153, 184-197, 217-223, 239-242, 245, 247, 251, 252, 257, 279-282, 317-318
Timbrh, 311
Tini, 243, 259
Tinya, 347
Tiple, 341
Tivra, 61
Toada, 352
To-ere, 243, 259
Togaku, 171, 175, 193
Tohono O'odham, 282
Tonada, 335, 352
Tonadero, 348
Tonal, 24
Tonality, 22, 23, 29, 335, 351, 352
Tonga, 242
Tonic, 18, 20, 21, 29, 63, 71, 78, 98, 138, 212, 213, 214, 215, 245
Tonic Chord (I), 29, 35, 336
Torimono, 176
Treble (g1) Clef, 15
Tres, 341
Triad, 28, 29, 298, 328, 352
Triple Time, 32, 303, 328, 349, 352
Triste, 349, 351
Trompong, 222
Tsume, 186
Tsuri-daiko, 195
Tsuyogin, 179
Tumbadora, 344
Twenesin, 307

U

'Ubudhiyya, 116
Uchi, 188
Ud, 94, 96, 100, 105-107, 114, 117
Ukeke, 242
Ukulele, 242, 247, 259
'Ulili, 240

Uli'uli, 240, 241, 259
Umayyad, 92, 93
Umkiki, 316
Ur, 37, 248
Uta, 308
Utai, 177, 185
Utamono, 188
Uttaranga, 57, 70
Uzal, 104

V

Vadi, 63, 64, 70, 71, 80
Vadya, 50
Vals, 333
Varnam, 81
Vedic, 54
Vibhaga, 66, 68
Vidalta, 351
Vihuela, 333, 340
Vilambita, 67
Vina, 74, 79
Vivadi, 63
Vocable, 270, 273, 277, 300, 313, 343

W

Wagon, 187, 197
Waila, 282
Waki, 178
Wasle, 105
Wayang, 224-228
Wayang Golek, 226
Wayang Kulit, 208, 224-226
Wayant Orang, 226
Whole-step, 16, 39, 41, 212, 213
Whole-tone Scale, 24
Woodwind Family, 39, 40

X

Xacara, 352
Xiao, 150, 151, 154, 193
Xuan, 151, 153

Y

Yamada, 187
Yamato-koto, 187, 197
Yangqin, 147-148, 151
Yang-yin, 131, 136, 140
Yaqui, 266, 267, 280, 281
Yei, 276
Yei-be-chai, 276, 277
Yoruba, 293, 308, 309, 317
Yosen, 173
Yowagin, 179
Yu, 150
Yueqin, 146, 151, 156
Yunluo, 149, 151

Z

Zahir, 98
Zaire, 293, 297, 299, 301, 309, 310, 311, 312
Zapateado, 330, 336, 337
Zapateo, 342, 343
Zheng, 142-143, 144, 151, 185
Zhou, 154
Zhu, 150
Zir, 106
Zither, 76, 107, 128, 141, 168, 184, 197, 217, 242, 301, 311, 312, 318
Zokra, 111
Zumari, 303
Zumbara, 316
Zurna, 110, 111, 114